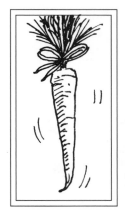

Old Russian Saying

There's an old Russian saying, "It isn't the horse that makes the wagon go. It's the carrot you put in front of his nose."

This book is full of "carrots" — ideas that will help you get people to want to do what you want them to. They will help you increase your skills in marketing, advertising, sales, small business management, and sales promotion. The suggestions in this book are designed to help you make more money.

We hope the ideas will work for you.

Al Whitman

Al Whitman

P.S. If you have any comments about this book, positive or negative, please write:

Al Whitman
1540 6th Avenue North
Long Lake, Minnesota 55356

What Makes This Book Special?

This book differs from others on the market in many ways:

1. It contains no untested theories. Everything in it has been learned on the job and has been proven to work.

2. All 69 chapters were written by an expert in his or her field.

3. This book was not authored by a single person, but by 18 authors.

4. This book was written for a broad audience: small business owners, entrepreneurs, salespeople, advertising agency people, marketing directors, product managers, sales promotion people, fundraisers for nonprofit organizations, and other worthy causes (such as art museums and orchestras), and volunteer workers. It was also written for people in publicity and market research.

5. Each chapter has been written simply, clearly, and with the fewest words needed to convey the author's message.

6. The effectivemess of this book was tested through the use of a laser-printed version, which was given to more than 100 people in many different occupations, who agreed to review the book and give comments in a questionnaire. As a result, many improvements were made.

7. This book contains pen-and-ink sketches and helpful charts in addition to photographs of ads.

IV

Special Remarks

You may be asking:

1. Why was this book written?
2. Are any chapters especially important?
3. Is this book written in any particular way?
4. How many different uses does this book have?

Why this Book was Written

This book was written because a great many people had at one time worked with, supervised, and taught everything they could to many of the authors. Many felt indebted to these mentors.

One way to repay the debt was to help train other people who are or will be engaged in marketing, advertising and selling.

What Subjects are not Included?

This book doesn't discuss industrial advertising, advertising to farmers or trade paper advertising.

Are any Chapters Especially Important?

It all depends on the interest of the reader. A small business owner would probably go right to Chapter 24. A marketing person would choose Chapter 1. A politician would gravitate to Chapter 29, and a research person to Chapters 20, 21 and 53. Finally, sales people would probably turn to Chapters 1, 20, 54, 55 and 57.

In my opinion, the most important chapter in the book is Chapter 11 on benefits.

Its content applies to almost everyone, and all salespersons, creative advertising people, small business owners, and marketing people should find this book invaluable.

How Many Different Uses Does This Book Have?

It can be used to improve your working skills, to make more money and to get faster promotions. In addition, it has other uses including:

a. Use as gifts at Christmas time, or any time, to suppliers and customers.

b. To use in sales training sessions on such subjects as how to do a better marketing or advertising job, how to improve your services to your customers and to your customers' customers, for use as a reference book on many of the subjects featured in each chapter, and for use in synectics and brainstorming sessions to help come up with new ideas.

Contributing Authors

Ray Mithun — Founder of Campbell-Mithun and a member of the Advertising Hall of Fame, has authored six chapters: Which Way Is North, Ten Ways to Pioneer in Marketing, How to Be a Good Leader, How to Motivate People Who Work for You, How to Get Ahead in Business, and How and Why the Job Is the Boss.

Jim Fish — Formerly Director of Advertising for General Mills, and a member of the Advertising Hall of Fame, has authored one chapter on how to get a job.

William Urseth — One of the country's leading sales promotion experts, has authored one chapter on that subject.

Pete Docherty — President of Northwestern Incentive Service authored one chapter on sales incentives.

William Wells — Executive Vice President and Director of Marketing Services at D.D.B. Needham in Chicago, has authored two chapters on market and creative research.

Richard Wilson
Steve Griak — Formed the Wilson-Griak Agency in Minneapolis some years ago, and each wrote a chapter. Wilson's chapter is on the importance of sound in radio and television, and Griak's tells you how to create and produce a television commercial.

Sonja Larsen — Former Senior Vice President of Advertising for the Target chain of discount stores, has authored a chapter on retail advertising.

Richard Shull — Product Manager and Buyer of Lands' End Co., Dodgeville, Wisconsin, has written a chapter on selling by direct mail catalog.

Bill Sorem — Founder and owner of the Computer Obedience School located outside Minneapolis, has written a chapter on the use of computers in marketing and advertising.

Richard Rundle   Former Advertising and Media Director for BBDO in Minneapolis, and later Director of Marketing at International Multifoods, has written the chapter on evaluating results.

Dean Thomas   Former Sales Manager of the Pillsbury Company, has written two chapters, one on tips for selling and one on sales management.

Bill Dunlap   CEO at Campbell-Mithun-Esty (Chicago, Mineapolis, Detroit, and New York) has written a chapter on how to get new business.

Carol Clemens   A direct mail expert has written a chapter on that subject.

Sue Eilertsen   Formerly with Random House, has written a chapter on publicity.

John Nelson   Vice Presicent of Marketing for Source/Inc. design. Now President of JRN Associates, a new business development consultancy for the design industry.

William Whitman   Senior Vice President at Leo Burnett and Account Director on the Kellogg Account, Battle Creek, Michigan has contributed a chapter on today's advertising media.

How to make people say "yes"

This book is dedicated to my wife Edie, without whose support and encouragement I'd never have written this book. And for over a year, she had to put up with seeing only my back as I dictated and wrote this book. She's a gem.

CONTENTS

*   Denotes chapter written by a contributing author

About The Author By Ray Mithun

Al Whitman is a graduate of Princeton. He joined Benton & Bowles Advertising in New York City as an office boy at the age of 21. He was elected Vice President at age 29, and set up the agency's first sales promotion department.

At Benton & Bowles he learned a lot about marketing from his primary mentor, Atherton Hobler, Chairman, and from two key clients, General Foods and Procter & Gamble.

After 18 years in New York, Al joined the Campbell-Mithun Agency, Minneapolis and Chicago, as a partner and executive Vice President, and head of the agency's Marketing Strategy Board. Some years later he became President. At the end of his Presidency, he was offered the job as Chairman but turned it down to take early retirement at the age of 59.

If you asked him what he did most, he'd say, "I taught."

I call Al just about the finest marketing man in the Midwest.

Al wrote 43 of the 69 chapters in this book, and created or supervised the marketing, advertising, publicity, direct mail and research plans for it.

CHAPTER 1

What Is Marketing?

By: Al Whitman

Marketing is the entire process needed to bring a product or service to the marketplace or to improve sales and profits of existing products or services.

The purpose of marketing is to make existing and potential customers *WANT* TO DO WHAT YOU WANT THEM TO.

Successful marketing calls for:

- Clear-cut goals.
- Careful planning.
- A strategy for each "key element," including "positioning."
- A clearcut definition of the "targets" or "market segments" you want to influence.
- Step by step execution of your plans.

The Starting Point

Every good marketing program is customer oriented. It is designed to meet *known* customer needs and wants and to offer benefits to customers.

The basis of every good marketing program lies in discovering what customers want and need, and then designing the product or service that will meet these wants and needs. Every decision made is based on the idea that the customer is number one.

What You Need to Know About Marketing

You need to know only two things to be a successful marketer:

1. The key elements of the marketing process.
2. Proven ways to make these elements really work.

The 14 Key Elements in an Integrated Marketing Program

1. The right information.

2. A high quality product or service with customer benefits built into it (see Chapter 11).

3. Good product or package design.

4. The right kind of pricing.

5. Marketing segments or targets that the product or service was designed for.

6. The known *needs* and *wants* that the product or service should meet.

7. "Positioning" for the product or service (see Chapter 16).

8. The *sales organization* needed to obtain the right kind of distribution.

9. The right kind of *distribution system* .

10. The right kind of marketing plans and marketing direction.

11. The right kind of an advertising plan, with
    » the right creative
    » the right media
    » the right budget

12. The right kind of sales promotion (if needed).

13. The right kind of publicity and direct mail plans.

14. A good research plan to evaluate results.

Each of the above elements is discussed in detail in this book.

Proven Ways to Make These Key Elements Really Work

Other chapters in this book spell out proven ways to get the most out of the 14 elements.

Here are specific examples:

• Chapters 2 and 4 on sales promotion and sales incentives

• Chapter 5 on information

• Chapters 6 , 7, and 8 on marketing plans

• Chapter 9 on blind product testing (for quality)

• Chapter 11 on benefits

• Chapter 12 on pioneering

• Chapter 15 on "positioning" new products

• Chapter 16 on "repositioning" existing products

• Chapters 15, 18, 30, and 56 on advertising

- Chapter 20 on market research
- Chapter 25 on pricing
- Chapter 26 on product and package design
- Chapter 29 on marketing and the small businessman
- Chapters 30 and 31 on ideas
- Chapter 32 on product names
- Chapters 19, 52, 54, and 55 on selling
- Chapter 69 on how this book is being marketed

Where Successful Marketing Starts

Have your marketing program serve your customer's needs and wants

Successful marketing starts with the *customer.* Your main objective is to have your marketing program serve your customer's needs and wants. Market research is a necessary tool for learning what those needs and wants are.

If you don't gear your marketing to satisfying the *known* needs and wants of the people you want to influence, your program will fail.

Base all marketing decisions on facts, not opinions.

Design all marketing programs to put customer needs, wants, and benefits ahead of corporate objectives.

Quality of a Product or Service

Chapter 30 of this book states that the quality of a product is more important than a gifted pen. In other words, the quality of the product is more important than the way it is advertised and promoted.

There are at least two key reasons why the quality of a product or service is so important.

1. When a person buys a product or uses a service and is satisfied with it, he or she often tells others about it. "Word of mouth" advertising is probably the finest and most productive advertising possible because it is believable.

2. When a user is satisfied with the quality of a product or service, chances are good that the person will use the product or service again and again, or use the service regularly or even exclusively. So when putting together a good marketing

program, the quality of the product or service is number one.

In a market oriented company operating in a competitive field, marketing is the heart of the company's operation.

Good marketing is not built solely by the marketing or sales and sales promotion or advertising personnel.

Product development, transportation and finance departments are all part of the picture.

You may wonder why the Japanese have surpassed the United States in technology in the past 10 years and why many Americans think Japanese products are better in quality than those made in this country and why Japanese products have obtained a sizable market share in the United States, particularly in cars and major appliances.

As a result, they are buying a substantial interest in many organizations in the United States.

What did the Japanese do that we didn't do?

A number of people offer different reasons but here are five:

1. The Japanese make products for the *long haul,* not for short-term reasons such as immediate sales.

2. Japanese workers work for the same company *all their lives.* They virtually "marry" the company and vice versa. The have lifetime job security.

3. In the United States, many companies select the suppliers who will give them the lowest price for parts and service. The Japanese consider quality far more important than price.

4. The Japanese don't run their businesses to make money for stockholders but to stay in business. This means they give total dedication to product quality and the productivity of their workers.

5. The Japanese never accept inferior work. Quality is their watchword. They turn out such marvelous products that the need for inspection is not as great as it is in many American plants.

Why Japanese products have obtained a sizable market share in the United States, particularly in cars and major appliances

Other Important Marketing Concepts

The market-oriented company trains its people to understand the vital role marketing plays in the company's operations, and communicates clearly how and why they are expected to contribute.

Smart marketers build products that offer wanted benefits to customers. When new products are involved, the customer's needs and wants are researched and the product tailored accordingly.

The market-oriented company understands that to succeed in the long run, its products or services must deliver complete satisfaction.

So once the new product or service is in use, the company talks to a cross-section of users to determine the degree of satisfaction and to discover ways to improve the product or service.

Some products are used infrequently or in small amounts. Flour, salt, window cleaners, floor polishes, and furniture polishes are good examples. Others are used frequently and produce excellent volume for the company. So customers can be divided into big users, small users, and average users.

When fast-turning consumer products are involved, such as soap, coffee, and cereal, usually 10 to 20 percent of the users will account for 50 percent or more of the total volume. So the "big users" are often the target of a marketing program.

Take the travel business. Travel agents, airlines, hotels, and car rental companies offer special programs and incentives to *business travelers*, who constitute a huge part of their market, particularly all flyers who travel 50,000 to 100,000 miles or more.

Marketing's Relationship to Advertising and Selling

Advertising and selling are *part of* marketing. So are sales promotion, market research, and product definition.

In consumer oriented companies, marketing plays a major role in a company's success.

If you're responsible for marketing, you have a big job and usually the following people report to you:

- Marketing and Product Managers
- Director of Sales

To succeed in the long run, its products or services must deliver complete satisfaction

5

- Director of Advertising
- Director of Sales Promotion
- Director of Publicity
- The Public Relations Director
- Research Director

Always Put Your Marketing Plan in Writing

There are several reasons why you'll want to take this important step:

1. It will help you think more clearly.

2. It will give you a ready reference.

3. It tells the others in top management what you plan to do and why. So if they approve, they're in the same boat with you.

4. It explains clearly to those who execute each part of your plan what they're expected to do and why.

What It Takes to Be a Marketer

1. You have to understand what marketing is.

2. You need an inquiring, analytical mind.

3. You need to understand the importance of information.

4. You think "customer" all the way.

5. You say to yourself, "What customer benefits can we put into each new product or service — benefits that'll make customers think or say "That's *my* kind of product or service." They must have designed that product with me in mind."

6. You never design a "me too" product or service, but use the power of ideas to build in easy-to-understand, wanted advantages that will make existing and new customers prefer your services over your competitors.

7. You always ask this question: "Does our service meet the needs and wants of our customers?" If it does not, or if it was really designed to accomplish some selfish corporate objective, then either go back to the drawing board or don't market it.

Marketing in Action — Example One

Let's suppose a company went into the cruise line business and asked us for a total marketing plan for that cruise line.

What would we do?

We'd give them our recommendations in a series of steps along the following lines:

Step #1

Learn everything about the market and put together a marketing resume or fact book on the cruise industry, including the size and rapid growth of the cruise line business, the importance of first-time cruisers to certain low-price lines, the importance of luxury lines like Royal Viking, Seabourne, and Cunard to people over 60.

The fact that no major cruise line flies the American flag.

Step #2

Strategy. Be different, stand out from a crowd. Make the kinds of moves that'll be remembered. Appeal to people over 60, because that's the kind of cruise line we're recommending, i.e., one that offers expensive luxury cruises.

Step #3

Position our line as the "All American Line." Make everything feature the American idea.

Step #4

Give it a great name like The American Line or America's Vacation Cruise Line.

Step #5

Price all cabins at luxury prices. Use at least three cruise ships that would carry about 750 people and one cruise ship that features nothing but suites for 150 to 200 passengers.

Step #6

Paint the cruise ships red, white, and blue. Give each stateroom a name of a state and a number. Design bedspreads that feature that state.

Step #7

With the exception of Vancouver, cruise exclusively to American ports, up and down the east and west coasts.

Step #8

If legal, hire only American employees and design training programs for them.

Step #9

Use an "All-American" menu. Include items such as Smithfield hams, Southern fried chicken, Maine lobster, Idaho potatoes, Indian River grapefruit, and fresh produce in season.

Step #10

Recommend "All-American" entertainment, one dance band playing the old favorites from the thirties and forties, and the other playing Dixieland and Ragtime.

Step #11

Feature songs and dances from outstanding American musicals such as Oklahoma and South Pacific.

Step #12

Show the latest popular movies and also old-time favorite American stars, such as Cary Grant, Clark Gable, and Fred Astaire.

Step #13

Have television actors and actresses as host/hostess on board, i.e. Burt Reynolds, Bill Cosby, Billy Crystal, Angela Lansbury, Gerald McRaney and Shanah Reed (Major Dad on TV).

Step #14

Feature "All-American" drinks at the ship's bars, such as Kentucky Mint Julep, a mint drink that might also be called "Minnesota Mint."

Step #15

Promote the business with travel agencies who book virtually all cruise business, and work out cooperative promotions with them, including "cruise nights." Offer a free cruise as a door prize.

Step #16

Hold a special weekend event in Miami for leading travel editors and top travel agency personnel. Give them fact sheets about our line and prepare special stories for other media, and arrange for interviews for important national TV shows like "Today."

Step #17

Advertise on national television appealing to people age 60 and over.

Advertise in magazines such as *Travel and Leisure* and *National Geographic.* Use direct mail made up of people who are members of business and country clubs in different cities.

Use double page magazine spreads in red, white, and blue. Send direct mail letters in the same colors.

Summary

So there you have the key elements in a complete marketing plan designed to reach a particular market segment in a memorable and distinctive way.

Marketing in Action—Example Two

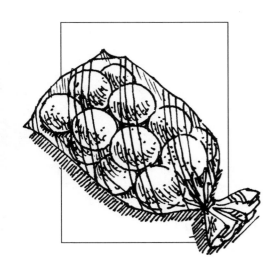

In the early 1980's, America's second largest food wholesaler wrapped, in cellophane or clear wrap, all produce it sold to its independent retailers and stores of its own. This made it easy for the produce to be handled and was ideal for packing more than one of an item, such as a dozen oranges.

However, several competitive food chains did *not* package their produce. A man on the board of directors of the food wholesaler urged the company's management not to package its produce.

He made this suggestion at least once a year for several years and finally persuaded the organization to have one store "test" the concept of unpackaged produce.

The test was an overwhelming success. The sales of produce in the store went up about 60 percent and overall food sales throughout the store rose several percentage points.

By the end of the year, 165 retailers associated with the wholesaler had chosen *not* to have prepackaged produce.

The next year, well over 1,000 of the outlets served by the wholesaler were using the same plan.

By this time consumers wanted to see the quality of what they were buying, and they didn't want bad spots covered up.

There you have a good example of a company that finally benefited by discovering what their retailers' customers really wanted instead of guessing what they might want. Had the company interviewed customers *before* they prepackaged their produce, they would not have prepackaged it in the first place.

An Important Additional Example

Turn to the last chapter. It tells you in detail how this book is being marketed using the marketing principles featured in this book. From it you should get an even better explanation of what a real marketing program is all about.

By the end of the year, 165 retailers associated with the wholesaler had chosen *not* to have prepackaged produce

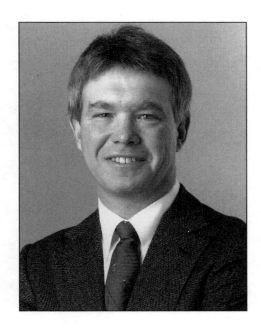

William Urseth is President of U.S. Directives and former President of U.S. Communications.

Bill is one of the country's leading sales promotion experts.

His hobbies include running, riding, shooting, golf, and skiing.

What You Should Know About Sales Promotion and How to Use It

By: William Urseth

What Is Sales Promotion?

Sales promotion is a key marketing element designed to give customers and producers an incentive to buy products or services within a specific period of time.

It's the vehicle of communication that differentiates one product or service from all other similar products at a chosen point in time.

A properly executed promotion causes a call to action that produces immediate and measurable sales results.

While advertising creates attitudes about products and services that cause people to consider them, promotional marketing picks up where advertising leaves off. It's intended to cause a person considering two or three different products to buy a particular one.

In 1978, the normal consumer goods company spent about 40 percent of its marketing budget in promotion, and about 60 percent in advertising. Today, it spends about 70 percent in promotion, and about 30 percent in advertising.

Sales promotion was born many years ago and used primarily for food products to give producers and customers an incentive to buy.

Today, sales promotion is no longer used only to increase sales of packaged goods. Today, any firm with a product to sell, whether it's a car, food item, sports team, or movie, uses promotion in one form or another.

Methodology

Each promotion is different in terms of objectives, timing, type of product or service and budgetary implications. These variables are taken into consideration in promotional planning stages to meet the objective of making a product or service stand out and to increase sales.

The methodology in promotional marketing includes four steps.

- The first step is *defining the objective(s).* Increase sales, in-store display placement, product positioning, and establishment of partnership relationships.

- The second step is *research.* Before developing a plan, extensive research is conducted.

- From the research, a promotional *marketing plan* is developed, expressing clear, measurable, and obtainable goals and strategies to achieve the goals plus a timetable for execution and a budget.

- The final step is *executing the tactics* defined in the strategic promotional marketing plan.

Levels of Implementation

Effective consumer promotional marketing programs often are executed on three levels, including the internal sales force, industry trade, and consumer levels.

Incentives to motivate the sales force are designed to increase product placement. Incentives to the trade, or retailer, provide motivation to stock a product in a store. When incentives to the consumer are provided sales increases are realized and the corporation gains market share. When promotion gives the consumer a reason for choosing a specific product they have a choice between several similar products.

Tactical Tools of Promotional Marketing

There are many tools commonly employed in the implementation of strategic consumer promotional plans. From them, endless forms of execution and creative variations are possible. Before reviewing the specific tools, let's review one of the fundamental keys to successful promotional marketing.

Innovative Creative Execution

Remember being taught to dress for success and that first impressions are made within the first five seconds of meeting? Packaging and package design, product name, display, and collateral materials are how a manufacturer "dresses" a product. In promotional marketing, the visuals and copy often *call for action*, and this is what motivates the customer to purchase.

An illustration of this is a coupon with a strategic headline, "Save $1.00" on the purchase of a box of breakfast cereal. Does the customer choose to spend the time and make the effort to use the coupon in purchasing this brand because he or she desires the flavor this cereal offers versus a similar cereal? Probably not.

The customer desires to save money. The copy, graphic design, and layout of the coupon address the consumer's self interest. The visuals feature the product, and the copy complements this through a call to action; "Save $1.00."

The customer, interested in saving money, makes a decision to choose this brand. The promotion communicated through the creative work highlights the point of differentiation and calls for the sale.

Although promotion picks up where advertising leaves off, the messages communicated via the two vehicles should not conflict in any way. They should present a consistent image.

Creative collateral materials are one of the most important tactical tools available to the promotional strategist and should be the finest available.

Common Characteristics of Promotional Tactics

Each promotional marketing tactic utilizes at least one of four primary types of consumer incentives or benefits. These include money, merchandise, product, and travel. The delivery of the consumer incentive or benefit can be either immediately, or delayed with either *assurance* or *chance* of receipt of the incentive or benefit by the consumer.

Consumer Promotion Stratification

Delivery Timing	Type of Incentive/Benefit Offered			
	Money	**Merchandise**	**Product**	**Travel**
Immediate	Allowances Price Packs	Premium Packs	Samples Bonus	Special Packaging
Delayed/Assurance	Coupons Refunds	Premium Mail-ins	Coupon Mail-ins	
Delayed/Chance	Contests Sweeps Games	Contests Sweeps Games		Contests Sweepstakes Games

Sampling

Sampling calls for delivering an actual product to a group of selected consumers, to induce trial of the product. Originally the samples are provided to the consumer at no cost. It's the most broadly effective and reliable method of promotion for generating trial among a targeted audience.

Sampling is particularly effective when some kind of product superiority exists. The size of the sample varies depending on the percentage of consumers using a brand in the product category, how much is needed for a trial, and the sampling costs.

In-store distribution — Samples are either handed out by a representative or are available in a display.

Direct sampling — Samples are mailed to individual homes or delivered door-to-door by a distribution crew.

Response sampling — Samples are made available by an offer in the media.

Cross-ruff sampling — A sample of one product is made available with the purchase of another product, in the same package, such as a toothbrush with a tube of toothpaste.

Media sampling — A flat sample is included in a piece of printed material, such as a magazine. Perfume is often promoted in this manner.

Professional sampling — A physician or veterinarian, for example, distributes free samples of medical products to the patient or customer.

Selective sampling — Samples are distributed through a facility that attracts consumers or individuals, such as hospitals, hotels, and restaurants.

Here is an example of how selective sampling can be used to increase sales:

Years ago, a drug manufacturer in Connecticut came out with a "new and improved" suntan lotion. At that time, the leading lotion had coloring in it (probably iodine). The manufacturer said to its promotional marketing firm, "Here are the facts about our new product, and our new label. It's 100% stain proof and smells like newly mown hay."

The agency took on this new account in December. They sent one of their smartest sales promotion people to Miami to see if he could come up with a plan.

For several days he roamed the beaches, talking to bathers about suntan lotions and asking what they liked and disliked about them. He noticed that most of the bathers were using the number one lotion on the market and that after a dip in the ocean the lotion stained the towels when bathers dried themselves off.

The promotional strategist called on a number of hotels in Miami Beach to find out if they were having problems in getting the stain out of their beach towels. Without exception, they were and had to give their towels special cleaning treatment at added cost.

As a result, the agency's sales promotion expert made the following deal with 12 of the largest and most important hotels on the beach:

1. During the winter season the manufacturer would give each hotel an almost unlimited supply of small sample bottles of its suntan lotion.

2. It would also prepare a tiny four-color advertisement (about three and one half inches square), which the hotel would place under the glass on top of the dressing tables in every hotel room.

3. The hotel would put the sample bottle of the suntan lotion in every room and replace it with a new bottle as soon as each guest checked out.

The hotel would put the sample bottle of the suntan lotion in every room and replace it with a new bottle as soon as each guest checked out

15

Then the promotional strategist called on all the drug stores and chains in and near these hotels and sold a supply of the client's suntan lotion in the regular size.

In April, the manufacturer started to receive letters and phone calls from wholesalers and retail druggists from all over the country wanting to buy this lotion, which the manufacturer had not yet started to market in other cities.

As a result, with very little cost, *national* distribution was obtained, and almost overnight the lotion reached second place in sales.

This is an example of sales promotion at its best. It dramatizes what the combination of a good idea and a smart sampling plan can do to build a manufacturer's business at relatively low cost.

As a result, with very little cost, *national* distribution was obtained, and almost overnight the lotion reached second place in sales

Coupons

A coupon is a printed piece that entitles a consumer to a specific price reduction on a specified product at the time of purchase.

After receiving a coupon on a product or service through one of a large variety of distribution vehicles, the consumer redeems it in lieu of the specified value of the coupon in cash when purchasing the product.

Six Reasons Why Coupons Are Used

1. As an incentive to get customers to buy a specific brand.
2. To get consumers to buy a new product.
3. To get new uses for an old product.
4. To increase market share.
5. To reduce heavy inventories of a brand.
6. To help sell retailers to take on a new brand.

Basic Methods of Distributing Coupons

Print Media — Coupons are distributed in a number of print media sources, including magazines, Sunday supplements, ROP's (run of paper, the sections run of daily newspapers), or FSI's (freestanding inserts) in newspapers. Freestanding inserts are a separate color section of the newspaper that is developed by the sponsors for the specific purpose of delivering coupons and other direct response offers.

Direct Mail — Cents-off coupons mailed directly to consumers' homes, either individually (for different products of the same manufacturer or on a co-op basis with other manufacturers) or in the same envelope with other coupons. Multiple couponing is the most cost-effective method of direct-mail couponing.

On-Package — There are three variations of on-package couponing:

a. *Cross Ruff* — A product coupon distributed via another product. The coupon is carried in or on the package of another brand.

This is useful to the carrier brand if it's announced on the front of the package. It also allows the couponed brand to reach the carrier's audience efficiently. Typically cross ruff coupons are used with complementary products.

An example of this is coupons for dryer sheets found in a box of laundry soap.

b. *Bounce-Back* — A product distributes a coupon good toward the next purchase of itself or an additional offer. This stimulates repeat purchase in the future. This type of couponing is often used by cereal manufacturers.

c. *Instant Redeeming* — There are two types of instant redeeming coupons.

The first is a coupon distributed on the outside of a package. It lowers the current purchase of the product. This coupon acts like a cents-off and is more efficient than a bounce-back in generating trial.

The second is distributed in conjunction with a sample. An example of this is when a distribution team passes out samples at a supermarket and provides a coupon, redeemable for the current purchase of the regular product.

Price Packs

A price pack, or cents-off pack, is a specially marked product package that carries a specific retail price.

A variation of this is a "pre-priced" package that identifies the special, temporarily reduced, retail price instead of the value of the price reduction. The value of the price reduction varies by product category and the product's share position within the category. Products with a relatively low share require higher value Typical price packs offer a 10 to 25 percent retail price reduction versus the customary retail price for that size of the product. An example of this is a bottle of shampoo that regularly retails for $1.99 and is offered for $1.49 on the package.

Price packs have proven to be one of the most effective and efficient forms of promotion. Inherent in price packs are two of the strongest consumer promotional benefits: appeal of the incentive money, and immediate delivery of the benefit. Through these consumer strengths price packs have been particularly successful in high volume-high repurchase product categories.

Bonus Packs

A bonus pack is a special factory pack that offers the consumer extra product at no additional cost. The amount of the "bonus" varies between 20 and 40 percent; "one-third more" is the most common. An example of this is a pack of soap bars with an additional bar being offered at no additional cost.

A bonus pack is similar to price packs. However, a bonus pack produces less trial and increases loading because it has such a strong appeal to present users.

In a period of price consciousness and inflation, the price pack promotion may prove very effective in generating extra business.

Merchandise Packs

Merchandise packs involve the use of an in-store display featuring visuals of the product and a headline calling for action by stating the offer: "Buy now and get a $3.49 value for only $2.98." The actual product is be stocked in the display for easy accessibility for purchase.

Merchandise packs call out the offer, increase visibility, and ultimately increase sales of the product.

Refunds and Coupon Mail-Ins

Refunds and coupon mail-ins offer consumers a return of part or all of the product purchase price by return mail. To receive a cash refund, the consumer simply sends in proof(s)-of-purchase together with name, address and a special refund certificate.

A special variation of cash refunds involves a high-value coupon on the sponsoring product(s) to the participating consumers. Such offers are becoming increasingly common as consumers show an eagerness to participate in such promotions.

There are two basic variations:

1. *High-Value Multiple Unit Refund Offer* — A consumer is offered a disproportionately large cash refund in return for the purchase of several units of a product. For instance, instead of offering a 25 cent refund on one unit, the product might instead offer a $1.00 refund on three units.

2. *Trade-Selected Item or Cash Register Tape Refund* —This is an incentive for the trade to merchandise the product aggressively.

   The consumer is required to purchase a number of units of the sponsoring product (or more typically several products) and then mail in the proofs-of-purchase plus the cash register tape, name and address.

   The refund is received by return mail.

Premium Mail-Ins

In a premium mail-in promotion, the consumer mails in a stipulated number of proofs-of-purchase and receives a free premium by return mail, with no money changing hands. Because free mail-ins represent a delayed value and require more consumer effort, the value of the premium offered as the incentive must generally be significantly higher than the value of the on-pack premiums to ensure widespread participation.

There are two basic variations of premium mail-ins:

1. *High-Value Free Premiums* — Premiums costing as much as $10.00 in the mail, with retail values of $20.00 or more,

have been offered with great success in return for large numbers of proofs-of-purchase.

2. *Multi-Product Offers* — One or more proofs-of-purchase from several different brands can be required.

Contests

Chance promotions are an entire category of rather unique promotion forms revolving around the utilization of three key elements:

- Chance
- Consideration
- Prize

The relationship between the key elements present within a promotion determines whether the promotion is a lottery, a contest, or a sweepstakes/game.

Chance Promotion Checklist			
	Chance	Consideration	Prize
Lottery	✔	✔	✔
Contest		✔	✔
Sweepstakes/Games	✔		✔

Contests offer the consumer an opportunity to "win" one or more prizes of significant value in return for the exercise of some skill plus the purchase of one or more units of product.

Contests differ from sweepstakes in that they are not based on chance.

It's extremely difficult to structure a contest to produce meaningful short-term business gains, and the promotion form is not broadly used by most manufacturers.

Sweepstakes

A sweepstakes is a promotion form involving chance and a prize but not specifically requiring a product purchase to win the prize offered.

In its basic form, the consumer sends in his or her name and address, together with a proof-of-purchase or facsimile, and one or more names are selected from the pool to determine who wins the prize(s) offered.

To generate a high percentage of participation in a sweepstakes, the grand prize must be perceived as "very valuable" by the targeted audience.

A lottery, for instance, is a form of a sweepstakes. The odds of winning are not very great, but many perceive the possibility of a several million dollar reward worth taking a chance.

Fast-food restaurants have used this form of promotion very successfully. It's an excellent way to sell more of a certain product. Many of the instant-win cards have 25 cents off a drink or burger. The chance of winning the $500,000 is usually detailed on the back of the card in tiny print. The odds of winning big are usually not very high. The objective is to increase sales, not make millionaires out of customers.

Games

A chance game promotion is a modification of a sweepstakes promotion. Game promotions have historically been designed and structured to motivate purchase continuity.

To accomplish purchase continuity, game promotions offer consumers the opportunity to win one or more high-value prizes through a progression of accomplishments leading to the potential winning of a prize.

Games have proven to be the most effective and efficient promotion form ever developed for generating volume/continuity of purchase for frequent repurchase cycle products

Games have proven to be the most effective and efficient promotion form ever developed for generating volume/continuity of purchase for frequent repurchase cycle products over an extended period of time.

Again, fast-food restaurants have been very successful with promotion games.

Special Packaging

Special packaging is the utilization of a special variation of the product purchase and trade merchandising support. Frequently such special packaging uses an old package label for the product (perhaps dating back 50 years or more) or a special seasonal product package to enable the product to be used in a Christmas stocking or Easter basket.

Assuming a product has a meaningful tie-in, special packaging can enable the product to generate merchandising support and incremental consumer purchases that tie in on a relatively efficient basis.

Event Marketing

The term "event marketing" is somewhat loosely defined.

To some it can mean simply buying media time on a sports show or offering a sports-related premium as a consumer promotion. However, it's generally thought of as an integrated marketing activity that capitalizes on an association with an event, person, or group (team) of people, and when the sponsor seeks to become identified with the event. Event marketing helps the sponsor:

1. Create an image (advertising/communications related).
2. Generate incremental volume (promotion related).

In 1986, U.S. Communications (a leading sales promotion firm) developed an extremely successful event promotion for Apple Computer.

"Apple Open House" was developed to generate excitement and increase consumer demand before the holiday selling period.

It marked the first traveling mall show in the history of the computer industry. Its objective: to encourage first-hand experimentation. The event was planned to include hands-on demonstrations of Apple products. The event premiered in 26 malls across the country during September, October, and November of 1986. The event was so successful that Apple doubled the number of malls participating in the program the following year.

In addition, the campaign received the 1987 Gold REGGIE Award, from the Promotion Marketing Association of America, on the basis of superior creativity, execution, and results.

"Apple Open House" marked the first traveling mall show in the history of the computer industry

Continuity Plans

Usually a multiple proof-of-purchase offer in which a customer receives a premium if he or she makes a number of buys within the specified time. A premium is an item offered to the consumer at little or no additional charge.

A common type of continuity plan is the frequent-flyer programs offered by major airlines.

Most of these programs follow a somewhat standard format. When a consumer enrolls, they receive a number of "enrollment points." With each subsequent flight they make on the designated airline, they receive additional points for their air mileage. The points accumulate over time and when the customer has flown a certain number of miles (often 20,000) with the airline, they receive a free flight coupon good for one round-trip flight.

The rules vary slightly according to the airline, but the basic premise is the same; Repeat purchases are induced by the incentive.

Borrowed Interest

Borrowed interest involves using the image of one product to help sell another product. U.S. Communications used the technique in 1983, when it put Star Wars characters on Oral B children's toothbrushes — which ended up doubling the sales of Oral B's children's toothbrush division that year.

Tie-Ins

Tie-ins, or joint promotional events, are common tools used in promotional marketing. They involve two products or companies participating jointly in the same promotion; one product is offered free with the purchase of another.

An example of this is Dolly Madison dessert products and the Minnesota North Stars hockey organization. Customers who purchased $5 worth of Dolly Madison dessert products received a free Minnesota North Stars hockey poster and an entry in a North Stars tickets sweepstakes.

These partnership arrangements are desirable because they usually result in increased sales or channels of distribution for both products involved.

Movie Tie-Ins

Movie tie-in promotions have linked major motion picture producers and corporate America. Promotion licensing allows many companies to use the magic of a major motion picture release as a uniquely powerful promotional marketing tool.

In turn, movie-makers have reaped huge rewards in terms of increased awareness by linking their movies with aggressively promoted products. Example: tie-ins with Star Wars.

Under What Conditions Do You Use Promotion?

1. **To increase sales.**

   Many companies employ promotional marketing as a temporary shot in the arm for sagging sales. They implement a promotional campaign when sales are down only to discontinue it as soon as the sales curve rises.

   Within a short time, however, sales again begin to slow and they find themselves reaching for another dose of promotion.

   The most effective way to increase and maintain sales growth is to establish a long-term promotional strategy and stick with it. By setting the tone early on, each promotion acts as another step toward achieving long-term objectives.

2. **To introduce a new product.**

   In planning for a new product introduction, a corporation must look to both advertising and promotion.

   As mentioned previously, promotion should never conflict with an advertising strategy. Promotion should be planned strategically, and tactical promotional tools should be considered that will complement the advertising product image. It's very important to present a consistent product image when the product is new to the marketplace.

3. **To increase market share.**

   A company may be interested in not only preserving, but increasing market share, after a new product introduction by a competitor. A new product is almost always escorted into the marketplace with both an advertising campaign and a promotional program. An equally appealing promotion of an existing brand, with established brand loyalty, will undoubtedly present the new competition with a significant challenge. Carefully thought-out strategies, including timing, are crucial for success.

Seasonal Considerations

Many consumer products have seasonal appeal. Ice cream sales in the north and midwest are, without question, considerably higher during summer months. On the flip side, merchants in these climates don't sell a whole lot of hats and mittens in August. Seasonality does have a major impact on certain types of products.

To compensate for the lag in sales during off seasons, some manufacturers have turned to promotional marketing. They offer incentives to motivate consumers to purchase when they might not even consider the product otherwise. Quaker Instant Oatmeal is one product that has successfully managed its off-season sales by instituting promotional marketing tactics. The fall months are capitalized upon against a backdrop of back-to-school preparations and dipping temperatures. These promotions set the stage for year-long repetitive purchases.

Another Example of Sales Promotion

If you shop for food in the same supermarket regularly, you know where everything is. However, if you have ever gone into a supermarket for the first time, you probably were confused as to the location of the items you wanted and had difficulty in shopping quickly.

Smart independent supermarket owners and chain store owners understand this fact.

Years ago they discovered that on average it takes seven visits to the same store week after week before the shopper feels "at home."

So when an individual or a chain opens a new supermarket it uses the following plan:

1. It gets a mailing list of the people in all or most of the homes in the area from which it realizes its customers must come from.

2. It prepares seven coupons for selected, popular items in the store, including products like lettuce, bananas, potatoes, milk, and eggs. The coupons either give a specific price for the item being featured or so many cents off.

Years ago supermarkets discovered that on average it takes 7 visits to the same store week after week before the shopper feels "at home"

The owner makes sure the savings to the consumer is substantial on each coupon.

Each coupon is good for purchases made during a specific week.

3. It then mails all seven coupons at one time to the names and homes on the mailing list.

This plan gives each shopper an incentive to shop at the new supermarket for seven consecutive weeks. By this time the customer feels at home in the store and very often continues as a regular shopper.

Summary

Here's a quick summary of what we've covered in this chapter:

1. We've defined sales promotion and the many kinds of sales promotion plans that have been and are being used today.

2. We've told you about the different steps that need to be taken to put together a good sales promotion plan.

3. We've told you what different sales promotion plans were designed to do, and that each is used to accomplish specific objectives.

4. We've discussed sampling, couponing, contests, sweepstakes, price bonus, merchandise packs, coupon mail-ins, and premium mail-ins.

5. We've told you about sales promotion programs with tie-ins to sports events and motion pictures, and given you three or four examples of successful promotion programs.

This plan gives each shopper an incentive to shop at the new supermarket for seven consecutive weeks. By this time the customer feels at home in the store and very often continues as a regular shopper

CHAPTER 3

What Is the Purpose of Advertising?

By: Al Whitman

The purpose of advertising varies by the job you want the advertising to do.

Many people think that the primary purpose of advertising is to persuade readers and listeners "to want to do what you want them to."

That *is* a very important purpose.

Another closely allied purpose is to increase sales, market share and profit for the advertiser.

Still another is to lower the cost of distribution per unit sold. This happens when the advertising is able to increase sales so successfully that the cost per unit comes down.

Additional Purposes

In addition to the above, at times the primary purpose of advertising is to *inform.*

An example is when you have an opportunity to write an advertisement that features news about an improved product or service that's full of benefits (see Chapter 11).

Another purpose is to *explain.* An example might be to explain why customers wanting to buy our product couldn't do so, because it sold out after the first ad appeared. Or to explain why we asked all wholesalers and retailers to return our product to us because of an improper formulation, or because some of our product had been tampered with in retail stores, resulting in illness or even death.

Remember, advertising is a key part of marketing, along with product quality, pricing, selling, sales promotion, positioning, distribution, publicity, package design, and personnel training. As such, the purpose is never to win an advertising award.

The only thing that counts is whether the advertising accomplishes its primary goal in the marketplace.

CHAPTER 4

What Are Sales Incentive Plans, and How Do You Use Them?

By: Peter B. Docherty

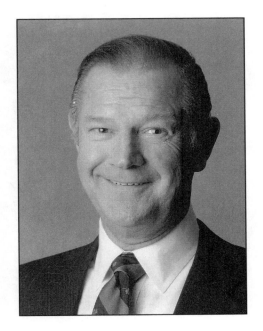

Peter Docherty is President of Northwestern Incentive Services, a sales incentive company specializing in creating and executing incentive plans for companies who want to offer incentives to their own sales organization, to distributors, to brokers, or to dealers.

Pete is a native of Glasgow, Scotland, and has traveled around the world several times and is recognized as an authority on destinations.

Prior to having his own incentive company, Incentives Unlimited, for 10 years, Pete worked with 3 leading incentive firms, E.F. MacDonald of Detroit, S & H Green Stamps, and the Carlson Marketing Group.

Sales incentive programs should should be designed so a company makes a profit

Sales incentives—the practice of offering special rewards for exceptional sales efforts—was conceived just prior to World War II.

The concept began modestly, with small items of merchandise being awarded to top salesmen in recognition of their accomplishments.

In 1947, travel incentive plans were introduced as an alternative choice to merchandise, and down through the years the volume of incentive sales has risen steadily.

In 1990, U.S. companies spent almost $10 billion taking their top achievers around the world or inundating them with everything from fishing equipment to mink coats.

The reason is simple: Incentives work.

In almost every instance, a properly structured, promoted, and implemented incentive program will achieve its intended results.

The purpose of most programs is to increase sales and profits, but in the last few years the emphasis of some campaigns has been to strengthen distributor and dealer networks and maintain market share.

Additionally, they offer a platform for superior performers to gain recognition from their superiors in the presence of their peers.

When Incentive Programs Were Initiated In The Auto Industry

Automobile companies are credited with being the catalytic force that first focused the attention of other industries on the value of sales incentives. In the late forties and early fifties, automotive sales soared as one incentive campaign after another proved its value.

Importantly, sales incentive programs should be designed so a company makes a profit. If there are no winners, there are no costs to pay. The only exception is the expense of the promotion to announce the campaign and produce monthly pieces aimed at maintaining a high level of excitement among all eligible participants.

In some cases, a sponsoring company will have its own writers assume this responsibility, thus making it a minimal internal expense.

Sales incentive companies maintain their own sales organizations, concentrating, for the most part, on new business.

Most of their salespeople work on commission or a combination of commission and salary.

They know travel destinations, the basics of how to put together an incentive program, and how to sell both the benefits of sponsoring an incentive plan and what specifics are required to achieve the desired results.

For companies that have never used incentive plans, the salesperson will explain how his or her company can design a successful program.

A good salesperson selling for a full-service incentive firm can earn between $60,000 and $150,000 per year. In some cases, account executives make much more.

The first step of any successful program begins with the salesperson (account executive) explaining to the prospective account what an incentive campaign can accomplish. The account executive must elaborate on five major facets: marketing, administration, promotion, merchandise and travel. Companies planning an incentive program may use one or more of these facets in a campaign. They may, for example, rely on their own marketing staffs to develop the rules structure (the assignment of points for each of the products sold or purchased in the campaign) or their own writers to produce the promotional copy.

The majority of organizations hire sales incentive companies to create and implement the entire program.

Each of the five facets requires expertise as described below:

1. **Marketing**

   Here is an actual plan used by a building supply company:

ABC Company 1990 Dealer Incentive Program Rules

Program Period:	January 1, 1990 through December 31, 1990
Participants:	All authorized and enrolled ABC Company Dealers
Eligible Purchases:	All net purchases from the ABC Company (less sales taxes, returns and delivery charges) of warehouse and direct purchase products.
Program Awards:	8 Day/7 Night Caribbean Cruise
	6 Day/5 Night Acapulco Trip
	Deluxe Merchandise Awards (illustrated in ABC Company Catalog)
How to Qualify:	To qualify, Dealer must be enrolled and equal their 1989 combined total of warehouse and direct purchases or $20,000, whichever is highest. In addition, Dealers must equal their 1989 total Warehouse Purchases.
How to Earn Prize Points:	Each month New Business in 1990 will earn Dealers Prize points toward Travel or Merchandise Awards.
	New Business is defined as 1990 monthly (warehouse, direct or combination) purchases that exceed the same months purchases in 1989.
	After equaling the same 1989 month total purchases, each $1000 of new Warehouse Purchases will earn 5800 prize points, and/or each $1000 of new Direct Purchases will earn 1800 prize points.

Program Structure:

1. Each enrolled Dealer will receive a Progress Report at the end of the first and second quarters and then monthly for the last six months of

the year. These reports will show monthly purchases and prize points earned, including year-to-date amounts.

2. Dealers' accounts must be in good credit standing throughout the program year to qualify for any of the program's awards.

3. Prize points cannot be sold and are non-transferable and are intended for use by the management and/or employees of the Dealership and their immediate families.

4. Prize points can be redeemed for the program trips and merchandise only. Prize points cannot be redeemed for cash, promotional allowance, rebates, or any other form of award.

5. After the first trip for one person is earned, partially earned or additional trips may be purchased.

6. All unredeemed prize points will be voided on March 31, 1991 and become the property of the ABC Company.

This is a basic program with simple rules that are easy to understand—and those are the most effective.

2. Administration

Administration is the electronic record-keeping of all eligible participants in the campaign. When sales or purchases are made, verified at the district level, and relayed to headquarters, they are fed into a computer and printed monthly. A copy of the participant's monthly purchases is mailed out with an indication of how the salesperson, distributor, or dealer is faring against goal, that is, whether the participant is on target, ahead, or behind.

Valuable marketing information can be elicited from this data. Here is an example:

The more a client
spends on promotion,
the greater the number
of winners

Let's say the sponsoring organization manufactures lawn equipment. Equivalent points are assigned to the units. The monthly data reports may show that dealers in the northeastern part of the country are purchasing more riding lawnmowers than power mowers, while the southeastern dealers are buying more push mowers than any other part of the country.

This enables the marketing department to know where to focus its efforts to increase sales of certain units in specific areas.

3. **Promotion and Communication**

Promotion plays a major role in determining the numbers of participants or recipients of merchandise in a campaign. There is a saying in the incentive industry: The more a client spends on promotion, the greater the number of winners. The success of the program is commensurate with the number of dollars spent on the monthly hype.

Creative communications are also of vital importance: The theme. The creativity in brochures or in letters. The way the incentive program is announced. Creative communications are as important to incentive plans as good advertising is to the sales performance of products in the marketplace.

A special letterhead is developed for each program so that when a participant sees the envelope in the mail, he or she immediately knows it's campaign literature.

Promotional pieces are mailed *to the home* and not to the office—and for a very good reason.

When a promotion piece is sent to the home, the spouse becomes involved and the most successful campaigns are those that include incentives for husbands *and wives.*

It's a proven fact that husbands and wives create a powerful impetus, a second motivation that's often more powerful than if the salesperson, distributor, or dealer is the sole recipient.

Some firms sponsoring incentive plans make a grave error in having their own writers perform the promotion function.

In all probability, their writers are accomplished wordsmiths, but they lack proper information on the destination, hotels, and car rental companies, which information is available to the writers in the creative departments of incentive companies who have access to travel staffs who are constantly traveling with groups to destinations around the world.

Would a writer in a company's public relations department know or be able to explain Beijing's Underground City? Would a writer in its advertising department have knowledge of the Chine lock that baffled modern engineers and archaeologists when they tried to open the door to an Emperor's burial site in the Ming Tombs?

The rule of thumb is to spend the equivalent of 5 percent to 8 percent of a travel or merchandise program on promotion and communications. The smart ones spend—and reap—more!

4. **Merchandise**

The bigger slice of the incentive dollar has always gone to merchandise.

Yet, it is a generally recognized fact that travel is the *better motivator*. The reasons why travel is more popular are manifold and are enumerated in the following chapter.

There are many small dealers who do not have the numbers to justify a trip to Rome or Las Vegas so merchandise is the viable alternative, In campaigns where small and medium-size dealers do not have the amount of business needed to earn a trip, they use their acquired points to select merchandise.

The rule of thumb is to spend the equivalent of 5 percent to 8 percent of a travel or merchandise program on promotion and communications

To keep the smaller dealers happy, sponsoring companies when offering a travel destination as the top prize will often make merchandise available, too

To keep the smaller dealers happy, sponsoring companies when offering a travel destination as the top prize will often make merchandise available, too. The companies provide each participant with a catalog from which he or she may select the desired items.

Some companies conduct only merchandise programs. Merchandise, therefore, has always gobbled up a steady 60 to 65 percent of the available incentive dollars.

5. **Travel**

The reasons why travel is conceded to be the better motivator are manifest.

The obvious are a glamorous destination with an itinerary that includes sightseeing, superb meals in top restaurants, opportunities to play golf in balmy weather when snow and freezing temperatures make it impossible at home, deep-sea fishing, an awards banquet where exceptional efforts are recognized by a top official (in most cases, the president) of the sponsoring company, an opportunity to take a spouse away from the drudgery of everyday life and be pampered in a luxurious setting.

A trip also makes available to winners an opportunity to converse with their peers and learn of advertising and sales ideas and business techniques that have been successfully implemented in other areas of the country.

New and lasting friendships are formed, and once these have been strengthened, it becomes an additional incentive to win a trip and enjoy their company in subsequent years.

But before an itinerary can be planned, the account executive must secure responses to many questions.

These details are usually "in-put" sessions with the clients and then relayed to the travel department.

For example:

1. Who is to participate in the incentive program? Company salespeople? Brokers? Distributors? Dealers?

2. How many participants are anticipated?

3. What do the participants have to do to qualify for the program, that is, what kind of sales increases are necessary?

4. Should the incentive plan feature travel or merchandise or both?

5. What should be the length of the travel program? (This is mostly determined by the budget.)

6. Will the program include spouses?

7. What destinations should be selected? (Occasionally, the client may have a site in mind. In most cases destinations are recommended by the incentive house.)

8. What company personnel will host the trip? Chairman, President, Sales Manager?

9. Will the group fly coach and will anyone be booked first or business class?

10. What entertainment will be required?

    a. golf, tennis, fishing, riding, or boating?

    b. sightseeing?

    c. theme parties?

    d. guest speakers?

There are many more, but the above should give you a good idea of what an incentive house has to do to plan and execute an incentive travel program:

After the trip is over, the sponsoring company can do other things including to capitalize on the program?

    a. Give all the winners a book of pictures featuring the highlights of the trip, including pictures of the winners and spouses.

b. Announce the destination for the next trip with a special slide or video presentation.

c. Write articles with quotes from winners for the company newsletter, employee magazine, or local newspaers.

SUMMARY

It is frequently difficult to determine with any degree of accuracy what percentage of a company's increased business is attributed to an incentive campaign. This largely is because year-round advertising and public relations programs as well as a plethora of similar efforts contribute to the overall success.

It is a well-known fact, however, that once a company implements its first incentive program, it is hooked to the point that incentives become an almost indispensable part of its way of doing business.

Destinations are selected according to interest, budget, and time of the year.

A company planning its first incentive campaign should choose a destination carefully, allowing it to build up to more exotic and appealing areas of the world in ensuing years.

The first trip may be to Phoenix, followed by Cancun, then perhaps Hawaii before the cornucopia of Europe keeps it busy for several years. Asian locales such as Hong Kong, Singapore, Thailand, and Bali are interspersed with Europe to keep the appeal at a high level.

When companies have traveled extensively around the world, they may repeat destinations (London, Hawaii, and Switzerland are most visited) or look for unusual locales. The latter may include the Galapagos Islands, or Machu Picchu in Peru.

Now that the Berlin Wall has come down and the satellite nations of eastern Europe are embracing democracy, companies that once were reluctant to take their people behind the Iron Curtain are now rushing to visit them.

Since the volume of incentive sales was first recorded in the late forties the annual total expenditures by U.S. companies have never failed to exceed the previous year's figures.

There's a reason: Incentives work.

Conclusion

While the idea of offering sales incentives is old hat to many companies, there are also others who know little, if anything, about them including the very important feature that you can design almost all incentive plans so that the sponsor is bound to make money.

CHAPTER 5

The Importance of Information and How to Use It

By: Al Whitman

There's an old saying that's very pertinent to marketing.

> NO ONE'S PLANS CAN BE BETTER THAN HIS/HER INFORMATION.

To do a good job in planning you need all the information available on the subject.

And you need to be sure the information is accurate.

When you have accurate information, it's possible to arrive at a definition of the sales and marketing *opportunities* for your product or service and the sales and marketing *problems* that your product faces.

The essence of a good marketing plan calls for capitalizing on as many of your strengths as possible and in developing ways to overcome your weaknesses

The essence of a good marketing plan calls for capitalizing on as many of your strengths as possible and in developing ways to overcome your weaknesses.

With some advertisers the basic marketing plans are prepared by the advertiser's marketing personnel, either with or without the help of the advertising agency.

In other instances the agency does the planning job and submits the plans to the client for changes and ultimate approval.

Either way, the right information is vital to a good marketing plan.

Without good information few marketing programs have any hope for success.

That's why the primary job in many advertising agencies is to compile all the available information into a marketing resume, which some people call a "fact book" (see Chapter 6).

One of the "must" items in the fact book is "what information we need to know that is *not* available." In such instances the solution lies in market re search.

How to Prepare a Fact Book for Use in Marketing Plans

By: Al Whitman

The fact book, or marketing resume, is a marketing document of great importance. It's the starting point for marketing plans and strategies.

It's the source of information required for good decision making and points the way to the right moves that should be made.

It provides valuable information for those in charge of creating ads and promotions.

It's an educational tool for the people who prepare it and facilitates top managements' review of proposed plans and strategies.

Who Prepares the Fact Book?

Usually the agency's account team works closely with the product and marketing managers to prepare the fact book. In some cases the director of sales and director of marketing must approve it.

How Is a Fact Book Prepared?

The person preparing the fact book takes these actions:

1. Prepares an outline as to what the book should contain.

2. Gathers all available information pertinent to a product, service, or company, and its marketing.

3. Analyzes the data to determine marketing problems or opportunities.

4. Determines if there's any important information that is not yet available, and takes the steps necessary to get it.

Where Does the Information Come From?

1. From industry sources, including associations, companies, suppliers

2. From existing research
3. From clients
4. From media
5. From libraries
6. From government data
7. From other companies in the industry

The author collects all information and keeps it in files for ready reference.

What Kind of Information Goes into a Marketing Resume "Fact Book?"

All information in a fact book should be pertinent to the development of the marketing plan and to the marketing strategies.

To illustrate what needs to be compiled in a marketing resume or fact book, let's suppose we're considering the introduction of a new product in the marketplace, a product that will compete with several established brands.

What kind of information pertinent to the market and to strategic conditions do we need to examine to market our product successfully?

Note: If our fact book was being written for a service it would obviously be different in certain aspects.

Here's an outline of a typical fact book that illustrates what needs to be included and examined carefully.

Fact Book Outline

1. *The Industry*
   - » Size in units or dollars
   - » Sales trend last three years
   - » Any unusual developments last three years

2. *Sales by geographic areas vs. percentage of sales by population*

   Area   Percent of population   Est. percent sales

3. *Same figures for city size*

   Size   Percent of population   Percent of sales

4. *The major companies in the marketplace and their brands.*

   Companies   Brands

   _____   _____

   _____   _____

   _____   _____

5. *The leading brands and their estimated dollar sales and share of market.*

   Brands   Est. $ Sales   Est. Market Share

6. *The fastest growing brands last three years and estimated increases.*

   Brands   Est. % Increase Last Three Years

7. *Reasons for an unusual increase (if any).*
   » Explain

8. *Package sizes and relative importance.*

   Sizes   Est. Market Share

9. *How are brands packed?*
   » to a case.

10. *Retail pricing by sizes.*

    Size   Average Retail Price

11. *Package Designs*
    » Show designs here, indicating any major changes last three years

12. *How leading products are "positioned" in the marketplace.*
    » Describe position for each brand.

13. *Explain any product advantages any brand offers.*

14. *What about sales promotion practices.*
    » Sampling?
    » Couponing?
    » Cents-off sale?

» Sweepstakes?

» Contests?

» Consumer Premium offers?

» In-store demonstrations?

Comment here if any promotion on any leading brand was particularly effective.

15. *Estimated dollars invested in advertising each of last three years.*

Brands   Est. Expenditures by Year

_____   _____

_____   _____

_____   _____

16. *Estimated dollars spent by key brands in advertising and sales promotion per case last year.*

Brand   Est. Adv.\Case   Est $ per Case

17. *Key advertising media use by key brands .*

Brand   Key Media

18. *Key advertising claims by brands.*

Brand   Claim

a._____   _____

b._____   _____

c._____   _____

19. *Have any key brands changed their claims within the past three years?*

20. *Have any brands made other investments not covered above?*

» Publicity?

» Trade paper advertising?

» Trade deals?

» If yes, please explain.

21. *Taking the above into consideration, what major problems face our brand? What major opportunities exist for our brand?*

Describe strengths and problems here.

22. *Does the above suggest a need to come up with any specific strategies?*
   - » Product improvement advantages?
   - » Packaging improvements?
   - » Package design?
   - » Package size?
   - » Pricing?
   - » Strength of sales organization and distribution system?
   - » Sales promotion?
   - » Positioning?
   - » Advertising Media?
   - » Creative advertising claims?

In short, a marketing resume is a key marketing device and the heart of planning a good marketing program.

Summary

In a nutshell, the right information is the key to a marketing plan.

CHAPTER 7

How to Write a Marketing Plan or Sales Plan

By: Al Whitman

Did you ever stop to think that when a marketing or advertising person writes a marketing plan he takes much the same steps as the doctor does when a patient comes to him or her for help?

The goal of the patient is to find out what's wrong and to get well. The goal of the marketing person is to attain his or her clients' marketing objectives.

The similarity between the doctor and the marketing person is illustrated in the following comparison:

DOCTOR	**MARKETING PERSON**
1. Gets all available information on the patient, i.e., reviews the patients' history and listens to patient describe the symptoms.	**1.** Lists all the key marketing facts pertaining to the problem.
2. Gives the patient a thorough exam and arrives at a list of possible ailments.	**2.** Analyzes the facts. Should more information be needed, recommends research.
3. Initiates a series of tests (blood, urine, etc.) to see if some of the possible ailments can be eliminated, or if a single ailment can be identified.	**3.** Lists the marketing opportunities and the marketing problems.
4. Perhaps would ask colleagues for their opinion.	**4.** Reviews thinking with supervisor or top management.
5. Prescribes for the patient what to do and what kinds of medicines, if any, to take.	**5.** Writes a plan to overcome the marketing problems and take full advantage of the opportunities.
6. Asks the patient to call at a later date so results can be checked.	**6.** Executes the plan assuring that all of the players know their responsibilities.
7. Writes a short case history for the record.	**7.** Sets up a system to check the results.

While the similarity between a doctor arriving at a prescription and a marketer preparing a plan is an apt one that may be helpful to you, it really doesn't describe all the key questions that a marketer has to answer before beginning to write the plan.

Most of these questions were reviewed in Chapter 6:

1. What part of the market are we going to sell — by sex, age, income, and other demographics?

2. What is competition doing in the areas of product development, packaging, pricing, sales promotion, and advertising?

3. What share of the market does each competitor have and what are the trends in this area?

4. How do competitors' sales and distributing operation compare with ours?

5. How much money does each key product in the industry spend for sales promotion and advertising?

6. Is there research available that suggests a certain course of action for us to take?

7. Are we planning to open the whole country or just sections?

8. What is the best advertising medium for us …daytime TV, prime time TV, spots, etc.

9. If ours is a new product, is any kind of special sales promotion indicated, i.e., sampling, coupons, etc.?

When you write a marketing plan and use the analogy of the doctor's prescription and also use information properly, you should come out with a very specific and workable plan for your product or service.

CHAPTER 8

How to Prepare a Test Marketing Plan for New Consumer Products

By: Al Whitman

New products are very important in today's marketing and have been for many years.

For some manufacturing companies that produce products for consumers, they are even the "life blood" of those companies.

Last year in food products alone, we are told that 12,000 new items, including some new sizes, were introduced into supermarkets.

You might be interested to know how much the major marketing and advertising companies know about the market that should exist for the new products they're planning to test market, and particularly about the people who need or want to buy the new products.

Through their own personal research and research information purchased from outside firms, they know what products the customer is presently using, how often each product is purchased, the television habits of the people, the kind of neighborhoods the best prospects are living in, and all about their buying habits.

They also know whether the consumers of products within the category of their new product have a tendency to use various types of sales promotion activities (see Chapter 2) and the estimated number of dollars used for sales promotion and for advertising.

Steps to Prepare a Test Market Plan for New Products

Start by preparing a *national* plan

1. Start by preparing a *national* plan, complete in every detail. Include in the plan:
   - » When the new product will be introduced.
   - » How it will be priced.
   - » The estimated sales goal.
   - » The type of distribution and sales organization that will be used.

- » How the product will be positioned.
- » Marketing targets, (i.e., demographics and psychographics).
- » Type and cost of advertising.
- » Details of advertising media.
- » Sales promotion activity and projected costs.
- » Publicity plans.
- » Incentive plans for the company's sales organization or the distributor's sales force.

2. Usually two to four test markets are selected, with each such market considered "typical" of the national market.

3. All elements of the national plan are put into the test market plan. The goal is to duplicate in the test markets all the elements of the national plan.

4. The national plan will often call for elements that are not possible to duplicate exactly in the test markets, so you do your best. For example, if the national plan calls for using national magazines, your test marketing plan might call for using Sunday magazine sections.

If your national plan calls for using television programs which the company is already sponsoring, the local plan may call for using locally purchased evening programs or locally delivered commercials "cut in" on the programs being used nationally by the company for other products.

Criteria for Selecting Test Markets

They'd call for a reasonably typical pattern of distribution. For example, you wouldn't use a test market for a new food or drug product where a single chain controls 35 percent or more of the food business. In addition, the ideal test market is one that doesn't receive more than an average amount of advertising emanating from competitive products in other cities.

Summary

The procedures outlined here are used by virtually all large marketing companies. We're sure that what works for them will work for you.

Remember to prepare your national plan first and then duplicate your plans as expertly as possible for use in your test markets.

CHAPTER 9

Blind Product Testing

By: Al Whitman

Blind product testing is a specialized form of research that's used when you need to know one of two things:

1. How a proposed new product compares in quality with the leading brand on the market.

2. How well a proposed product improvement of an existing product is received by consumers (without telling them about the improvement), and whether or not the improved product is preferred to the leading brand.

In either case, the firm doing the testing takes these steps:

1. Buys a supply of the leading seller and repackages that product in a "nameless" container (no brand identification). This is where the name "blind product" comes from.

2. Puts the product being tested in an identical package.

3. Identifies each with a letter such as K, O, Q, or W, (but not two letters like A and B. Such labeling creates a built-in advantage for "A.")

4. Prepares a letter and questionnaire to be mailed out with the two packages.

5. Mails all testing materials to a carefully selected sample of homes large enough to minimize probabilities of error due to sample size.

6. Reports on results and indicates the predictable margin for error of plus or minus ___%.

Blind product testing is another way to ensure that the quality of product being offered is as high as, and hopefully better than, the quality of its leading competitor. The importance of quality as the number one element in good marketing is discussed in Chapter 1.

Note: This type of research can be very helpful to marketing. It can sometimes turn up information leading to product claims for the advertising and the best kind of sales promotion for the product. It cna also turn up ideas for other new products.

However, in most instances the brand new or improved product was produced on a *small scale* in test kitchens or development labs.

As a result, when a product is produced on a large scale in the factory, it's possible that the resulting product will not be equal in quality to what was "blind product tested." So whenever there is any evidence that this problem may exist it is often a good idea to test the two products again before going into natinal distribution.

Summary

Blind product testing is an important part of marketing and almost essential in the development of new products or product improvements.

Blind product testing is an important part of marketing...

CHAPTER 10

Ray Mithun was the co-founder of Campbell-Mithun, Inc. (Minneapolis and Chicago) in 1933 after working for two years at BBDO, Minneapolis, as Ralph Campbell's assistant.

Ray was a brilliant student, a great teacher of advertising, a visionary, a fine creative man, a fierce competitor, a superb salesman and a great businessman whose advice was valued greatly by his clients.

His first three accounts (Andersen Windows, Land O' Lakes and Northwestern National Bank) are still with his former agency, which is now called Campbell-Mithun-Esty, a $750 million agency and one of the largest in the United States.

After retiring from Campbell Mithun, Ray entered the banking business as the owner of three suburban banks. He has had great success in this new field.

Ray was elected to the Advertising Hall Of Fame in 1990, and is the author of six chapters in this book.

Which Way Is North?

By: Ray Mithun

This question can be asked of almost any person, in any job, in every business or industry. The answer illustrates an important concept in marketing a product or service.

I used to tell this story: "Imagine you're in a forest. You want to get out but there's no sun to tell you which way is north. To get out of the forest, you've got to have a compass."

In pioneer days every caravan of wagons needed a guide. It was the guide's job to chart the course, and he had better know his stuff. If he got lost, or worse yet if he led the caravan astray, he'd be replaced—or lynched.

How does this story apply to business?

It means that you have to know what direction to take and what moves to make.

If you have no compass to guide you, it's tough to find your way out of the forest. You've got to know which way is north.

To dramatize this concept, I had a designer create a stylized compass. Then I went to a famous tie maker and had ties designed with the initials "CM" on them and the stylized compass. Finally, I had coffee cups imprinted with a compass pointing north, and I gave the cups to people in our agency to use at coffee breaks.

Do you know what your job is? What's expected of you? What kind of advertising to prepare? What kind of marketing plans to write? Do you know which way is north? If you do, chances are you're really on top of your job.

CHAPTER 11

How to Use Benefits in Advertising, Personal Selling, and Supervising People

By: Al Whitman

This is the most important chapter in this book for salespeople, and those who create advertising, for marketing people, for marketing directors and their marketing and product managers, for small business entrepreneurs and money raisers.

Why? Because it contains the essentials for persuading people to say, "yes".

It also gives copywriters one of the keys to writing headlines that interest people and make them want to buy.

It provides salespeople with the key to good salesmanship — the way to make customers and prospects *want* to do what they want them to.

Some years ago I learned about benefits from a sales and personnel training company in New Canaan, Connecticut. This company had been hired by one of my former clients (The Prudential Insurance Company) for the twofold purpose of

1. Training better salespeople

2. Improving the communications of supervisors and helping them communicate more effectively with those who worked with them so they'd want to do what the supervisor wanted them to.

In my opinion there are three main motivators in the life of the average person:

1. Instinct, such as the instinct for survival.

2. Ideas (see Chapters 12, 30 and 31)

3. Benefits.

When you use benefits properly, you invariably make the person you're communicating with say "yes"

When you use benefits properly, you invariably make the person you're communicating with say "yes."

Every product or service provides *benefits* and *qualities*, as follows:

- A *benefit* is what a product or service *does* for a customer or prospect.
- A *quality* is what the product or service *is*.

Benefits are *active* (does). Benefits motivate people into action.

Qualities (which often are the reason why for a benefit) are *passive. Qualities are inactive. They just "sit."*

NOTE: The verb used most frequently in books written for young children learning to read is "is."

To adults, passive verbs are dull and uninteresting.

In advertising and in personal selling, many cub copywriters and new salespeople use qualities in their headlines or opening remarks and *not* benefits. Sometimes the reader or listener is able to translate that quality into a benefit. If not, the advertising or sales efforts are heavily diluted.

What Is a Benefit?

The *American College Dictionary* defines a benefit as "anything that is good for a person." I always describe a benefit as what the product or service *does* for the customer in helping to meet known customer needs or wants. I emphasize *known* needs, not opinions as to what is needed or wanted.

If we do not know what customers want or need, we go to them directly and solicit their opinion.

When you offer a needed or wanted benefit to a customer, you help bring about the action or decision you want from that customer. Offering needed or wanted benefits appeals to the self-interest of the customer and motivates him or her to buy.

Obviously, then, benefits are one of the secrets of successful advertising and personal selling. The merit of the old adages, "Use a carrot instead of a stick," or "Sell the sizzle instead of the steak," was proven long ago.

Other Uses of Benefits

Benefits can help a person in charge of a company's labor relations persuade a labor union to accept the company's point of view. For example: "When you accept this proposal you'll help the

Benefits are one of the secrets of successful advertising and personal selling. The merit of the old adages, "Use a carrot instead of a stick," or "Sell the sizzle instead of the steak," were proven long ago

company create more jobs, and more jobs will increase the size of your union."

Benefits can help a supervisor persuade his or her people to change or improve their work habits.

Using benefits is worthwhile when individuals try to sell the idea that they deserve a raise or a promotion.

A good benefit is an "activator" to help current and potential customers see things *your way* and a "motivator" to get them to buy.

Another way to arrive at benefits is to start with the qualities of a product or service and translate them into benefits. This is not difficult to do.

To illustrate, let's use the example of a small electrically powered orange juice squeezer.

In the following comparison we list four qualities. We then show their translation into benefits. Actually, the qualities are the "reasons why" for the benefits.

Qualities	Benefits
1. Less than 6 inches wide.	1. Fits on any counter near an electrical outlet.
2. Made of tough plastic.	2. Won't break.
3. Has a removable plastic squeezer that fits over an electrical base which turns the squeezer.	3. Easy to use.
4. Has electrical cord and plug.	4. Just plug it in and it's ready for use instantly.

Examples of Benefits

Every day you're exposed to all kinds of benefits offered on the radio, TV, in newspapers and magazines. Here are some examples:

» Here's how to save $_____ on _____.

» This gadget will cut preparation time in half.

» Here's a new party recipe your guests will rave about.

» This time-tested plan will increase your income by 20 to 50 percent.

> » 17 proven ways to make a hit with your boss.
>
> » Four delicious meal ideas that'll make your husband say, "I married the greatest gal in all the world."
>
> » Each one of these four new dresses will make your girl friends turn green with envy.

At times people will suggest marketing moves whose benefits are unclear or debatable.

In such a case, ask yourself, "If we make this move, what benefit (s) would we offer the customer?" If the answer is "none," or if the reason is not customer oriented, forget about making the proposed move. Benefits must always provide something the customer wants or needs.

Additional Examples of Benefits

1. For Andersen Windows
   > » They *enhance the beauty* of your home.
   > » They're easy to *install.*
   > » They're easy to *clean.*
   > » They *increase the value* of your home.

2. For a business travel company (see Chapter 4 written by the president of Northwestern Incentives Services):
   > » We offer our business travelers peace of mind (no worries).
   > » We book your flight to depart when you want and arrive when you want (convenience).
   > » If you want low calorie or kosher meals, we arrange for them, if available (extra service).
   > » We guarantee to book every traveler at the *lowest fare* (saves money for his or her company) unless he or she specifies a different arrangement or a different airline.

3. For brands of toothpaste:
   > » It cleans your breath as it cleans your teeth (Colgate).
   > » "Look, Ma, no cavities" (tartar-control Crest).

Who can improve
your employee benefits
without increasing costs?

Summary

A benefit is what a product or service *does* for the customer…something desirable, something he or she wants or needs.

A product quality is what a product or service *is*. If you describe a lead pencil, you might say, "It's 7 inches long, has an eraser, and is yellow." But if the eraser was a particular kind that lasted indefinitely and erased as clean as a whistle, that's a benefit, because it does something you want.

When you talk about benefits, you're talking actively (does). When you talk about qualities, you're talking passively (is).

When you offer a juicy benefit, it motivates people to buy or want to do what you want them to. Qualities just sort of "sit" and get little or no response from the person you're talking to. Often qualities are "a reason why" for the benefits, as was illustrated by the example of the orange juice squeezer.

So, when you want to bring about an action in advertising or personal selling or to persuade people to "want to do what you want them to," you lead with benefits.

Unfortunately, scores of advertisements are written with qualities in their headlines instead of benefits.

You motivate people in ads, in selling, and in personal relationships by using benefits such as the "carrots" you put under the prospect's nose. When you write an ad or sell a product you always sell with news and benefits. This is the way to *interest* prospects and to *motivate* them to say yes.

You'll find this counsel worth its weight in gold. You'll create better ads, and you'll be a better salesperson. You'll make people *want* to do what you want them to.

Here are three ads taken from a recent issue of *Sports Illustrated*. All feature benefits.

The center ad doesn't show the name of the insurance company that ran it (UNUM Insurance Company of Portland Maine), because this ad ran as the first of two right-hand pages. The second page featured the company name and its copy expanded on the headline shown here.

Note from Al Whitman: For many years I've been telling young advertising copywriters about benefits, and I've also stressed these two points:

1. The proper use of benefits in the ads you write may not ever make you a great copywriter, but if you don't use them, and use them properly, you'll never be a good one.

2. If you are a good copywriter and you continue to create advertising for perhaps 20 years or more, you'll make at least $250,000 to $500,000 more in salary and bonuses during that period than you would have if you had not understood and used benefits properly. Understanding benefits might even mean the difference between keeping your job and losing it.

Summary

Benefits are the key to good selling, and to making people say "yes."

To motivate them to want to do what you want them to, all ad headlines and face-to-face selling should feature a benefit, plus news if it exists.

CHAPTER 12

Ten Ways to Pioneer in Marketing

By: Ray Mithun

1. You can pioneer a unique, *first-of-its-kind product:*
    - the first computer
    - penicillin
    - the first microwave oven
    - the first product for home pregnancy tests
    - the first laundry detergent (Tide)
2. You can pioneer a *product improvement*:
    - Duncan Hines Cookie Mix, the first product in this category with a special packet of liquid vegetable oil in its cookie mix
    - Boeing's 757 aircraft
    - Raytheon's Patriot Missiles
    - Gillette Sensor Razor Blades
    - Ziplock Bags
3. You can pioneer a *new package* or a *packaging improvement*:
    - dispensing packages for Scotch Tape
    - packages with handles, such as Downy fabric softener
    - the fruit juice line named "Juice in a Box"
4. You can pioneer a type of *distribution* new to an industry:
    - fast-food chains (probably the first of these chains was the White Castle hamburger outlets)
    - Federal Express's *new,* lower cost distribution system under which they pick up the mail in the afternoon and deliver it to the destination the next morning
5. You can pioneer the way your product is positioned (see Chapter 15):
    - Carnival Cruises for people who like to have fun
    - Marlboro cigarettes (originally a cigarette for *women*), now the largest

cigarette seller, repositioned as the cigarette for outdoor-loving *men*

6. You can pioneer a new *product use:*
   - » Arm and Hammer baking soda as a refrigerator deodorizer
   - » Philadelphia cream cheese for use in cake frostings, and now as a substitute for butter or margarine
   - » Stove Top Stuffing instead of potatoes

7. You can pioneer in *pricing:*
   - » Cub Foods lower supermarket prices and excellent quality
   - » the *high*-priced Polo brand of Ralph Lauren

8. You can pioneer in *customer service*:
   - » Betty Crocker Kitchens
   - » the AARP health-insurance program for senior citizens

9. You can pioneer in *sales promotion:*
   - » McDonald's Dick Tracy promotion
   - » Super Bowl promotions
   - » frequent-flyer programs
   - » rebates on new car purchases.

10. You can pioneer in *advertising* with TV commercials:
    - » Nike athletic commercials
    - » Duracell Energizer batteries, with their animated commercials demonstrating "They keep on going and going and going"
    - » The Prudential commercials featuring a young married couple whose problems always have a happy ending, as in the movies of yesteryear
    - » Bartles & James wine cooler advertising, made memorably different by two colorful personalities

When you pioneer in one or more of the first nine ways listed above, you provide pioneering values for *your advertising.*

So in an important sense, this "marketing" philosophy is also an "advertising" philosophy.

Almost anyone can write a pretty good ad if he or she has a pioneering advantage to work with.

If you're among the many who consider Procter & Gamble one of the finest marketers of consumer

When you pioneer in one or more of the first nine ways listed above, you provide pioneering values for *your advertising*.

So in an important sense, this "marketing" philosophy is also an "advertising" philosophy

goods in America (see Chapter 17), you'll be interested to know that for years the company taught its marketing people to use a number of the same principles listed above to build pioneering values for the marketing of its products—product improvements, packaging improvements, sales promotion, and advertising advantages.

CHAPTER 13

Why Pioneering Ideas are Usually the Best Ideas

By: Al Whitman

In the previous chapter, we discussed a marketing philosophy, under the title "Ten Ways to Pioneer." This marketing philosophy was used by Ray Mithun (the author of six chapters in this book) as a marketing and advertising philosophy for his advertising agency and its many clients.

When an advertiser pioneers a new product or product improvement or a new use or a new form of consumer service, it gives the creative writer a huge advantage. It gives them something to say that no other advertiser in the industry can offer.

> When Procter & Gamble created a special packet of vegetable oil to go into Duncan Hines cookie mixes, it made a product far superior to any cookie mix ever marketed before.
>
> When General Mills created Betty Crocker and her kitchens, it created a new, wanted consumer service concept.
>
> When 3M created Scotch Tape dispensers, it created another wanted benefit.

When you have pioneering advantages like these to work with, it's almost impossible not to be able to come up with advertising that works

When you have pioneering advantages like these to work with, it's almost impossible not to be able to come up with advertising that works.

CHAPTER 14

A Few Important Creative Thoughts and Convictions of David Ogilvy

By: Al Whitman

A year or two before I retired from Campbell-Mithun, Ray Mithun invited David Ogilvy, head of the famous New York agency Ogilvy & Mather, to make a presentation to our creative department, plus a few of the agency's top executives. Using a series of slides that he had prepared for his own agency, Ogilvy made an excellent presentation, of which certain points stand out in my memory.

The most interesting and probably the most valuable was a list of key words for use in headlines. Here's a partial list:

- Amazing
- Bargain
- How to
- New
- Sale
- Wanted
- Announcing
- Free
- Introducing
- Now
- Suddenly

I also remember that one word, which I thought belonged on this list was missing, i.e., the word "Only."

Ogilvy stressed that the two *most powerful* words to use in headlines are *free* and *new*

Ogilvy stressed that the two *most powerful* words to use in headlines are *free* and *new*.

Other points he made included the following:

a. The headline is the most important element in an advertisement.

b. A change in headline can make a big difference in the sales effectiveness of an ad.

c. Every headline should promise the consumer a benefit (see Chapter 11).

d. Use easy-to-understand words, short sentences, and short paragraphs.

e. Write colloquially — as if you're talking to a friend face to face.

f. Most good headlines contain at least eight words.

g. Don't be afraid to write longer headlines (see Ogilvy's famous ad for Rolls Royce, shown below) or long copy. Use whatever number of words you think are needed to do the job, and break up your copy with subheads.

AUTHOR'S NOTE: If you don't know who David Ogilvy is, here's some information about him.

1. He was one of the great creative writers and leaders of all time.

2. He authored many famous campaigns, including:
    » Hathaway shirts (featuring the man with the eye patch).
    » The campaign that introduced Schweppes to America.
    » A famous campaign on Puerto Rico.
    » Campaigns for Dove Soap and Pepperidge Farm Bread.

    I don't know if he wrote the famous "bubbling percolator" television commercials for Maxwell House Coffee (see Chapter 38), but he was the agency's creative leader when it was created and produced.

3. At different times Ogilvy was a chef in a well-known Paris hotel and ran a well-known research organization specializing in motion pictures.

4. He was the author of at least three books, including the well-known, "Confessions of an Advertising Man," published in 1963.

5. Last, but not least, he was elected to the Advertising Hall of Fame in 1976.

Ogilvy believed that the ad shown on the right with 18 words in the headline was one of the finest ads he ever wrote. He stated that after the chief engineer at Rolls Royce read the ad, he commented, "We'll have to do something about that damn clock!"

"At 60 miles an hour the loudest noise in this new Rolls-Royce comes from the electric clock"

CHAPTER 15

The Importance of Creating Alternate Positions for New Products or Services

By: Al Whitman

What Is a "Position"?

When we speak of alternative "positions" for a brand or service, or of "positioning" a brand, what do we really mean?

You won't find the answer in a dictionary. Perhaps the closest dictionary definition of "position" is "a point of view."

Here's the author's definition:

> A position for a product or service is how a customer perceives the product or service when he or she uses it, sees it in the store, or reads or hears about it in an advertisement.

The way the customer perceives the product or service can come from a number of elements:

a. The name of the product or service

b. The package

c. The product's qualities

d. The product's benefits

e. The product's uses

f. Occasions when the product or what it makes should be used

A Simple Example

Let's consider a box of cake mix.

Because of its name, you understand the food *category* in which it belongs. From the name and picture on the box you know the brand and the *flavor*.

If it makes a product claim on the package front, you know at least one benefit it offers. The instructions on the package tell you how to make it.

With a familiar product like a cake mix, its been "positioned" in your mind as So-and-So's brand of cake mix in a familiar or a brand-new flavor.

But what about a *brand-new* product or service? It's *this* kind of product or service that this chapter is all about.

When you think about the new product or service for the first time, you examine:

- alternative markets for a product — that is, different groups of people who might be most interested in it.

- alternative names for the product or services

- alternative packaging possibilities

- alternative benefits

- alternative uses and occasions for using the product or service

When you think about the new product or service for the first time, examine alternative ways to position it

Other Examples of Alternative Positions

Let's consider a new premium coffee and examine some alternative positions.

Here are some "people" alternatives:

- For people over 65

- For people who want a mild coffee

- For people who drink their coffee black

- For people who drink six or more cups per day

Here are some alternative names:

_____'s party coffee

_____'s (brand) Colombian coffee.

_____'s roaster-fresh coffee.

_____'s finely ground coffee.

Here are some alternative *packages:*

- Vacuum-packed in tins

- Vacuum-packed in cardboard

- Freeze-dried coffee

- Whole bean coffee packaged in a paper bag and "dated" (to be ground at home)

Here are some alternative benefits:

- For friendly stimulation

- Picks you up; never lets you down

- Gives you fresher coffee every time

- Makes 15 percent more cups per pound

- Makes the kind of coffee guests will rave about

Here are some alternative uses and serving occasions:

- Makes delicious *iced* coffee
- As a flavoring for cakes or ice cream
- For drop-in guests
- For coffee breaks
- For after-dinner coffee

The above examples were quickly arrived at. None are new or even very inventive, but they do dramatize that there are alternative ways to position almost every new product or service.

The important thing is to find the best alternatives and then the *single best* way to position the brand or service. Later in this chapter we show you how to accomplish both goals.

Why Position Your Product and What Are You Looking For?

You're looking for the one best way to make prospective customers think, "That's *my* kind of product or service".

You examine alternative names and packaging possibilities, benefits, uses, and occasions for use because there usually are several *options* in each category. The ones you want are those that most prospects can relate to.

At Campbell-Mithun, we had our own way of arriving at alternative positions, which could be described as follows:

Think of the product as a certain kind of product for *certain kind of people.* Specify the kind of product or the kind of people. Example: This is a mild Colombian coffee (type of product) designed for people who like their coffee black (a certain kind of people). Or think of the way Procter & Gamble used to describe a certain kind of people for whom they advertised their Gleem toothpaste years ago: "For people who can't brush their teeth after every meal."

Or, arrive at a position by examining alternative uses:

This is a certain kind of product designed for breakfast.

> "Position" a brand in the minds of prospective customers so they'll think, "That's *my* kind of product or service," and will want to try it.

Again, describe the kind of product and list alternative potential uses. Example: This is an all-purpose baking mix that makes it easy to make wonderful homemade biscuits, pancakes, or waffles (types of uses).

Or describe a certain kind of product designed to be used for a *specific occasion.* Example: This blueberry muffin mix (type of product) is designed to make muffins for serving any time you serve coffee (a specific occasion).

Or describe a specific kind of product that offers a specific kind of customer *benefit.* Example: You get richer, moister cakes (specific benefit) when you use our cake mix with pudding in the mix (specific kind of product).

In groups of five or six creative people, we would go through the exercises of filling in statements like these with alternative kinds of people, uses, occasions, and benefits. We might come up with 10 or 15 different "positions" that we thought would be practical. Then we would go to the consumer and learn which position he or she preferred.

Very often one position would come out far ahead of any other. We use this information for new products to help determine product name, the way the package should be illustrated, and the kind of advertising that should be prepared to dramatize the position. Finally, we would put the selling idea, such as "for people who drink coffee black," on the package.

How to Choose the "One Best" Position

Some years ago a client gave an agency a new product assignment. The product was powdered drink mix with a wide variety of flavors. To make the product, all you had to do was add water. The product was designed to appeal to both adults and children. The basic flavors were lemon, orange, lime, pineapple, and cherry.

We could take liberties with these flavors to enable us to use a unique name or design or to make it more fun or different from the competition. Our new product team was made up of highly creative writers and account people.

Here's what the team did:

1. Created alternative names for the line of products and alternative names for each individual flavor in each product line.

    The fundamental position was built around a fairly orthodox name.

    Under this position, the line was named "Tart 'N Tangy."

2. A package design and TV story board were prepared for each line.

    The illustration on the package front was of two glasses with fruit slices and a bowl of ice alongside it.

    The line name appeared on the top of the package and the flavor at the bottom.

    All alternative positions were measured against "Tart 'N Tangy."

3. There were five alternative positions.

    A. A line called Colonel Q, a "Smashingly Sour" drink mix.

        The major illustration on the package for this line and for the advertising was a typical colonial British officer called Colonel Q.
        Here were the flavors in this line.

        • East Injah Orange
        • Calcutta Cooler
        • Ruddy Red Smash
        • Liverpool Lime

    B. The next line was called Forbidden Fruit, a fairly sophisticated position featuring five devil- may- care flavors:

        • Sinfully Sour Lemon
        • Sinfully Sour Red Berry
        • Sinfully Sour Lime
        • Sinfully Sour Pineapple Coconut
        • Sinfully Sour Orange

    C. The next alternative position was a young adult position. The line name was Take Five, and was described as having a big driving taste that would cut across your thirst. We don't remember the specific flavor names but they were in character with the line name.

D. The next alternative was given the name "Seven Seas." It was a romantic position featuring exciting drinks from faraway places. The flavors were named:

- Hong Kong Lime Cooler
- Tangier Lemon Tingle
- Singapore Red Sender
- Samoan Coco Sling
- Rio Orange Ricky

4. To select the best position, the research was carried out with carefully selected groups of women. Each was shown a copy of the package, a typical ad, and a TV story board. Each was given a list of alternative names in each line.

Using Tart 'N Tangy as the "control," each line was compared against it and each person in the research group rated each position against Tart 'N Tangy.

That concept was arbitrarily given a rating of 5, on a scale of 1 to 10. The clear-cut winner was Seven Seas.

We wish we could tell you that Seven Seas was a smashing success. Actually, after plans were made to introduce it in test markets, a decision was made by the client to introduce Funny Face drinks instead (see Chapter 30).

Another Example of Positioning

The owner and manager of one of the nation's fastest growing property and casualty insurance companies uses a formula like this to get business:

1. Offer rock-bottom prices.
2. Minimize risk by avoiding the upscale market.
3. Sell policies direct to consumers.
4. Refuse to sell to owners of expensive cars such as Rolls Royce, Porsche or BMW. Go for the Chevy, Ford, Plymouth, and

small Buick owners, and go for people who've been with their company for many years.

This company, which operates primarily in the South Carolina market, has earned an average 23 percent rate on equity for some time.

Each day 2,500 callers seek lower auto and home insurance rates that will save them money.

The company not only steers clear of insuring expensive cars but avoids people with poor driving records and those who've never carried auto insurance before.

NOTE FROM AUTHOR: The United States Marine Corps has always believed in "positioning." This is evident from the kind of television advertising the corps runs, along the lines of "We have openings for a few good men."

What the Marine Corps is saying in these commercials is obvious. When it comes to the fighting services, the Marine Corps is positioning itself as the creme de la creme. They are suggesting to the listener that service in the corps is a great privilege.

Position a product or service one way, and it can lay an egg. Position it another way and it can be a howling success.

Summary

Creating alternative positions for a product or service is one the the most important elements in a good marketing plan, particularly for new or improved products and services. If you position a product or service one way it can lay an egg. Position it another way and it can be a howling success.

CHAPTER 16

When and How to "Reposition" An Existing Product

By: Al Whitman

When you've had an existing product on the market for several years and perhaps sales are leveling out or going down, it's a good idea to examine the possibilities of creating a *new position* for that product. Sometimes you go through the same system as described in the previous chapter for arriving at alternative positions for new products. At other times a certain type of repositioning makes good sense.

Here are a couple of examples and a story.

There's a product on the market today called Snowy Bleach. This product is white powdered bleach you put in the washing machine when you wash clothes. Initially, the product was introduced years ago and positioned as a "fine fabrics bleach" to wash and bleach delicate washables, such as slips, undies, and bras in the washbowl in the bathroom.

After a few years on the market, during a marketing strategy board meeting at Campbell-Mithun, we came up with the idea of repositioning the product's use to bleach clothes *in the washing machine.* This new use called for the use of far more bleach than the tablespoon called for washing fine fabrics in the washbowl.

When we printed the line "The One Right Bleach for Automatic Washing Machines" on the front of the package, sales went up 15 percent

The result of the repositioning effort was an almost instant increase in sales. In fact, when we printed the line "The One Right Bleach for Automatic Washing Machines" on the front of the package, sales went up 15 percent. This increase took place *before* advertising of the new use was initiated.

Another example: The product Listerine has been repositioned again and again. At one time as a gargle and disinfectant for colds. Another for bad breath. Another for getting rid of dandruff. Today its latest position is for gingivitis.

A Specific Example of Repositioning

When we taught repositioning in seminars at Campbell-Mithun, I used a little story that helped people understand and remember the concept.

A company had a number of salesmen, one of whom was very clearly at the bottom of the list. The sales manager called him in and told him that if he didn't find a way to change his method of selling, he'd be fired. The sales manager gave him three months to improve.

Before the three months were up, the salesman had become *number one* in sales for the company. The sales manager called him in and asked him the secrets of his success. The salesman replied that he had discovered a magic word. The word was "fantastic."

He explained to the sales manager that when a customer, a golfer, told him he had shot a 73 over the weekend, and the salesman knew he'd never come close to breaking 80, the salesman exclaimed "That's fantastic."

When another customer bragged about catching a four-and-a-half-pound small mouth bass when it was known the lake contained only *large* mouth bass, the salesman said he'd say, "That's fantastic."

When a third customer brought up the three different women he said he'd dated over the weekend, even though the salesman knew this couldn't be true because the customer was so shy with women, he still replied, "That's fantastic."

The sales manager then asked, "What did you *used to say*?"

The salesman responded, "I used to say…'That's bullshit.'"

That's repositioning.

Summary

When sales have run down on an existing product and it needs a shot in the arm, good repositioning can be as important as creating an alternative position is for a new product or a product that has been improved.

CHAPTER 17

Some Ideas Worth Learning from Procter & Gamble's Marketing

By: Al Whitman

Perhaps the greatest compliment that can be paid to a company and its management is to have competitors and suppliers single out the company for its superior marketing. This is the reputation the Procter & Gamble Company has earned for years. The company is probably the greatest marketing organization of fast-turning products in America.

The following is a list of some of the brands Procter & Gamble created or purchased:

TIDE (detergent)	DUNCAN HINES (mixes)
CHEER (detergent)	CRISCO (shortening)
OXYDOL (detergent)	FOLGERS (coffee)
CREST (toothpaste)	PRELL and HEAD & SHOULDERS (shampoo)
PAMPERS and LUVS (diapers)	PRINGLES (potato chips in a can)
PEPTO BISMOL (medicine)	CITRUS HILL (orange juice in a carton)
CHARMIN, WHITE CLOUD, PUFFS (paper products)	

As you can see from this list it's widely and superbly diversified. Its sales in 1990 amounted to $24 billion.

Elements in Procter & Gamble's Marketing

Procter & Gamble has superb product development people working on new products and product improvements. It has a reputation for creating excellent packages and package designs that generally feature selling ideas on the front.

It has a top-notch, well-trained sales organization. It knows as much as or more about sales promotion than the very best market-oriented companies.

It has developed and pioneered many new products, such as:

IVORY SOAP (first floating bar soap)

TIDE (first laundry detergent)

PRELL (first shampoo in a tube)

PRINGLES (first potato chips in a can)

It has also purchased many outstanding companies with long-established successful brands. Among these are Duncan Hines, Pepto Bismol, Noxell (Noxema), Cover Girl Cosmetics, and recently Revlon Cosmetics.

Procter & Gamble has more brands that are number one in the market-place than any other company.

Other Marketing Strengths

Procter & Gamble invests heavily in advertising and marketing. They are the only company I've ever heard of ask, "Are we spending enough?"

For many years, Procter & Gamble has had its own media department, one whose ability is equivalent to or actually surpasses that of most leading advertising agencies.

This department operates through its agencies and does not compete with them. It simply helps them do a better job.

Procter & Gamble invests heavily in advertising and marketing, and is the only company I've ever heard of ask, "Are we spending enough?"

Radio and Television

Procter & Gamble's record in purchasing media has been outstanding over the years.

It pioneered five-times a week daytime radio programs for women, which became known as "soap operas."

And when television came into being in the 1950's it did the same thing for daytime television shows aimed at women.

Its record has been almost as good in its buys for evening shows. Historically it has bought situation comedies and good, clean shows.

Its media department asks its agencies to consider outstanding new shows as soon as they hear about them. When one really appeals to the company, it buys it and makes it available to that brand or those brands that can use it best, even if no such brand is the responsibility of the agency that suggests the show.

In addition to its own media department, Procter & Gamble maintains its own copy department. This department does not tell any agency what to write. It makes suggestions or asks questions.

Like the media department, its responsibility is to be helpful to its agency and to help them do a better job in the company's behalf.

Legal Department

As with many other companies, all advertising copy must be approved by the lawyer in the legal department assigned to the brand.

Compared to other companies, the lawyers at Procter & Gamble work in a different way when they review the legality of proposed advertising. When copy is clearly not legal or when the legality is questionable, they work closely with the product manager and the agency to help them find a way to say what they want to say, but in a legal manner.

In many other companies, the lawyers believe they have done their job when they disapprove the copy.

Procter & Gamble's Marketing Setup

Procter & Gamble started the concept of having the product manager, who works on a single brand, report to a marketing manager, who works on several brands, and in turn reports to a vice president and top manager, who work on many brands.

I believe that Procter & Gamble started the concept of having the product manager, who works on a single brand, report to a marketing manager, who works on several brands, and in turn reports to a vice president and top manager, who work on many brands.

This system was copied by at least one major food company that patterned its marketing department along the same lines as Procter & Gamble. In that company, too, this system has been a great success.

Procter & Gamble's Thoroughness

If you work at an advertising agency on one of Procter & Gamble's many brands, one of the first things you learn about is the company's thoroughness.

We've just explained the line of authority the company uses — the product manager, then the marketing manager, and then the vice president or top manager.

We've also told you about its media service, its helpfulness in making television shows available to whatever brand can use them best, its on-staff copy department, and its legal department.

Procter & Gamble is so thorough that it can be exasperating.

I remember walking into a colleague's office at Benton & Bowles, where I had worked for a time on Ivory Snow, and I found him practically pulling out his hair. When I asked what the problem was, he told me that one of the company's product managers asked him to critique a proposal he wanted to send to his boss.

So he did.

Then, believe it or not, he received a letter that morning asking him to critique the manager's own critique of his original proposal. Of course, the above is an exception and not the rule.

Other Marketing Principles

Perhaps by luck, but we suspect by design, Procter & Gamble has often introduced new products in fields in which a good share of market will produce huge sales and profit for the company.

For example:

- In the laundry detergent field with Tide.
- In the potato chip field with Pringles.
- In the toothpaste field with Crest.
- In the huge diaper market with Pampers and Luvs.

It has also bought leading brands in very substantial markets. Folgers Coffee, Duncan Hines, and Citrus Hill orange juice in a carton are other examples.

The profits P & G has earned over the years must have been quite substantial. In some cases huge.

When you consider P & G's marketing capabilities, it's obvious why only a few companies have been successful in competing with P & G's brands.

It might interest you to know that when we worked on part of their account, one of the most important assignments every product manager was given each year was this:

> Assume your major competitor is going to spare no cost to come up with a marketing

Procter & Gamble has often introduced new products in fields in which a good share of market will produce huge sales and profit for the company

84

Each year every P & G product manager was told to work with his product and packaging people in such a way that his present product would be *obsolete*.

edge over your products, an advantage that would provide marketing superiority for the competitor.

With this in mind, each year every P & G product manager was told to work with his product and packaging people in such a way that his present product would be *obsolete*.

This was the company's way of continually beating competition to the punch and keeping its products out ahead of the field.

When a company comes out with a "new and improved" product that offers important new benefits to the consumer (see Chapter 11), this adds extra power and a pioneer advantage (see Chapter 10) to the advertising and sales promotion.

New Products

When it came to introducing *new* products, the P & G we knew would not permit an introduction into the marketplace unless its entry offered advantages to the consumer in at least *two* marketing categories.

P & G believed the relative success or failure of its products depended partly on the dollar power the company supplied for promotion and, perhaps more importantly, on the power of its marketing plans and strategies and ideas (see Chapter 30).

That's why it has always employed a *well-trained* sales organization—the finest *product development people*, an unusually *gifted marketing* and advertising department, and the best couponing and sampling efforts in the food and soap business.

That's why the company always demanded clear-cut accountability from all its executives and insisted on having all plans put *in writing*.

When it came to attracting marketing personnel, for years P & G got the "cream of the crop" and has always been recognized as the number one training ground for marketing and advertising talent in the United States.

Small wonder P & G has been one of America's leading food, soap and cosmetic manufacturers and marketers since the 1930s.

Three Important Benefits Each Procter & Gamble Agency Receives

One of the benefits the agency and its people receive when it works with P & G is that the company's methods help train the agency and its personnel to be better at marketing and advertising.

The second benefit is that other large advertisers know that any agency P & G appoints to work with them is one of the best in the business. So the fact that it works for P & G is a great selling point for the agency's new business.

Third, P & G usually takes on a new agency only after a great deal of consideration. When it picks an agency, it considers the agency as a partner and never appoints a new agency on a short-term basis.

It wants to "marry" its agency and have it grow with them over a period of time.

An Extra Benefit for Agency People Who Have Worked with the Company

If you've worked on one or more P & G brands for a reasonable period of time, you receive another big advantage. You'll find you're "in demand."

It's easy for an agency to promote a P & G – trained account person to work on another account because of their experience with P & G.

But they are also in demand *without* the agency, i.e. companies who are looking for superbly trained personnel.

In leading agency after agency, you'll find key personnel who worked on P & G brands.

And you'll find many marketing, advertising, and consulting companies run by people who either worked for P & G or as an advertising person who spent some years working on P & G brands.

Conclusion

No one can expect other competitors or non-competitors to be able to match the dollars and marketing power that P & G is able to put behind its brands. But even advertisers who are much smaller can benefit by creating solid marketing plans and strategies based on the fundamentals P & G has used.

You'll find these fundamentals explained in quite a few chapters in this book:

CHAPTER 18

How to Market by Product Lines

By: Al Whitman

In this chapter we talk about another important way American companies use to market and advertise their products, by product lines.

Here are a few examples:

In the food field, all Pillsbury products are marketed under the *Pillsbury* label. So are Campbell's soups and Kellogg products.

The Kraft Company markets most of its products under the name *Kraft,* with a few exceptions, such as Philadelphia cream cheese and Velveeta.

General Foods follows a different philosophy.

It markets its products under *individual* names such as Maxwell House, Yuban and Brim for coffees, Jello, Gaines for dog food, and Post cereals.

General Mills has its own philosophy. It markets its products under several line names such as Cheerios and Total for cereals, Betty Crocker for mixes, and Gold Medal flour. However, there is a difference; both Cheerios and Total have subproducts under each of those two names.

When lines of products are used, there are virtually no companies in the food field that advertise the line *as a line*. They run advertising for each individual product

When lines of products are used, there are virtually no companies in the food field that advertise the line *as a line*. They run advertising for each individual product.

The Proctor & Gamble Company combines philosophies. The products in most of its lines, including Duncan Hines and Ivory, are advertised individually and with other products carrying the same name, giving a free *rub* off. And all or most of its individual products used in the home are marketed under individual brands. For instance, Tide, Oxydol, Crest, Pampers, Luvs, Pringles, Folgers Coffee, and Cover Girl cosmetics, are promoted individually.

What About Product Lines in Non-Food Fields?

One of the smartest marketing moves that any automobile company ever made was the product and pricing strategy employed by General Motors some years ago. The company offered the consumer a series of individual cars ranging from Cadillac (as the most expensive) to Chevrolet (least expensive) with each category *overlapping* the one just above it in price and just below it in price. So you have

Cadillacs

Buicks

Oldsmobiles

Pontiacs

Chevrolets

Geo

Chrysler pursues a different philosophy. It has three lines of regular cars: Plymouth and Dodge plus Jeep and Eagle. There's little difference between the Plymouth and Dodge cars in one line and its counterpart in the other. They all have different names, and each line is sold by separate dealerships. The same is true for Jeep and Eagle.

In the drug field, Tylenol started as a single product, competitive with plain and buffered aspirins. Today there are more Tylenol products, such as Tylenol-Cold, Tylenol-Sinus, and children's Tylenol.

General Electric and Westinghouse appliance divisions are examples of both philosophies of advertising being used. Some of their products are promoted individually; others are supported by more general advertising, which features a selling idea for the names General Electric and Westinghouse.

Finally, in hardware and farm-supply stores you can often find a line of Ortho packages of herbicide-related products. They are packaged in distinctive red and yellow packages. They look like a "line," so they stand out on the shelf.

In department, discount, and appliance stores, you'll find a line of West Bend appliances, such as coffee makers, electric fry pans, and deep fryers. These products are advertised individually and often found in different sections of the store, and the major resemblance in packaging is the name and trademark "West Bend."

The examples above help to illustrate the key marketing principle, that there are many ways to "skin a cat," many ways to persuade people to say "yes."

CHAPTER 19

How To Sell Successfully By Phone

By: Al Whitman

When It's a Pleasure to Use the Phone and When It's Not

The phone is a wonderful invention, probably the greatest means of communicating with friends and relatives that has ever been invented.

It has hundreds of other uses, many of which are highly beneficial and simplify our lives. But there are times when you hate to hear the phone ring.

For example, you're talking to a good friend at his house when the phone rings. He answers, and hears something like this: "Good evening David, my name is Carl McGowan. I represent the Speedy Carpet Co. We have a special offer on rug cleaning and shampooing. Give us your business and we'll save you during our one-week-only sale."

Sounds okay to you? Well, my friend doesn't like to be called "David." He prefers "Dave." But at age 70, he wants to be called "Mister" by someone like Carl McGowan, who is obviously young and whom he doesn't know. The rugs in his home don't need to be cleaned or shampooed and if they did, his wife would be in charge of having them done.

Night after night, people like Dave or you and I get calls like this from people selling products such as light bulbs, house painting, aluminum windows, etc. or from life insurance or real estate people or services such as cutting lawns, washing windows or offering loans.

Perhaps your phone rang last night about half an hour after you'd gone to bed and you heard something like this: "Is this Bill Vincent? You are? Well this is George Carey calling for the XYZ National Committee in Washington, D.C.

"We didn't hear from you last year, but we hope you'll support Senator Smith and send him a gift of five hundred dollars.

Oh, you aren't a member of the XYZ Party. You've never voted for Senator Smith and you've never given any politician five hundred dollars?"

Week after week don't you receive calls like this from both national parties? From Senators and Congressmen? From political parties in your state, city, and county? From council members, etc.?

We're sure you do, and in addition to the piles of junk mail you throw in the wastebasket, you get phone calls from all kinds of financial services offering you a system for making a fortune.

From broker after broker soliciting your purchase of stocks and bonds, T bills and notes. Plus additional calls from banks you'd never use suggesting you buy C.D.'s from them.

Few try to learn what you want or need. Few say something that piques your curiosity or interest. Few suggest specific benefits (see Chapter 11) to you for considering what they have to sell.

When you get calls asking you to buy what you don't want or need, and call after call for political contributions and to help welfare institutions, colleges, and graduate schools, we suspect you then hate the phone and wish it had never been invented.

How Important Is Selling By Phone?

As you can imagine, selling by phone is big business.

It is estimated that each year Americans invest approximately $92 billion in local and long distance phone calls. A large part of these expenditures are involved with the use of 800 numbers to purchase goods and services which are charged to credit cards. During an average year about eight billion phone calls are made by prospective buyers using an 800 number.

Often the charges for handling and postage are included in the price to the person who ordered the product or service that was described in the advertisement or direct-mail letter that contained the 800 number.

On some occasions, the seller used a two-step process to sell goods or services. First, the person interested in the offer used an 800 number to ask in for literature, which is mailed out by the sponsors, usually with an order blank, and sometimes simply with a reminder of the 800 number.

If the prospect wants to buy, he or she simply fills in and mails the coupon and check or money order, or calls the 800 number to place an order.

Why The Cost Of Sales By Phone Are Low Cost Sales

It costs a lot less to sell by phone than to sell with a personal call. Even if you call long distance, the call will probably cost less than $2.00.

Compare these costs to those contained in Chapter 53, "Essential Tips for Selling." The author, who was probably the greatest sales manager the Pillsbury Co. ever had, shows you that the average salesperson selling consumer products can only make two to four calls per day and the average call costs about $16.00. With these low selling costs, no wonder selling by phone has become so popular.

What the Phone Is Used For

1. To raise monies for worthwhile causes and nonprofit organizations (see Chapter 23).

2. To raise monies for schools, colleges, universities, and graduate schools, both public and private.

3. To sell products via 800 numbers:
   » Records
   » Cars
   » Steaks
   » Cassettes
   » Book-of-the month clubs
   » Tickets to sporting events and shows
   » Items in mail-order catalog
   » Premiums

4. To sell financial and other customer services:
   » Life insurance
   » Health insurance
   » Real estate
   » Stocks and bonds
   » Mutual funds
   » Airline tickets
   » Hotel reservations
   » Rent-a-car reservations
   » Banking services, etc.

5. To conduct polls and market research (see Chapter 20).

6. To place orders for products or services featured in direct-mail advertising or in direct-mail letters (see Chapters 46 and 47).

7. In sales promotion projects (see Chapter 2)

8. To pay for products or services charged to credit card companies

A Hypothetical Sales Pitch by Phone to a Small Business Entrepreneur

In using the phone to make a sale, follow the 11 basic principles of marketing:

1. Your product or service must offer good quality and value

2. You must have all the facts about your product (Chapters 5 and 6).

3. You carefully outline what you want to say.

4. Your opening remarks (like a speech; see Chapter 56) must capture the listener's attention.

5. After explaining, tell why you're calling and offer benefits (Chapter 11).

6. Be believable and convincing. Never oversell. Offer proof of the benefits and a solid reason why.

7. If testimonials are available, give a few.

8. Never sound like you're reading what you're saying.

9. Always be prepared to answer objections and sometimes raise and answer possible objections yourself.

10. Before you close, summarize what you've said, particularly the benefits.

11. In closing:

   a. Ask for the order. There are 3 ways to "ask for the order":

      1. The "direct" approach, ie., just ask for the order;

      2. The "assumptive" approach, ie. just assume the prospect will buy;

      3. The "puppy dog" approach, ie. offer a free trial, or money back if not satisfied;

In using the phone to make a sale, follow the 11 basic principles of marketing

  b . If possible, give the listener a good reason to make a deal right now.

Let's suppose I, as the author and publisher of the book HOW TO MAKE PEOPLE SAY "YES", have the job of selling or marketing copies of the book to a small business entrepreneur.

To illustrate how to use the phone properly in a sales pitch, we are going to have a *hypothetical* conversation between myself and a small business owner following the principles explained above.

"Good morning, is this Mr. Egan, the company's president?

"My name is Al Whitman, author of a book that is popular with small business owners. Its title is HOW TO MAKE PEOPLE SAY "YES".

"Many small business owners have used this book to increase their volume and profits.

"You're in the business of selling a unique service to supermarkets, aren't you? And you use food brokers to sell this service?

"In addition to increasing your profits, my book shows you how to differentiate your product or service from your competitors and how to position it in the marketplace.

"There's a chapter on pricing, another on distribution, another on sales promotion, and one on sales incentive plans.

"At least 27 of the chapters are important to small business entrepreneurs such as yourself. There's a great chapter on marketing and the small business owner, two on marketing, one on salesmanship and how to be a good sales manager, one on how to use benefits to make customers and prospects say "yes", two on ideas, several on selling, including how to write a good sales letter and one on how to sell successfully by phone.

"The chapters on sales and sales incentive plans are very authoritative as are other chapters; one on information, two on how to prepare marketing plans, one on 10 ways to pioneer in marketing, one on some ideas from Procter & Gamble, one on publicity and public relations, another on pricing, and one on how products and services are distributed.

"Also, the chapters on direct mail letters, how to motivate people, how to be a good leader, and how to be a great teacher are very good.

"Those are the reasons why so many small business owners have bought this book, as have many small business investment companies, who are using it themselves or buying it to give to their small business clients.

"Perhaps you remember Tom Kleppe who headed the Small Business Administration in Washington, D.C., during the Nixon administration and who was in President Ford's Cabinet as Secretary of the Interior. "After reading this book he described it as 'simply outstanding.'

"In summary, this book has almost 30 chapters written, in large part, for small business owners, to help them make more money, improve their products or services, dramatize differences from competition, and position their company and its products or services in a unique way in the marketplace.

"You may wonder, Mr. Egan, how much this book costs and how you can get it. You can order it in a book store for $29.95, or if you prefer to buy it by calling a toll free 800 number, the cost is $33.00, including postage and handling charges.

"You can get it by calling this number: 000-000-0000 – Dept. SB.

"We guarantee you'll like this book and find it of benefit to you or we'll send you your money back, plus postage.

"So as you can understand, you can't possibly lose.

"How many books would you like to start with, Mr. Egan? The retail price is $29.95. When you order one book via an 800 number you pay $33.00, including postage and handling. You can buy three books for $30.00 per book, a case of twelve books for about $19.00 per book and if you order a case of 36 books, the cost is $12.15 per book.

"Which of these amounts would you want to consider, Mr. Egan?

"So you want to buy three at $30.00 per book. Just call the 800 number as we explained and they'll send your copies out immediately.

"Finally, and this could be important to you, if you place your order immediately, or in the next ten days, we'll reduce the price of each book another $3.00.

"We make this offer simply as an incentive to get you to buy the book as soon as possible.

"Since you already told me you want three copies, why not call 1-800-000-0000 right now and save an extra $3.00.

"Thanks ever so much, Mr. Egan, for listening to my proposal to you. I'm sure you'll love the book and find it helpful. If not, remember you'll get your money back, plus postage, immediately.

"It was nice talking with you, Mr. Egan. Thank you very much."

You'll recall the 11 principles for marketing and using the telephone successfully.

You may have noticed that all of these principles, except one, were followed in this phone conversation.

The one principle about which we said nothing had to do with bringing up and answering objections in advance. We didn't address this because in this instance objections didn't apply.

Three Case Histories on Selling Successfully by Phone

Case History 1

This concerns a chain of hamburger houses operating in seven or eight midwestern states.

This chain was the first fast-food chain to sell hamburgers. It started its business sometime before McDonald's, Burger King, or Wendy's existed.

In its operating territory, the chain sold millions of hamburgers at a relatively low price to customers who came into its stores. It not only has a rushing business on hamburgers, but a huge share of market.

Over the years, the chain's management recognized that many families in its original territory had moved to other states such as California and Florida. It knew this because many former customers living in other states in which the chain did *not* operate wrote in to inquire about whether they could order and receive hamburgers *by mail.*

As a result, the chain had sold several thousand hamburgers a week by mail.

So about 10 or 15 years ago the chain decided to create and sponsor television commercials, each giving an 800 number that people could call to order a minimum number of hamburgers by mail — charging the cost to a credit card.

The chain received more than a million orders a year that were billed at a sizable price, thus giving the chain an extra gross annual profit exceeding $50 million a year.

Case History 2

A major automobile manufacturer made a sales analysis of dealer sales per capita in each dealer's territory in each state. In one midwestern state there were two dealers operating side by side in dealerships that had approximately the same per capita population. One of these dealers ranked *first* in sales in the state and the other ranked *last*. The automobile manufacturer sent one of its top marketing executives to visit these two dealers to see if he could discover why the sales discrepancy existed, particularly in territories right next to one another.

When he returned, he reported that the ability of the dealers was not the reason for the success of the leading company. It was an unusual telephone sales plan that had been developed by one of the salesmen in the dealership which ranked number one.

The salesman had thought of the plan, tested it himself, and then taught it to other salespeople who were on the ball and wanted to increase their sales and were willing to work to do so.

The successful sales technique that the salesman and the number one dealer were using involved selling by phone.

How the Plan Worked

- Step 1 — Each week the dealer's salesman went out on the street and into parking lots and took license numbers of competitive makes of cars that were in good condition because they were only two or three years old and sold for nearly the same retail price as the dealer's comparable car.
- Step 2 — The salesman then went to the appropriate government body and obtained

In one midwestern state there were two dealers operating side by side in dealerships that had approximately the same per capita population. One of these dealers ranked *first* in sales in the state and the other ranked *last*

the names and addresses of the owners of the cars.

- Step 3 — He looked up the phone number and called each of them in the daytime, when the lady of the house would be most likely to be home.

- Step 4 — He talked to each lady along these lines: "I understand you own such-and-such make of car that came on the market in such-and-such year. I actually saw your car the other day at such-and-such parking place and could see it was in better condition than most cars of the same make and age.
  At our dealership we're making excellent offers on cars like these for a limited period. May I suggest that at your convenience I pick up your _____ year old car and replace it for two or three days with our brand new_____ model, which retails for about the same price as a new model of your make.
  You drive our car, fully insured, as though it were your own, and we'll take your car into our shop for a fair inspection and to establish our most favorable trade-in price, which we're sure you'll consider a real bargain.

- Step 5 — For those who agreed, the salesman would phone the lady once again and make an appointment to return the car after dinner at a time when he could talk to her husband as well.
  By this time both the lady and her husband had perceived the superiority of this new car over their older one. So when the salesman gave them a report on their present car's condition and made a trade-in offer, the result was often the sale of the new car.

As a result of the discovery of this plan, the car manufacturer made a movie of this telephone selling plan, using the star salesman, along with several actors in the film. It then took the film throughout the United States and played it for every dealer in the country, hoping that some of the salesmen would adopt this technique for themselves.

It's a beautiful example of a creative idea that depended in large part on phone selling, and it worked like a charm for the car manufacturer.

Case History 3

This book is going to be sold through media advertising and direct-mail letters using an 800 number (see Chapters 46 and 47).

In the market research plan used to get people in a number of occupations to read the book, a laser-printed version of the book and a questionnaire to fill in would be sent to them.

I made a mistake in how I asked people to get their people (salespeople, advertising people, marketing people, small business entrepreneurs) to read the book.

I wrote about 100 such people a letter outlining the benefits of their reading it. With the letter I enclosed a self-addressed, stamped postcard on which they were asked to check "yes" or "no" as to whether they would or wouldn't read the book and fill out the questionnaire. After doing so, we asked each to mail the postcard back.

This letter was written on my personal stationery and bore my name on the letterhead. I later discovered, much too late in the process, that the recipients never heard of A.R. Whitman, so quite a number threw the letter into the wastebasket.

Originally I had planned to use the telephone as a way of getting readers to read the book and fill out the questionnaire, but concluded it would be too costly and would require too many call-backs, mostly at long-distance, daytime rates.

I couldn't have been more wrong.

At the tail end, I called 16 different people by phone: 5 advertising creative directors, 2 advertising managers, 4 account supervisors, an agency president, the president of Metropolitan Life Insurance Company, and several heads of small business investment companies plus a well-known automobile company owner's spokesman for his company. Without exception, all agreed to read the book.

I shudder to think of the effort wasted by using the mail instead of the phone.

The phone was not only three or four times as productive, but much more successful in accomplishing our research objectives

The phone was not only three or four times as productive, but much more successful in accomplishing our research objectives.

Obviously in this case we have illustrated the meaning of telecommunications by showing how to sell successfully by telephone.

CHAPTER 20

William D. Wells, Executive Vice President and Director of Market Research Services for DDB — Needham Advertising Agency in Chicago.

Bill is one of the industry's leading marketing and research authorities, and is the only representative of the advertising business elected to the Attitude Research Hall Of Fame.

He received an M.A. and PH.D from Stanford University, and was a professor of Psychology at Rutgers and Professor of Psychology and Marketing at the University of Chicago.

A consultant to Leo Burnett and Benton & Bowles, Bill has authored over 60 books and articles.

How and When to Use Market Research

By: William Wells

Whether you're introducing a new product, repositioning an old product, or defending your market share, your decisions will be improved by information about the 3 Cs—your company, your competitors, and your customers.[1]

The first C includes your company's history, marketing philosophy, and marketing resources.

It also includes current, accurate, and objective feedback about how current and prospective customers evaluate your brands.

The second C includes comparable information about your competitors. Most importantly, it also includes the strengths and weaknesses of all the brands that compete directly with yours.

The third C includes customers' buying habits, financial resources, attitudes, and preferences. If you're going to make customers say "yes", you'll need in-depth understanding of how they decide whether and what to buy.

Getting information about the 3 Cs is the task of market researchers.

When market research is timely and accurate, and when it focuses exactly on the problem at hand, it gives you a strategic advantage over competitors who are not equally prepared.

Information about the 3 Cs comes from three major sources:

1. Many companies maintain large, professional *market research departments.* Even though some of these departments were reduced during the downsizing of the 1980s, they still remain an important source of marketing intelligence.

---

[1]   Kenichi Ohmae, *The Mind of the Strategist*, New York: Penguin Books, 1982.

2. Some advertising agencies and public relations firms maintain fine research departments. Professionals in these departments can provide outside perspective, information, and advice.

3. Today, however, the most important 3C information source is the *research supplier industry.* The companies in this industry range in size from A.C. Nielsen, with more than 4,500 employees in the United States alone, to hundreds of one-person research and consulting firms.

   Research suppliers also vary greatly in competence and expertise. Some specialize in computer-based analysis of government statistics. Others specialize in collection and syndication of market data. Some specialize in large-scale surveys that attempt to uncover all the factors that influence choices among brands. Others specialize in small- scale, intense, qualitative investigations of consumers' personalities, habits, attitudes, and beliefs.

Directories of Research

The most inclusive general directory of research suppliers is the "Greenbook"—the *International Directory of Marketing Research Companies and Services,* published by the American Marketing Association. This directory includes the names, addresses, and telephone numbers of virtually all the major research firms, along with names of their principals and lists of their services. A similar, less inclusive directory is published by the American Association of Public Opinion Research. This directory can be obtained from the Association's New York headquarters.

When you're selecting a research supplier, these directories can provide a rough first cut, but they cannot substitute for direct experience. Like doctors, lawyers, accountants, and electricians, research suppliers differ greatly in personality and work style. The right supplier can make your life much easier. The wrong supplier can be worse than no supplier at all.

The best source of information about a research supplier is the supplier's reputation. Because marketing research is a close-knit service industry, satisfied and dissatisfied customers are more than willing to talk in detail about how suppliers have performed.

In seeking 3C information, engaging the wrong research supplier is the second-biggest error you can make. The biggest error is asking the wrong research question. One wrong question is, "Let's find out as much as we can about X"—X being a product or service, a competitor or a customer.

Market research has only one valid justification

The right question comes in two parts: (1) "What decisions am I going to make?" and (2) "What information will change those decisions?" This is the right question because marketing research has one and only one valid justification: *to affect significant decisions.* "Nice to know," "generally interesting," or "possibly useful some time in the future" might be valid reasons for academic research, but they are not valid reasons for investing the marketing resources of your firm.

Start your market research by specifying the decisions that need to be made and the information needed to make those decisions

How To Start Your Market Research Projects

If a marketing research project is started *at the back end,* by first specifying the decisions that'll be affected, and then identifying the exact information that'll affect those decisions, then practically all the information collected in the course of the project will turn out to be useful.

If the project is started in the traditional fashion, by attempting to "find out as much as possible" about a general topic, then many of the findings, though "interesting" in some general sense, will not be used because no one will be able to figure out what to do with them. Furthermore, when a research project is started in the usual way, potentially critical information will often turn out to be missing.

Here's a specific example. The title of this book is *How to Make People Say "Yes".* Translated into a marketing strategy question, that title might be, How Can I Increase My Market Share? Let's suppose you're a food marketer. A marketing research project designed in the traditional fashion would attempt to isolate prospective purchasers and then "find out as much as possible" about how they decide what and when to buy. Such a project might well reveal, for instance, that price is very important, and that one of the principal reasons for brand choice is "It tastes better."

Suppose further, as often is the case, that price cuts are instantly met by competitors, and that taste is now as good as it can get, within existing technological limitations. In this rather typical situation, a finding that price and taste are key motivators, though valid, would not be of much help.

Suppose, on the other hand, that the package is going to be redesigned, and you can make a change in the advertising. A project designed from the back end, focused on decisions that actually can be made, might measure consumers' reactions to new package concepts or to new advertising ideas. Even without being absolutely conclusive, results from this "backward" approach to market research would surely be more relevant than the results of a shotgun effort to "find out as much as possible" about the customer and the brand.

The single most important requirement for any 3C project is to start at the back end, to *focus on the decisions that the project can affect* and to focus on those decisions exclusively.

Even though this rule may seem so obvious as to be trivial, it's often violated. Even today, far too many very expensive marketing research projects are designed without a clear end use in mind.

Quantitative vs. Qualitative Research Methods

A second critical distinction in 3C research has to do with the distinction between "quantitative" and "qualitative" methods.

Quantitative methods include large-scale surveys, large-scale field experiments and tests in which consumers react to marketing stimuli (such as packages or advertisements) under relatively controlled conditions. The key results of quantitative projects are usually expressed in numbers.

Qualitative methods include focus groups (a group of carefully selected people, usually interviewed together in a single room), individual "depth" interviews and various indirect approaches to understanding consumers' attitudes and personalities.

The single most important requirement for any market research project is to start at the back end, to *focus on the decisions that the project can affect* and to focus on those decisions exclusively

The key results of qualitative projects are usually expressed in words rather than statistics.

Quantitative methods lay claim to being "scientific," largely because a substantial body of technical knowledge underpins the sampling and statistical procedures these methods employ. The "scientific" aura is especially important when research is liable to be challenged, as when it's presented as evidence in litigation, or when it's used to sell media to advertisers.

By contrast, qualitative methods are much less formal. Inspired in part by the theories and techniques of psychotherapy, most of the qualitative methods are disarmingly understandable. When qualitative researchers want to find out what people think about some topic, they ask them, sometimes directly and sometimes indirectly, If they don't fully understand the answer, they ask them again in some other way.

Qualitative methods have often been criticized as being "unscientific" and "not real research." Nevertheless, they continue to grow in popularity, and they now influence many day-to-day marketing decisions.

In part, this popularity is due to time and cost. A few focus groups may take only a few weeks and cost less than $10,000. A large-scale survey may require several months and run into the hundreds of thousands of dollars. In these days of tight budgets and quick decisions, time and cost constraints alone will often favor qualitative over quantitative work.

The most important advantage of the qualitative approach harks back to the "backward" versus "frontward" distinction. Most qualitative projects focus on immediate decisions. Being designed backward, they seem and often are directly relevant.

But the popularity of qualitative methods goes considerably beyond time and cost considerations. The results of qualitative projects are usually presented in respondents' *own words,* a mode of presentation that makes them seem real, immediate, and easy to understand.

By contrast, the results of quantitative projects are often presented in *lifeless tables,* complete with obscure statistics and arcane symbols. The format difference alone tends to make qualitative studies seem easier to work with.

The most important advantage of the qualitative approach harks back to the "backward" versus "frontward" distinction discussed earlier. Most qualitative projects focus on immediate decisions.

Being designed backward, they seem and often are directly relevant. By contrast, a great many quantitative projects attempt to be comprehensive, and they end by not being directly relevant to much of anything.

This is not to say that quantitative methods have no value. When small differences have major consequences, as when a decision depends upon an exact market share, or when the fate of a TV program depends upon its Nielsen rating, projectionable statistics are absolutely necessary. And even the most quantitative of quantitative projects can be designed to have immediate effect. In deciding between the qualitative and the quantitative approach, the basic question is, as always (1) What decisions are going to be made? and (2) What information will bear on those decisions most directly?

The title of this chapter is *"How and When to Use Market Research."* In a general sense, the "when" is fairly obvious: You should use market research whenever information about the 3Cs will help you make the difficult and complex decisions that marketers must make. But in the specific case, the matter is not quite that simple. Marketing research is never without cost, and sometimes it can be very expensive. The real issue is the cost of getting relevant information versus the cost of making a specific error. While you can never calculate that trade-off exactly, you should never ignore it. Some decisions are so consequential that even a large research investment will pay off, providing timely and decisive information can in fact be made available. But many decisions are relatively trivial. They don't need research. And still other decisions, though important, are irrevocable. They don't need research either. In either of these cases, research is a waste of scare resources that should be invested in some other way.

Always Plan Your Research Backwards

The single most important guide to the "how" part of "How and When to Use Market Research" is *research backward!* Start with a set of near-term decisions, and focus exclusively upon obtaining the information that will influence those decisions one way or another. That way of looking at the problem will show whether you can get along with relatively

The single most important guide to the "how" part of "How and When to Use Market Research" is *research backward!*

inexpensive secondary data, or whether you must go out and collect new data. If you need new data, it will tell you whether qualitative or quantitative information will offer more help. And, once the method is selected, it will focus the questions on the most critical answers, thereby cutting sharply into time and cost.

Market research is not an act of faith; it is a business proposition. As with any other business proposition, you need to think very carefully about exactly what you really need, and then seek out the most efficient way of bringing that about.

Note: The market research program for this book (mailing a preliminary version and a questionnaire to about 100 people who are in occupations for which this book was written) was designed "backwards" to accomplish certain objectives.

One was to obtain helpful comments about the contents of the book plus suggestions for improving it. Those received resulted in our improving the quality of the book. This was our number one marketing objective. Another was to obtain information that could be used in selling the book via direct-mail letters and mail-order advertising.

CHAPTER 21

The What, When, and How of Copy Testing

By: William D. Wells

It is natural for advertisers to long for reassurance: "What will I get for all that money? How do I know that a different campaign might not have provided a higher return on my investment?"

It may be hard to believe, but a television commercial costs as much as $175,000 or more to produce. If the commercial appears on network television, its sponsor may put several million dollars behind it. Even though print ads don't cost quite as much, they can still consume a major share of marketing resources.

With costs that high, it is natural for advertisers to long for reassurance: "What will I get for all that money? How do I know that a different campaign might not have provided a higher return on my investment?"

Those questions are the motivation for copy testing.

The best possible kind of reassurance would be an accurate prediction of sales effectiveness — before thousands have been spent on final production and millions have been spent on media.

Advertisers can long for such decisive reassurance, but they can't get it. Despite occasional claims to the contrary, no copy test can accurately predict sales effectiveness.

If advertisers can't have an accurate prediction of sales effectiveness, what can they have? They can have several quite different kinds of copy tests, any of which, depending upon total real cost, can prove to be a good investment.

After the Fact Measurements

Among the oldest copy tests are direct, after-the-fact measures of sales effectiveness. A mail-order coupon is placed in a print ad, or an 800 number is placed in a television commercial and sales records show exactly how much revenue each ad generated.

Sometimes, alternative versions of print ads are "split run" in alternative copies of magazines or newspapers, or alternative versions of television commercials are "split run" on alternate days of daily television programs. This procedure compares the pulling power of the advertisements while holding constant the effect contributed by the media.

When the sale is less direct—as when a print ad or television commercial is intended to persuade the prospect to request further information—a coupon, an 800 number, or an offer hidden in a print ad's body copy can provide an excellent index of the ad's ability to meet its objective.

Valuable as they are, all these measures do come after the fact. The cost of creating finished ads has been incurred, as have all the (much greater) costs of running the ads in the media. Although these after-the-fact tests are useful scorecards and can help guide development of subsequent advertising, they do not provide what advertisers want most: accurate *predictions* of sales effectiveness.

Predictive Copy Tests

Among the predictive copy tests, two of the oldest are based on the plausible assumption that, if an advertisement is to have any effect at all, it must make some impression on the prospect's memory. The object, therefore, is to gain access to a sample of prospects, expose them to an advertisement, and then examine their memories.

Recall Tests

One memory test depends upon recall. Some time after exposure to an advertisement, prospects are contacted—often by telephone—and asked which advertisements they remember. Respondents who can remember the advertisement being tested are counted toward the advertisement's "unaided recall" score. Respondents who can't remember are prompted with the brand name. If they can remember after this prompt, they are counted toward the advertisement's "aided recall" score. Respondents who claim either "unaided" or "aided" recall are asked further questions about the advertisement's content. If their answers indicate that they remember the ad being tested, and not some other ad, they are counted toward the ad's "proven recall" score.

In recall tests of TV commercials, ad exposure can take many forms. The ads may appear on regular television channels in test cities. They may be seen on cable television by prerecruited panels of respondents. They may be shown to large audiences in theaters, or to small groups gathered around television sets. The settings and the methods of contact all influence the reliability and validity of the results.

In recall tests of print ads, the ads may appear in regular magazines, with test interviews in homes after respondents have had an opportunity to read the magazine under normal conditions. Or the ads may be "tipped in" to special test magazines, with the test interview occurring some time later. Again, methods affect outcomes. Recall test scores generated by different contact and interviewing methods are not interchangeable.

An advertiser who uses a recall test will need to answer two vital questions. First, is the test reliable? That is, when the same ad is tested over and over again, do the recall scores remain consistent, or do they jump around at random due to measurement errors that occur in the course of testing? Some recall testing systems are quite reliable; they yield virtually the same score every time. Others are quite unreliable; their scores jump around so much that score differences from test to test are almost as great as differences between advertisements.

Reliability

Some recall testing systems are quite reliable. Others are not

The reliability question can be answered only by skeptical examination of past work by the research supplier. It is a vital question because an unreliable copy test has negative worth. An unreliable copy test will not improve copy decisions, it will consume valuable resources, and it will demoralize the professionals who created the advertising.

The other question recall test users need to ask is "Do I really want a high recall score?" The recall test gives high scores to hard-sell ads with memorable characters like Charmin's notorious Mr. Whipple, and it gives low scores to soft-sell image-building ads that depend on positive emotion. Advertisers who want advertising that their customers will like should not use a recall test to select their advertisements for them.

Recognition Tests

The other common memory test depends on the respondent's ability to recognize rather than recall the ad. In a recognition test of print ads, respondents who have had an opportunity to look through a magazine at home are taken through the magazine again, one page at a time, and asked whether they noticed each ad previously. Respondents who say they had noticed the ad are asked whether they saw the part of the ad that identified the advertiser, and whether they read most of the body copy.

This procedure produces three recognition scores: "noted," "seen-associated," and "read most." Compared with recall scores of magazine ads, recognition scores are generally higher. They also tend to discriminate between ads somewhat better and to be less sensitive to random measurement error.

In the TV version of the recognition test, respondents receive, through the mail, questionnaires that show key frames and dialogue from commercials that have recently appeared on television. The questionnaire asks respondents whether they remember having seen each of these commercials on the air. If respondents claim recognition, the questionnaire asks them to complete a brief adjective checklist giving their reactions. This test produces both a recognition score for each ad and a brief evaluation.

Compared with recall tests, recognition tests are not as likely to favor hard-sell advertisements. Recognition test respondents who say they remember seeing an ad are also saying, "Yes, I usually notice ads like this." Compared with recall tests, recognition tests are less likely to eliminate ads that appeal to positive emotions.

Costs of Recall and Recognition Tests

Recall and recognition tests differ greatly in cost. Recall tests of television commercials cost between $12,000 and $20,000, depending upon the details of the methodology and the nature of the sample. Print recall tests range from $10,000 to $17,000 per ad. Recognition tests of television commercials cost about $7,500 per commercial, and recognition tests of print ads cost about $1,000 per ad.

Recall and recognition tests also differ in stage of finish required. Depending upon exactly how the test is conducted, some recall tests accept rough print ads or "animatic" versions of TV commercial executions. Others require finished advertisements. Recognition tests require that the advertisement has been finished and has run in the media. Thus, the results of some recall tests become available early in the game, while improvements can still be made. Other recall tests, and all recognition tests, come after the fact. They are useful as scorecards, and as guidance for the next round of creative development.

Memory tests measure memory, which is not to be confused with sales effectiveness. Everyone can remember ads for brands they do not purchase; and everyone can remember purchases that have no obvious link to specific advertisements.

Copy Tests

Quite different from memory tests are copy tests, which measure change in attitude or change in intention to purchase. The basic scheme in this approach is to ask respondents, "How much would you like to buy this brand?" then show them an advertisement for the brand, and then ask them, "Now, how much would you like to buy it?"

As with memory tests, executional details differ greatly from one testing company to another. Some testers expose the advertisements in a theater setting. Some use individual interviews in a mall research facility. Some use cable television. Because these details influence the nature of the sample and how respondents interpret the interview, results differ greatly in reliability, and test scores differ greatly in range and level, from one testing company to another. Again, test scores from different testing companies are not interchangeable.

Of all the factors that influence the results of attitude change copy tests, two are most important. First, results depend greatly on whether the commercial is for a new brand or for a brand that is already well known in the market. If the brand is new, the "before" score should be near zero, and one exposure to one advertisement can reasonably be expected to produce a meaningful change in intention to purchase the product.

However, if the brand is well known, the "before" score should not be zero. Consumers already have brand preferences based (at least in part) on personal experience. Under these conditions, one exposure to one commercial is unlikely to produce a large real change in intention to purchase, and any change that does occur is liable to be mostly random measurement error. So, while attitude-change copy tests may be capable of producing dependable findings for new brands, they are unlikely to produce dependable findings for brands that are in widespread use.

The second factor that affects the usefulness of attitude change copy tests is the size and nature of the sample. Results from large samples are more reliable and more representative than results from small samples. Results from users of the product category are worth much more serious attention than are results obtained from nonusers.

Attitude-Change Copy Test

Attitude-change copy tests are relatively costly: $10,000 to $15,000 per commercial. Pressures to keep costs down keep sample sizes undesirably small. As a consequence, aberrations due to random measurement error are an ever-present danger. Cost pressures also increase the temptation to test as many commercials as possible with the same group of respondents. Since users of one product category are not necessarily users of another, a sample of respondents that is exactly appropriate for one commercial may well be entirely inappropriate for at least some of the others.

Although having the right respondents is important in any copy test (including all of the memory test discussed earlier), having the right respondents is critically important when the test asks about intention to purchase. It makes no sense, for example, to ask respondents who do not own dogs about intentions to purchase various brands of dog food, or to ask people who never drink about intentions to purchase various brands of beer. Astonishingly, some copy test suppliers have tried to pretend that this fundamental distinction does not matter!

So, users of attitude change copy tests need to ask themselves two questions:

First, "Is the brand already well known in the market?" If the answer is yes, the results of the test are likely to be subject to excessive amounts of random error. Second, "Are all the respondents in my target audience?" If the answer is no, the results may be virtually meaningless. Users of attitude-change copy tests should also ask themselves, "Is the test executed in such a way that I can take the findings seriously?" Because copy test suppliers differ so greatly from each other, an unannounced personal visit to a testing session will do much to put test results into proper perspective.

What does the ad communicate, and how do consumers react to it?

We have discussed memory tests and attitude-change tests, two of the three major types of copy testing. The third major approach is the "communication and reaction" test. This approach asks, in effect, "What does the ad communicate, and how do consumers react to it?"

Communication and Reaction Tests

In a typical communication and reaction test, respondents are recruited in a shopping mall and interviewed in the mall's research facility. If the screening requirements are hard to meet (e.g., owners of high-priced cars, purchasing agents, frequent air travelers), recruiting may be done ahead of time by telephone.

After having viewed an advertisement, respondents are asked a set of open-end questions, such as:

1. As you were looking at the commercial, what thoughts or ideas went through your mind and what did you feel?

2. Did anything else come to your mind while looking at the commercial?

3. In you own words, please describe *what went on* and *what was said* in the commercial.

4. Do you remember anything else that was said or shown?

5. Besides trying to sell the product, what was the main point of the commercial?

6. What was the name of the product advertised? Please be as specific as possible.

7. Was there anything in this commercial that you found confusing or hard to understand?

8. Was there anything in this commercial that you found hard to believe?

9. What, if anything, did you *like* about this commercial?

10. What, if anything, did you dislike about this commercial?

Respondents may also fill out a set of rating scales intended to pick up any points the open-end questions may have omitted.

Communication and reaction tests address three basic question areas:

- Did the audience get the intended message?

- Did they get any message not intended?

- How did they react to the message, the characters (if any), and the other details of the advertisement?

While answers to these questions are a long way from a quantitative prediction of sales effectiveness, they can be very useful. Advertisers can fail to convey the message they intended. They can also deliver messages they didn't intend to deliver. Such misunderstandings can be costly.

Communication and reaction tests are relatively inexpensive: $3,000 to $5,000 per ad. Although they do not provide all the answers, they do provide valuable insurance.

Moment-to-Moment Testing

Memory tests, attitude-change tests, and communication and reaction tests—all measure reactions to the advertisement as a whole unit. Recently, some copy test suppliers have begun to experiment with moment-to-moment or scene-by-scene evaluations of television commercials, treating the commercial as a series of episodes, like a movie or a play.

In moment-to-moment tests, respondents use computer key-pads or dials to indicate their reactions while viewing the commercial. They may be asked to indicate whether they like or dislike what they are seeing, or whether anything they see makes them want to buy the brand.

The results of moment-to-moment tests are usually presented as line graphs that gradually emerge as the commercials unfold. The peaks and valleys of

Advertisers can fail to convey the message they intended. They can also deliver messages they didn't intend to deliver. Such misunderstandings can be costly

these graphs show how the audience reacted to what was happening on the screen.

Compared with memory tests, attitude-change tests, or communication and reaction tests, moment-to-moment tests make diagnosis somewhat easier. When test scores refer to the commercial as a whole, it may be difficult to locate the source of any problem. When the test produces a line graph, the problem is likely to be located where the line moves suddenly from positive to negative.

Many suppliers of moment-to-moment tests conduct communication and reaction tests as part of the testing session. Thus, moment-to-moment testing and communication and reaction testing may complement and supplement each other.

Physiological Tests

Finally, mention should be made of physiological tests. Over the years, copy test suppliers have made many attempts to measure emotional responses by tapping into viewers' physiological reactions. Brain waves, heart rate, pupil dilation, voice pitch, skin conductivity—all have been used in these experiments. The hope has been that involuntary emotional reactions would prove more reliable or provide greater insights that the more commonly used paper-and-pencil methods.

However, the physiological experiments have not yet fulfilled this promise. They have generally proved very costly, largely because they require expensive equipment, expert operators, and long testing sessions. They have also proved to be extremely sensitive to extraneous input, such as unexpected noises or even random thoughts that occur to respondents during testing sessions. At this point, the physiological approaches remain an interesting possibility for the future.

Why Copy Tests Are a Mixed Bag

Copy testing is definitely a mixed bag. What advertisers would like to have is an inexpensive, accurate prediction of an advertisement's ultimate sales effect. No copy test comes close to that, despite inflated claims from some suppliers of copy tests.

Advertisers can have a reasonably reliable measure of memorability. Note, however, that the relationship

Copy testing is definitely a mixed bag. What advertisers would like to have is an inexpensive, accurate prediction of an advertisement's ultimate sales effect. No copy test comes close to that

between memorability and effectiveness is at best indirect and is always highly questionable.

For new brands, advertisers can have a reasonably reliable measure of persuasiveness. For well-known brands, persuasiveness measures are subject to very large amounts of random variation and are therefore liable to be much less dependable. Whether the brand is new or old, the size and nature of the sample can drastically reduce the value of the findings.

Advertisers can learn whether consumers understand their messages, and they can learn whether their messages are appealing and believable. While far from an accurate prediction of sales effectiveness, this feedback can help advertisers avoid some possibly serious problems.

In evaluating copy testing options, advertisers owe themselves a skeptical evaluation of promised benefits. Copy tests are not magic; many deliver considerably less than their suppliers promise.

Advertisers also owe themselves a balanced look at costs. Because out-of-pocket costs vary so greatly, an inexpensive test may well turn out to be a better value than an expensive test, even though it may not supply as much information.

Finally, in considering costs, advertisers should always remember the effect the test will have upon their advertising. If the test rejects advertisements they would like to run and passes advertisements they would rather not run, the total real cost of the copy test will far exceed the dollars paid to the research supplier.

Copy tests are not magic; many deliver considerably less than their suppliers promise

CHAPTER 22

What You Need to Know About Publicity and Public Relations

By: Susan Eilertsen

For the past 5 years, Sue, who is highly skilled in publicity and public relations, has been President of WORD OF MOUTH, a publicity and public relations firm which she founded in 1986 and owns.

Prior to that date, Sue was a Publicist or Publicity Associate for A. W. Publishers, New York City, St. Martin's Press, New York City, and Publicity Manager for Berkley Publishing Corporation in New York.

She was a freelance Publicist for publishers, including Simon & Schuster and Seaview Books, and was Publicity Director for a division of Random House, Inc., New York. And, was Associate Director of Publicity for the Crown Publishing Group, New York.

Public relations is the well-established grandfather of public information; publicity is the fiery young offspring who likes attention

Publicity is what you do to get people talking about your product, service, or company, or about an individual.

It can be carried out through a method as conventional as sending out a press release or as unconventional as decorating an old school bus and driving it cross- country to promote a book like *The Electric Kool-Aid Acid Test,* promoted years ago. It could include a press party at the zoo in Central Park, a chartered boat ride around a lake, or a visit to a children's hospital by the popular Sesame Street characters, Big Bird, Bert and Ernie.

It might involve a cross-country media tour, with an authoritative spokesperson giving television, radio, and press interviews in the top 25 markets.

Through publicity, you can capture the imagination of the public, start a trend, get attention for your company, raise money, and sell your product.

What About Public Relations?

Public relations is a broad term that refers to all the functions within a corporation designed to maintain good relations with the public, its employees, and stockholders.

Public relations programs are created to inform them about a company's purpose, activities, and policies, and to create favorable opinion about the company. Public relations is the well-established grandfather of public information; publicity is the fiery young offspring who likes attention.

A good publicity campaign is clearly focused, goal-oriented, creative, and thorough. The first and most important question you must ask yourself before planning a publicity campaign is: "Whom do I want to reach?"

The second question you must ask yourself is: "What do they read, watch, and listen to?"

Once you've identified your media targets, you should figure out how you're going to reach them.

The only way to appeal to a reporter, editor, television, or radio producer is to interest him or her in a story that will interest his or her readers, viewers, or listeners.

The Golden Rule of Publicity

This is the golden rule of publicity, all too often forgotten by both professional and amateur publicists.

Remember, no reporter or producer is interested in selling your product. He or she is only interested in writing stories that will interest the readers or in producing programs that will inform, educate, and help viewers or listeners. If a reporter thinks you're trying to sell a product, he or she will tell you to call the advertising department and then will hang up on you.

Your challenge is to figure out what the story is that you have to tell, and then to package it in a way that will prove irresistible to the media. That package is called a *press kit*, and it could include:

- A feature story
- A fact sheet
- A backgrounder (story behind a story)
- A biography of your spokesperson
- Graphs, illustrations, or reproducible photographs
- Other relevant data that helps tell your story

How To Write a Press Release

Your main press release should be written like a newspaper story. Here are some key rules for writing a good press release:

1. The opening sentence is the most important sentence in the release. It must *grab the reader,* or it will probably be thrown into the wastebasket.

2. It should answer the questions *who, what, when, where, and why,* and answer them quickly.

3. It should be *double-spaced,* and never longer than *two pages.* The best press releases are

The only way to appeal to a reporter, editor, television, or radio producer is to interest him or her in a story that will interest his or her readers, viewers, or listeners

concise and fit onto one page. Remember: You don't have to tell them everything.

4. There should always be a *contact name* and *telephone number* at the upper right-hand corner of the front page of each release. It is written like this:

Contact: Susan Eilertsen

(612) 729-2778

5. There should always be a *headline,* that states the main point of the press release. Examples of headlines are:

SIMON AND SCHUSTER
TO PUBLISH UNAUTHORIZED BIOGRAPHY
OF NANCY REAGAN

APPLE COMPUTER INTRODUCES
NEW SUPERCOMPUTER TO USSR
FOR THE FIRST TIME

ROCCO ALTOBELLI
BRINGS BACK GLAMOROUS HAIR
IN A RETURN TO THE SIXTIES

AIR SYSTEMS, INC. RECEIVES PATENT
FOR AIR FILTER THAT PREVENTS
ALLERGIES IN CHILDREN

A fact sheet is just what it says: a list of facts about the product, service, organization or company you are promoting. It is used as a *reference source* by reporters when they are writing a story about your product or service, so it's an opportunity for you to emphasize the characteristics that distinguish your product or service from others on the market.

It's a good idea to include survey results and statistics wherever possible, because it adds weight to your story ("In a national survey, 85% of homeowners questioned said they would switch from the use of chemicals to an environmentally safe lawn fertilizer if given the option"). It also makes your story more believable.

A "backgrounder" is a story behind the story. It might include a brief history of the company launching a new product or a "story behind a book," explaining the interesting and unusual circumstances that led the author to write a book.

If you are introducing a new style of clothing, it might include a brief history of how fashions have changed. A backgrounder should be included only if it's an interesting and important part of the larger story. In many cases, a simple press release and a fact sheet will do.

Once you've prepared your press material and created a target media list, send the material to the media outlets you think might have an interest in your story.

Know Your Media

The second golden rule of publicity is "know your media." Study the magazine, radio or television program you wish to have cover your product. Only send your story to a media target if the story seems genuinely appropriate for that magazine or program. If you send a story that doesn't fit with the direction of a particular media outlet, you'll not only succeed in wasting time, but you'll manage to annoy somebody in the press. And that's bad public relations for your company.

Professional publicists spend years developing target media lists for different areas of interest, and, as in other areas of marketing, you'll always benefit from working with a professional.

Professional publicists also have the advantage of strong connections with the media, so they can often get a story placed because of whom they know, in addition to how good the story is.

Should you decide to create your own media list, the best way to start is to determine the media placements that would have the most impact on the growth of your company, on sales of your product or service, and go after them. The library is filled with reference books that contain the names of addresses of magazines and newspapers. So, with some old-fashioned library research, you can create your own media list.

The Importance of Follow-up

The next step is an essential ingredient of all successful publicity campaigns: *follow-up*. Editors, reporters, and producers receive hundreds of press releases every day, and if you don't follow up your mailing with a phone call, you might as well not bother sending the press release out.

When you follow up with a phone call, always keep in mind that editors, reporters, and producers are very busy people and do not have time for you to beat around the bush. Be prepared to tell your story, make your main points, and try to close the sale, or get a commitment for an interview, within two to four minutes. I use a "cheat sheet," to keep my main messages in front of me so that I never stammer or waste time.

Take an index card and write your four main messages; then tape it in a visible spot next to the telephone. That way, you'll never forget to say the things you want to say.

A newspaper story in the right place, an appearance on the "Phil Donahue Show," or an interview on a popular local radio program can be the single most important ingredient in getting your sales moving. I've seen hundreds of examples where television, radio, or press coverage was the critical kickoff for marketing campaigns that turned books into best-sellers, a good idea into a national trend, and products into multi-million-dollar profit centers.

Of course, a good publicity campaign is most successful when it's a part of a larger plan that includes advertising, promotion, sales efforts, and distribution.

There's no point in getting an appearance on the "Oprah Winfrey Show," an article in *USA Today,* or a story in *House Beautiful* if the product under discussion is not widely available to the consumer.

The Importance of a Company "Spokesperson"

It's important to have a *company spokesperson* for every publicity campaign

It's important to have a *company spokesperson* for every publicity campaign. A spokesperson might be the president of a company, a doctor or nurse, a psychologist, a person with a doctorate in economics, or an inventor; the critical factor is that the individual is a qualified authority and is articulate. Lee Iacocca is a wonderful sales-person for Chrysler-made cars and jeeps.

Once you've chosen a spokesperson, make sure that he or she is well equipped to handle questions from the media. The spokesperson must know the main messages to communicate about a given product, service, or company inside and out. It's vitally important that the spokesperson be able to communicate the company's message with precision and punch.

If you have any doubts about the spokesperson's ability to handle interviews, consider hiring a professional media coach. There are media coaches in almost every major city in the country, and they can prepare you or your spokesperson to handle interviews with confidence and authority.

Purpose Of Publicity

The purpose of publicity is to get attention for your product, service, or company, and the more creative you can be in getting that attention, the more successful your publicity campaign is likely to be. "Brainstorming" — getting together with a group of individuals and free-associating about your product — is a good way to generate creative ideas for publicity campaigns.

I started my career as a publicist in the publicity departments of publishing companies in New York, and we came up with some terrific techniques for starting a good word-of-mouth publicity campaign on different books.

How To Get Word-Of-Mouth Publicity

Before Alexandra Penny's book *How to Make Love to a Man* was published, we sent advance copies of the book to editors at *Self, Cosmopolitan, Glamour, Vogue,* and other magazines. On top of each advance copy was a giant chocolate kiss, and the package was hand-delivered to all of the magazine editors on the same morning. The chocolate kisses were so big that everyone on the staff at each magazine couldn't help but notice them, and the magazine world buzzed for days. Two and three years later I had magazine editors say to me, "I remember that giant chocolate kiss you sent me with Alexandra Penny's book." Incidentally, the book became a multi-million copy best-seller.

When Martha Stewart's first book, *Entertaining,* was published, she threw a spectacular publicity party at her farmhouse in Connecticut. We hired a bus for all the magazine and newspaper reporters, and served them Martha Stewart's ginger cookies and apple cider on the way to her farmhouse. Once they arrived, the media could sample different kinds of food in each of Martha's seven kitchens. One chef made homemade pumpkin pasta in a barn. A second barn was filled with mouth-watering pastries. Wild mushrooms were flown in from California. Squab were roasting on an outdoor grill. In an upstairs kitchen, three or four homemade soups were simmering on an old-fashioned stove. A long table outdoors was laden with fresh oysters from New England. In the basement, Martha's mother was hand-rolling Polish pierogies and piroshkis. Goat cheese and tomato pizzas were pulled from the brick pizza oven in Martha's regular kitchen. And so on. Martha Stewart was hailed as the quintessential new American hostess. It was a party that everybody wrote about, including *Vogue* and the *Associated Press.* Nobody ever forgot it. *Entertaining* was to become a gold mine for both publisher and author.

When Little Richard's autobiography was published, we contacted the mayor of Atlanta, and Richard was inducted into the Georgia Hall of Fame. That honor, along with the recognition of Little Richard's contribution to contemporary American Music, a press party, and a tremendous amount of advance publicity, led to coverage of Richard's life on CBS-TV's "Sixty Minutes."

When Bette Midler's book *The Saga of Baby Devine* was published, the Gay Marching Band of San Francisco met her at the bookstore where she was scheduled to autograph copies of her book. All three local television network affiliates ran the story at the top of their six o'clock news programs.

Lyndon Johnson changed the face of politics when, in his 1948 senatorial race against Adlai Stevenson, he used a helicopter to land in small towns all over Texas. It was the first time a helicopter had ever been used that way. The voters went wild, and the press covered him all across the state. I think you know the rest of the story. Now *that* was publicity!

You don't have to be famous to get publicity; just creative. With a little imagination, you can create your own publicity stunts. Offering something special is a good way to get people to talk about your product or service. The more unusual and the more carefully planned, the more successful your campaign is likely to be.

To summarize, a good publicity campaign is a vital component of any good marketing program.

Publicity increases the visibility of your product through media exposure.

Publicity brings public attention to your company.

Publicity has a different kind of impact than advertising and is best used in conjunction with an ad campaign.

Publicity As Part Of Marketing

Publicity works best when it's part of a comprehensive marketing strategy. These are the important points to remember:

- Identify your target market.
- Define your main messages.
- As for your spokesperson, choose a well qualified authority who is well informed, articulate, and well prepared.
- Write press material that is factual and concise, with a good opening paragraph.
- Try to connect your story to the right person at the right place at the right time.
- Follow up all press mailings with a phone call.
- Do something special to attract attention for your product.
- Hire a professional publicist whenever possible to help you create the right kind of press package, plan a strong publicity campaign, and connect with key media.

Remember, it doesn't matter if you've invented the greatest mousetrap ever if nobody knows about it.

In the next two pages you'll find:

1. A publicity release and caption
2. A fact sheet, each prepared for two different products.

Publicity works best when it's part of a comprehensive marketing strategy

GYP-CRETE CORPORATION
P.O. BOX 253
HAMEL, MINNESOTA 55340
PHONE (612) 478-6072

Contact: Susan Eilertsen

Word of Mouth
612-729-2778

WARM BATHROOM FLOOR KIT IS NEWEST RAGE
FOR DO-IT-YOURSELFERS

The newest project for the tireless do-it-yourselfers — that growing group of people from seniors to baby boomers to first-time home buyers who are always looking for ways to improve their homes — is a warm bathroom floor kit. With the Infloor Kit, from the Gyp-Crete Corporation, the do-it-yourselfer can install radiant floor heating in her own bathroom for as little as three hundred dollars.

As easy as closing your eyes, imagining yourself relaxing in your own hot tub, and then stepping out onto warm bathroom tiles? Well, not quite, but almost, according to the team of designers who created the Infloor Kit. First, heating cables are attached to the subfloor of a new or renovated bathroom area and connected to a thermostat. A heat sensor fastened on the subfloor permits easy adjustment of floor warmth.

Next, the bagged Therma-Floor Easy-Mix is blended with water and poured over the cables. Nearly any type of floor goods can be applied over the Therma-Floor Easy-Mix, including tile, marble and wood. Therma-Floor is poured thinner than concrete so floors heat fast and transfer warmth more evenly. The entire process from start to finish takes approximately four hours.

The infloor kits come in three sizes and range in price from $199-349. The infloor method of heating a bathroom floor — or any floor — is unusually energy efficient, so homeowners can have comfortably warm floors for a few cents a day. The Infloor Kit was created with bathroom floors in mind, but it can just as easily be used to heat floors in kitchens, entry ways, or anywhere comfort is a priority.

"New home buyers and people who are renovating older homes are increasingly turning to radiant floor heating as the heating method of choice for their homes," says Jim Ervin, Product Manager for the Gyp-Crete Corporation. "Infloor doesn't waste energy trying to warm tremendous volumes of air, as in a forced air system. There are no drafts or hot-air surges; heating throughout the home is uniform, with very little temperature difference between the floor and the ceiling. Utility bills for a home heated by radiant floor heating average 15% - 30% less than the identical home using a forced air furnace."

"There are no registers or cold-air returns to circulate dust or allergens, and as homeowners and home buyers are becoming increasingly health conscious, this feature will probably become more important," said Ervin.

WORD OF MOUTH
A SUSAN EILERTSEN COMPANY

FACT SHEET: THE ALTOBELLA CLAYPACK™

-The Altobella ClayPac™ is a hair treatment used in salons to repair and revitalize hair that has been damaged by the environment or by chemical processing.

-It is a 'first of its kind' treatment, and it is patented.

-ClayPac™ leaves all types of hair with a natural fullness, lightness, and shine — signifying that the hair is in superb basic condition.

-ClayPac™ works by combining the body's own moisturizer, Hyaluronic Acid, with a blend of clay and protein. The Hyaluronic Acid penetrates deeply while the clay locks in moisture and the protein seals the cuticle layer.

-ClayPack™ has been proven effective as a conditioning treatment in the following situations:

. When the hair feels dry and appears dull.

. When the hair lacks shine, bounce, or life.

. Before and after permanent waving.

. Before and after any haircoloring process, including permanent tints, highlighting, bleaching and toning.

-There is a recommended procedure for the proper application of the Altobella ClayPac™, and that technique is also patented. To obtain the correct application of the ClayPack™, the consumer must have the treatment in a qualified salon.

-The ClayPac™ is produced by Altobella Hair Products, Altobella Business Plaza, 1408 Northland Drive, Suite 106, Mendota Heights, Minnesota, 55120.

-The ClayPac™ treatment is offered at fine salons throughout the United States. To locate the salon nearest you where the ClayPac™ is available, call 1-800-435-9000.

4342 Longfellow Ave. S. - Minneapolis, Minnesota 55407
Office: (612) 729-2778 - Fax: (612) 729-5740

Summary

If you have legitimate news about your company or a new product or service to report, consider publicity and if you succeed in obtaining it in the printed media, use the publicity story in brochures or attach to sales literature just like the stories were your advertisements.

CHAPTER 23

How to Raise Money for Worthwhile Causes and NonProfit Organizations

By: Al Whitman

The Importance of the Fund-raising Industry

Fund-raising is the third-largest industry in the United States. About 900,000 different organizations are involved in money raising.

Each year over $100 billion is raised by nonprofit groups from nongovernment sources. Most of the money is raised by millions of volunteer workers in an average year.

The Two Kinds of Money-Raising Campaigns

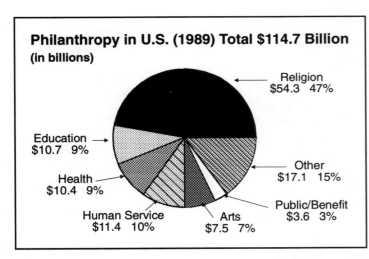

Philanthropy in U.S. (1989) Total $114.7 Billion
(in billions)

Religion $54.3 47%
Education $10.7 9%
Health $10.4 9%
Human Service $11.4 10%
Arts $7.5 7%
Public/Benefit $3.6 3%
Other $17.1 15%

The first type of money raising campaign is a *capital* campaign which seeks to raise money for endowment, buildings, libraries, and other major needs. This kind of a campaign usually is run by the organization no more than once in a decade.

The second type of campaign is *annual giving*. This kind of a campaign isusually conducted each year by the same organization at the same time. Perhaps the best-known annual giving programs are carried out for educational institutions, such as colleges and graduate schools.

A capital campaign contributes in important ways to strengthen annual giving programs. It gets people who have never given to the institution on the list of givers and helps educate new givers about the institution for which money is being raised.

An example of an annual giving campaign is the United Way. It's a very important campaign conducted each year at the same time in more than 2,000 cities. In 1990 $3.1 billion was raised in these cities.

There's a major difference. The United Way works to raise monies for a wide number of charities and welfare institutions and distributes most of the monies it raises to *other* institutions.

However, annual giving campaigns run for colleges, schools, and other institutions are used for *their own* specific purposes.

How Are the Monies Raised?

There are many ways of raising money for worthwhile charitable causes.

Some institutions raise money with bingo games, or a day at the ballpark, through charity balls, telethons, second-hand auctions, Girl Scout cookies, Salvation Army Christmas "Bell Ringers," celebrity cookbooks, celebrity golf and tennis tournaments, and other events.

But monies raised in this way generally are used for small money-raising causes or are part of the monies raised for large institutions that use more formal programs.

What Kind Of Charitable Institutions Raise Money Via Full-Fledged Campaigns?

Here's at least a partial list: the United Way, the Salvation Army, the American Red Cross, welfare institutions (blindness, cancer, Alzheimer's, cerebral palsy), colleges and schools, churches, arts and humanities, symphonies.

On the previous page we showed you a chart prepared by AAFRC Trust for Philanthropy for 1989.

This chart shows the amount and percentage of all monies raised by churches, education, health, human services, public benefits, arts and humanities, and other institutions for these two years.

The Importance of Bequests and Matching Gifts

A great deal of money is raised, particularly in capital gift campaigns, via bequests. Many money-raising institutions, particularly colleges, have an expert on their development staff who specializes in soliciting bequests.

Many businesses offer a matching-gifts program. Under such a program, the business will match any gift given by any employee to an acceptable welfare or charitable organization.

The Use of the Phone in Fund-raising

Many fund-raisers use the phone to support a direct-mail campaign or in place of it.

When pledges are made, you can expect that 20 to 25 percent will not be collected. When a telephone campaign is executed properly to a list of prospects and givers, the pledge rate can be as much as 10 to 12 times that of direct mail.

Total pledges tend to be considerably greater when a multipayment plan is offered.

Challenge Grants

There's another technique used to raise more money for a deserving institution or charity.

It calls for persuading a big giver to agree to add a substantial sum to the money-raising pot when the solicitors have raised a certain sum of money.

A simple example:

Let's suppose a college was conducting a capital campaign for $50 million. It arranges for one of its big givers to say that he would donate an additional $2 million if the campaign has reached three-fourths of its goal by a specific date.

This technique puts substantial pressure on the selling organization. But it also gives them an additional selling tool, because it helps them convince repeat and prospective donors to give more money than they might have planned, and to do so by a specific date.

In other words, the donor is "challenging" the solicitors to get on the ball.

Keys to a Good Money-Raising Program

Assuming you already have a good product, a favorable feasibility study, and good leadership, you must also have:

1. The right kind of organization.
2. Someone who can describe the "product" so it's understood and liked.
3. The kind of an organization that can sell it.
4. Good communications.

When a telephone campaign is executed properly to a list of prospects and givers, the pledge rate can be as much as 10 to 12 times that of direct mail

5. The professional services of a money- raising organization like Ketchun of Pittsburgh; Brakeley John Price Jones of Stamford, Connecticut; the Community Council Services, New York City; and Donald A. Campbell and Company of Chicago.

Feasibility Study

For capital campaigns, a feasibility study can be very important. Here's the key question involved. How feasible is the goal we have in mind? Should it be a certain dollar amount?

The answer lies in making a feasibility study with a cross-section of previous givers and prospective givers. If a professional money-raising company is used, it will probably charge about $5,000 to do this study. We know of very few major campaigns that have not taken this very important step.

If the study indicates the amount of money that can probably be raised is somewhat less than hoped for, then the goal should be adjusted downward, or some additional important element that can help raise more money should be added to the money raising effort.

How to Organize for a Campaign

1. Determine the operations budget (try to keep operating costs at 10% or less of your goal).

2. Prepare your case. Ask
   a. Why monies are needed
   b. In what areas or for what purposes

3. Set the goal.

4. Make your lists of past and prospective users. Be sure to update them.

5. "Rate" each key prospect, using a committee to set a figure for each prospect.

*6. Lay out a "pyramid of giving" (capital campaign). You must expect you can raise a lot of money from only a few givers, no more than 6 to 10 and often less.

   * (see pyramid example that follows).

7. Build the organization.

8. Prepare a publicity plan in writing.

For capital campaigns, a feasibility study can be very important. Here's the key question involved. How feasible is the goal we have in mind?

9. Solicit the trustees and division heads first.

10. Set up the right kind of a money-raising organization. Have a division for each of the following:
   a. Large givers
   b. Corporate givers
   c. Gifts by the employees who work in these corporations
   d. Foundations
   e. Bequests
   f. Special groups, such as alumni, parents, teachers, etc.

To be successful in a campaign for raising capital you must be able to raise an important percentage of your goal from relatively few gifts

Explanation of Pyramid Giving

This is a way of dramatizing that to be successful in a campaign for raising capital you must be able to raise an important percentage of your goal from relatively few gifts. Never more than 10 gifts. Often from only 3 to 5 gifts.

Here's an example for a $30 million capital drive:

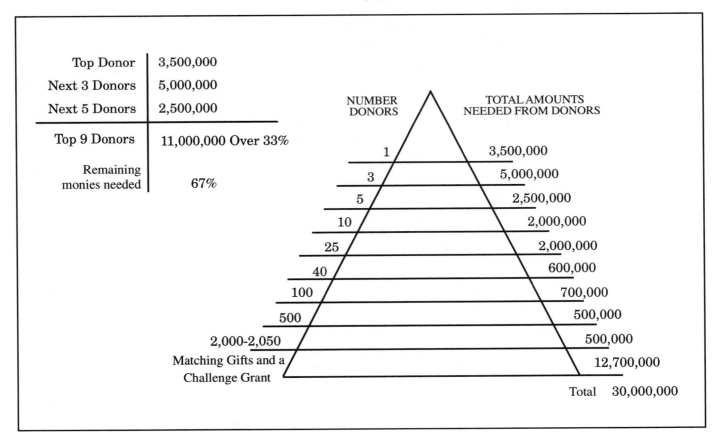

Top Donor	3,500,000	
Next 3 Donors	5,000,000	
Next 5 Donors	2,500,000	
Top 9 Donors	11,000,000	Over 33%
Remaining monies needed	67%	

NUMBER DONORS	TOTAL AMOUNTS NEEDED FROM DONORS
1	3,500,000
3	5,000,000
5	2,500,000
10	2,000,000
25	2,000,000
40	600,000
100	700,000
500	500,000
2,000-2,050	500,000
Matching Gifts and a Challenge Grant	12,700,000
Total	30,000,000

According to this particular pyramid, the top giver would supply more than 10 percent of the total goal, 3 more another 15 percent, and 5 more about 7.5 percent.

This means that almost 33 percent of the monies would have to come from just nine gifts!

No wonder advance feasibility studies are so important in the money-raising process.

Here again, every emphasis should be placed on employee matching gifts and for the use of payroll deductions for employee contributions.

What Does The Volunteer Chairperson Do?

- Appoints the key division leaders and committees; i.e., publicity, speakers bureau.
- Double-checks all key activities.
- Calls on large givers, usually with the special gifts division heads.
- If creative, helps decide on the theme for the drive.
- Chairs all key report meetings.
- Whenever possible, attends key organization meetings, gives a talk, and answers questions.
- Is always available to newspaper, radio, and T.V. reporters.

How To Execute a Campaign

1. Announce how much the trustees and a few large givers have pedged.
2. Call on your giving constituencies:
   a. Large givers
   b. Corporations
   c. Foundations
3. Provide for soliciting matching gifts, bequests, and challenge grants.
4. Turn on the publicity program and the speaker's bureau.
5. Set up a system for reporting results to date, to honor unusual performance by givers and to recognize unusually fine work by specific solicitors.
6. Publicize the results.
7. Meet with the media to review the future.

How to "Kick Off" a Campaign.

After having your proposed program approved by the trustees of the organization, and after taking all the other steps necessary to attain the goal, the next step is to announce the campaign to the general public and to the various media.

The announcement is generally made by the voluntary chairperson or by the full-time executive director of the institution for whom the money is being raised.

At this meeting, the chairperson announces how much money the trustees have pledged in total. They also announce certain pledges that have been made by selected individuals and groups of large givers. Such a move is not only good publicity, but can be very encouraging to the solicitors. It also adds credibility to the program by other givers on the theory that "if it's good enough for these people, it is good enough for us."

At the "kick off" meeting, the chairperson announces the goal, and the dates the money-raising program will start and end. Publicity releases are handed out to the media, and these people are told whom they can call for additional information.

The Role of the Professional Fund-raiser

When a money-raising organization hires a professional fund-raising company to work with them, the right person assigned to a campaign can be very important to its success. After all, it is his or her business and supposedly is something at which he or she is truly an expert.

What professional fund-raisers really do is supply knowledgeable, worthwhile advice and counsel all along the line. They would suggest, for example, "Get this type of person as the voluntary head," "Conduct a feasibility study," "Plan your campaign this way," "Execute it this way." The larger and more important the campaign, the greater the chances that a professional fund-raiser will be an important part of the picture.

No one outside the money-raising organization may ever know that the professional fund-raiser exists, but the professional's contributions are felt every day.

The Report Meetings

Once underway, most campaigns have periodic report meetings. A campaign lasting for six weeks will probably have about six report meetings. These meetings are headed by the chairperson. He or she usually has each division head report on the amount of money each division has raised to date. The meetings also accomplish several other purposes.

1. They tell the money-raising organization, the public, and the media how much money has been raised and the percentage of the goal attained to date.

2. They give the money-raising organization an opportunity to honor certain businesses or foundations or special groups of people who've donated significant amounts. They give the organization a chance to recognize the work of volunteer workers who have produced above and beyond what could be normally expected.

   In each case, the groups who've been honored, or the workers who've been recognized will be present at the meeting, where they can be seen by their peers and often photographed or filmed for use by newspapers and television news programs.

   In most cases, the money-raising organization will be smart enough to have read publicity releases ready for media use.

Role of The Volunteer

Some people may wonder why a money-raising organization uses volunteer workers to answer phones, write letters, and so forth, inside the money-raising organization, and others to solicit monies from past givers and new prospects.

Reasons why volunteer workers are so important

Here are some of the reasons:

1. Volunteer workers who get involved in projects become enthusiastic.

2. They give of themselves and can help you raise a lot of money from others.

3. They help spread the word about the campaign, and they add credibility to the organization because people know they

140

are not paid. Most appreciate help and direction and are pleasant to work with.

4. They help you learn about misconceptions or problems the people they called on may have about the organization and its campaign.

How Do You Select Volunteer Workers?

Be sure that they

1. Want the job.
2. Have time to do it right.
3. Make a good impression, are outgoing, and like people.
4. Have raised money for other organizations.
5. Ask good questions about the organization, its needs and plans.
6. Have a record of getting things done.

Also make sure the recruiter has guidance as to what to look for and has high selection standards.

What Do Good Volunteer Solicitors Have in common?

1. They know the need and goal.
2. They learn as much about each prospect as possible.
3. They make an appointment for all key solicitations.
4. They plan each interview in advance.
5. They listen during each interview.
6. They ask good questions.
7. They use the right benefits and the right opening remarks.
8. They know how to close.
9. They ask for a specific amount in a way that does not antagonize the prospect.

How to Train Volunteers

1. The better the preparation, the better the meeting.
2. Make sure the volunteers understand the organization and the need. Encourage questions.
3. Keep the meetings small, short, and to the point.

4. Explain what to say on all cold calls and how to say it (see selling approach example).

5. Help the volunteer understand what benefits the institution for which money is being raised offers to the community or its users.

6. Make sure each volunteer is coached to listen carefully to what each prospect has to say.

7. Make sure each volunteer has a pledge card for those to be called on and knows how to use the card. Make sure each knows how to use any pertinent printed material the organization has furnished.

8. Explain how to tell a prospect what others who are in comparable situations give.

9. Explain how to close the sale.

10. If time permits, hold a brief question and answer session, and ask a volunteer to say what he or she believes is the best way to open. Then have others critique the opening. Do the same thing for the close.

11. Close with a quick recap by the trainers. Then thank them for coming.

12. Give all volunteers a sheet highlighting the important points and the names and numbers to call in case the volunteer wants other questions answered.

The content of each training will vary by the division the volunteers are in, but the principles should not.

The Importance of Volunteer Solicitors

The importance of volunteer solicitors cannot be over-emphasized. There are millions who solicit for charities and nonprofit organizations each year and more than 4,000,000 for the United Way campaign alone. The better the group of volunteers, the more the monies that will be raised. They can make or break a campaign.

That's why they have to be selected so carefully and be trained as expertly as possible.

EXAMPLE OF A SELLING APPROACH FOR VOLUNTEER SOLICITORS MAKING A COLD CALL FOR A UNITED WAY CAMPAIGN

Establishes you as someone who's familiar with the company.	"Good morning. I'm Betsy Ross, volunteer worker for the United Way. I work for the _____ company in this area and know quite a few people in your company, and we use several of your products."
Tells your prospect what you want to talk about, and what organizations are helped.	"I'm sure you're familiar with the United Way. But do you know the many organizations it supports?" "You don't? Well here's a list of all 63 of them (give list to prospect). You can also see how much money was allocated to each last year."
Shows that United Way keeps its work up to date.	"You can see that some of these furnish food, clothing and temporary housing to the poor and the elderly...those who truly have basic needs."
Lays the groundwork for an increase in giving.	"This year's United Way Campaign seeks to raise $20 million in this city and county. That's $2 million dollars more than last year, or an increase of 10%."
Spells out how each gift benefits the community (see Chapter 11).	"Have you any idea how your gift to the United Way benefits your community?" "It helps people to help themselves." "It helps make our city a better place to live." "You help people who're really in need, and give them a better life."

How a Typical United Way Is Organized

We can't tell you how all United Way campaigns are organized. But we can give you a specific example of the organization used each year in one large midwestern city.

First of all, there is a permanent paid staff headed by an executive director who has been carefully selected and who is a very important figure in the whole process.

The executive director is the staff counterpart to the voluntary chairperson.

Under the executive director are people who are counterparts to the volunteer heads of key divisions: a division for special gifts, a division for corporate giving, a division for employee giving, a division for foundations, etc.

In addition, the director of the United Way usually has on staff an experienced publicity person who has a substantial background in publicity and public relations.

He, too, has a counterpart in the volunteer organization. In a sense, the only key person in the organization that does not have an alter ego in the paid staff is the volunteer head of a speakers bureau, who is appointed by the volunteer chairperson.

United Way's organization in this city also has an administrative setup headed by a community leader who knows the organization. Different groups of paid staff and volunteer citizens allocate the monies the United Way raises to the various deserving institutions for which the United Way raises the monies. It also has a staff that keeps records, keeps track of pledges and their due dates, and sends out bills.

Miscellaneous

Here are a few other thoughts worth remembering about money raising:

1. A very large part of the monies raised in almost any campaign will come from *individuals* — perhaps 80 percent or more. Employee giving via payroll deductions is one reason, and the monies raised from large individual givers is another.

2. A capital giving program will strengthen annual giving programs, and vice versa. People once believed you should not have both in the same year, but that has proved to be absolute nonsense.

Summary

You may wonder which people are most important to a successful money-raising drive.

First is the executive director employed full time by the money-raising institution. Next is the volunteer chairperson. Next are the key division heads.

Another person whose contributions can be very important is the one who creates the theme for the

A very large part of the monies raised in almost any campaign will come from *individuals*

campaign, the brochures, and the selling tools. It's always great to have a truly creative person on the team. As an aside, many years ago an advertising man had the job of collecting class dues from as many of his classmates as possible. During most of his five-year stint as the class treasurer, the country was in an economic depression, and it was difficult to get members to pay the class dues. One day he had lunch with the father of one of his close friends. The father had been a class treasurer for a number of years, and mentioned that each April he sent everyone in the class a money-raising "valentine." So my friend adopted the idea and, in addition to his regular collection letter, sent out a valentine of his own in April. Twenty classmates who had never before paid their dues, paid up.

Next there are persons or organizations who train the volunteers.

And last, but not least, are the volunteer workers who are so tremendously important to the success of the campaign.

An Example of a Highly Successful Money-Raising Campaign

This example has to do with the annual giving program of a rather good country day school.

> The trustees decided that the school needed to increase the amount of its annual giving program.

> During the previous year, they had raised more money than ever before.

> But, as a result of adopting the program of a trustee who was skilled at raising money, three times as much money was raised, and in less that eight weeks!

> With that program as the starting point, the school is now raising nearly half a million dollars in annual giving each year.

> Here's a point-by-point description of the program that was adopted:

> 1. The trustee had recommended that before the annual giving program was to start, the school conduct a substantial campaign for capital gifts. This was done.

2. He also recommended that several study committees be put together, each headed by a trustee.

    There were about 10 of these committees, including committees for:

    - The curriculum
    - The faculty
    - The buildings and grounds
    - Athletics and athletic facilities
    - Extra-curricular activities, such as plays, debating, student community projects, and several other committees, plus a priority committee headed by the trustee in charge of the money-raising programs.

3. The findings of these committees were put in writing for the committee on priorities, and each carried a recommendation as to what was needed in the areas they had studied and the estimated cost of supplying these needs.

    The interesting fact was that a number of their findings and recommendations were so obviously correct that they were put into effect almost immediately (long before the campaign started).

4. Once the campaign started with the various constituencies, the soliciting organization used a brochure written and illustrated by the head of the program.

    The theme was "Blueprint For Greatness."

This campaign met and slightly exceeded its goal, which represented at that time an all-time high for comparable country day schools in the area.

Here's what the annual giving program entailed:

1. The chairman was a gifted, creative man and a marvelous organizer.

146

2. He set up a "sales" organization along these lines:

   a. There would be a trustee in charge of solicitors for raising money from parents.

   There would be a similar organization for alumni.

   b. There would be another such organization for corporations and foundations.

   c. There would be a fourth for soliciting "friends" of the school.

The heads of each of these groups set their own goals, and a brass spittoon was the first prize for the chairman who raised the most money in excess of the approved budget.

The chairman wrote a speech to be given by different trustees to the parents at father-and-son class dinners, which were held once a year.

In these talks it was stressed that the more parents gave, the less the need for raising tuition. That, plus the fact that part of each gift was tax deductible, resulted in the brass spittoon going to the head of the parent division.

This was the most successful annual giving program in the school's history, and when word of it got out, the fundamentals were used in two other schools with almost equally good results.

CHAPTER 24

How to Market Via Direct-Mail Catalogs

By: Richard Shull

"Rick" Shull is a Product Manager and Buyer for the Lands' End Co., in Dodgeville, Wisconsin.

Prior to joining Lands' End in 1982, Rick has graduated from the University of Minnesota with a BA in Business Administration. Rick spent several years in media and as account executive of an advertising agency, then he spent 3 years in the advertising department of Minnesota's largest bank.

In 1974, Rick joined the famous mail-order and retail store, Gokey Co., known the world over for its famous sportsman's boots, BOTTE SAUVAGE, where he managed the company's first expansion store. Here he became involved in product selection and buying men's and women's clothing, gift merchandise, and sporting goods for both the retail and mail-order divisions of the company.

All this led quite naturally to his move to Lands' End.

Selling products by mailing out catalogs containing order blanks is big business. An estimated 12 billion catalogs are mailed out each year by hundreds of different companies offering many different kinds of merchandise.

One of the best-known catalogs is the one used by Sears Roebuck.

Regular customers who make most or all of their purchases from catalogs receive big catalogs featuring all or most of the items Sears sells.

Numerous other companies in widely different fields use smaller catalogs at different times of the year, such as spring, summer, fall, and Christmas catalogs.

Who Receives These Catalogs?

- People who are occasional or regular customers.
- Prospects who qualify on the basis of demographics or psychographics.

What About Using Catalogs for Special Sales?

A number of companies feature "clearance sales." The company may be overstocked or wish to move seasonal merchandise or merchandise left over from a peak selling period, such as the Christmas holidays.

What Kinds of Companies Are in the Catalog Business?

- Big national companies like, Sears, Spiegel, and Penneys.
- Companies selling plants, seeds, bulbs, and shrubs, like Jackson & Perkins and Burpee.
- Companies selling printed products, like Miles Kimball.

- Companies selling kitchen items, like Williams-Sonoma.
- Companies selling fishing and hunting equipment, like Orvis.
- Companies selling skiing and hunting apparel, like Eddie Bauer.
- Companies selling clothing, like Lands' End, Spiegel, Blair, and L. L. Bean.

Marketing by direct mail presents challenges that are different from those of retail methods, but direct mail also offers boundless opportunities that are not available through other marketing methods.

The challenges to mail-order marketing are reach, react, respond, and retain. The opportunities are reward, repeat, realistic, and predictable.

To market by mail, one must determine a means of reaching the right potential customer. The costs of preparing and mailing a catalog are continually increasing at 15 percent to 20 percent a year. Therefore, sending a catalog to an unlikely prospect is expensive.

However, a great deal of demographic and psychographic data is available to define one's target market.

Mailing Lists

One of the best and most reliable sources of customer names is lists rented from other mail-order companies. List brokers perform this service for a negotiated fee based on volume and the cost to use net names (about $85.00 per thousand).

A customer who responds to your mailing becomes your customer and should be retained in your file.

If he or she does not respond, you may choose not to mail future catalogs to that person.

Once a catalog has been issued, the next challenge is to stimulate the recipient to react.

Catalog competition is fierce. For a first-time recipient to react to a catalog, several things must be in your favor. More specifically, you should have done some groundwork.

Several companies have found that *image* advertising preconditions a catalog shopper. This dramatizes the competitive edge XYZ company has over alternative shopping opportunities. In addition, the product catalog itself must be enticing, appealing, and most of all *involving*.

Assuming your catalog interests your prospect and he or she has delved into the contents, the challenge remains to get a response. There are unlimited ways to entice people to respond.

The best results seem to come from a combination of product, price, and presentation. That is, build the best product, price it fairly, and present it with a strong selling message.

All products should offer an advantage to the customer or prospect (see Chapter 11) and a reason why the benefits exist. These benefits should have a recognizable value.

The Importance of a Good Positioning Statement

To convey all this, the product should have a "positioning" statement… the characteristics of what is being offered, why, and for what price.

The headline should be the selling message… price/value/benefits, product improvements, or whatever sets these items apart from the competition. The visual should represent the product in a realistic manner.

To perform these functions, the mail-order company must have available a staff of buyers for product development and positioning, a staff of copywriters and art directors to develop the art and copy, and a staff or source for the technical preparation of the book.

Merchants should be well versed in product development, i.e., sourcing, materials, construction, negotiating, and marketing.

The creative staff should be well trained in product presentation. They should be able to select the best way to describe benefits and features not apparent in the visual presentation. The art director must know what features of the product are most important to illustrate the product (e.g. on figures, in use, as a still life).

Most catalog creative personnel have had advertising agency or department store experience, providing the background of in-depth research to learn about a variety of products and the ability to sell them properly. This merchandising teamwork is an integral part of the success of any cataloger.

When the preparation process is executed correctly, the results should be rewarding. An involving cover, proper order and sequence of the product, enticing headlines, and arresting visual presentations will stimulate a response.

Rate of Response is Usually Predictable

Based on past experiences, the cataloger can predict the rate of response overall for most items. Rate of response is based on circulation, space allocation, price, sizes, and color offerings, and other things. With the availibility of toll-free telephone ordering, the catalog could expect 60 percent of the orders to come by telephone and 40 percent by mail.

The cataloger must be prepared to service the customer as efficiently and expeditiously as possible. Having accomplished the most difficult process to generate a response, it's imperative that the customer receive *immediate satisfaction*. Delays, lost orders, or inaccurate fulfillment of a customer's order will have more long-term, far-reaching negative effects than not accepting an order in the first place.

The Importance of Customer Satisfaction

Customers who have a pleasurable experience and who like what they've ordered will become life-long, loyal patrons. They may change jobs or lifestyle, move or grow older; but the cataloger can always reach them and they can always reach the cataloger. But any negative experience could permanently sever that relationship.

This core list of customers becomes the cataloger's life blood. These customers will become the basis of a predictable business. And as more come into the fold, the cataloger can plan and program the future. He or she can plan the product offering, the size of the mailing, the response rate, and the book's productivity and profit.

A Brief Example of One Mail-Order Company's Operation

The Lands' End Company of Dodgeville, Wisconsin, has been in the mail order business for many years and has sold various types of clothing by catalog since 1976.

Based on past experiences, the cataloger can predict the rate of response overall for most items

With the availibility of toll-free telephone ordering, the catalog could expect 60 percent of the orders to come by telephone and 40 percent by mail

This core list of customers becomes the cataloger's life blood. These customers will become the basis of a predictable business

It is dependent on catalogs for 100 percent of its business. The average catalog is more than 200 pages long, with mostly four-color illustrations of the merchandise.

It contains clothing for men, women and teens, with some items for children.

Type of Merchandise

Most items are of the classic type — the old standbys, such as men's shirts and sweaters, made in a variety of fabrics, styles, and colors

Most items are of the classic type — the old standbys, such as men's shirts and sweaters, made in a variety of fabrics, styles, and colors.

Basic items are featured year-round and seasonal items at appropriate times of the year, i.e., swimsuits or winter clothing. Seasonal issues also feature basic items in different weights and designs and colors.

In addition to the classic basics, the company keeps a close tab on new products and includes the most promising items as regular policy.

What About Pricing?

Prices are set to be good values to the customer, usually between department store and discount store prices

Prices are set to be good values to the customer, usually between department store and discount store prices. Product margins are generally set in the area of 45 percent to 65 percent of the sales price to the customer. They are somewhat higher for slower moving items purchased infrequently. A delivery and handling charge is added to all orders.

How Does the Customer Order?

- Using the order blank in the catalog.
- Via an 800 number.

CHAPTER 25

Some Important Thoughts on Pricing

By: Al Whitman

Proper pricing of products or services is a key element in marketing.

If you can do the pricing properly, or if you have someone in your company who has pricing capability, any pricing problems are usually minor.

But, if you're a neophyte, proper pricing can be full of pitfalls.

This is particularly true in small businesses.

Many individuals who've founded their own small business are experts in product development but not in other areas of marketing. Often they don't understand what marketing really is (see Chapter 1). Most think of it as being synonymous with selling.

Quite often, they are in the dark about the fundamentals of pricing, without which knowledge you can lose your shirt and your business. Many of them know little about pricing, selling, sales promotion, packaging, publicity, or advertising, etc.

What Are Some of These Fundamentals?

1. You should have an accurate fix on costs, including overhead. In many small businesses it's surprising how often overhead figures are not included or estimated accurately.

2. You must know how your product will be priced for the ultimate consumers and you must know the margins each factor in the distributive process is expected to earn.

   Example: When you sell a product to a department store, discount store or drug outlet, expect them to price your product on the shelf for twice what they were charged by the wholesaler.

   In food distribution the margins are lower.

If you sell direct to the consumer (house-to-house or via mail-order, letters, catalogs or advertising) you realize far higher margins than you do selling to wholesalers, chains, and retailers, because the customer pays the full retail price plus postage and handling.

Neophytes in mail order often price their product *too low* to the consumer, at less than five to six times their production and packaging costs, not including postage and handling charges.

When you're pricing a product, you should think about quantity discounts and the cost of any promotional deals you have to make.

You must allow for selling, promotion, and publicity costs, as well as overhead and operational costs.

There's a big difference in the way products used in the home are priced (usually firm pricing), and the way *services* are priced (usually variable).

In the area of consumer goods there's little variation in pricing, except for deals and other promotions. However, in the area of *services* (airlines, hotels or car rentals for example), prices can vary daily, up and down and all over the lot.

Recommendation

When it comes to pricing you have to know your stuff. If you don't you need help.

At minimum you need a good financial person to know how to control and budget costs accurately. You also need a person who really knows the pricing principles of your industry.

If you can't afford such people on your payroll, get a pair of knowledgeable part-time experts as consultants. Without them you can really get hurt.

Summary

Proper pricing is an integral part of marketing and it is of particular importance to small business executives who are not well trained in marketing.

Neophytes in mail order often price their product *too low* to the consumer

There's a big difference in the way products used in the home are priced (usually firm pricing), and the way *services* are priced (usually variable)

CHAPTER 26

For the past 11 years, John Nelson has been Vice President of Marketing for Source/Inc., a package design agency in Chicago, Illinois.

In July 1991, he opened a new business consulting firm called JRN Associates.

Nelson has an advertising background. He worked for Tathan, Laird and Kudner, and Clinton Frank Agencies in Chicago.

The he was a Director of Business Plans for Design Planning Group in Chicago.

He was Marketing Manager of Columbia Broadcasting Stations (CBS) in Chicago, in the late '70's.

For Source/Inc., he was in charge of new business, client administration, marketing plans, and participated in setting the strategy for package design work for client companies, including General Mills, Pillsbury, S.C. Johnson, Oscar Mayer, Eli Lilly and Land O' Lakes.

The Importance of Package Design. . . and Designers

By: John R. Nelson

Package design is an important element in the marketing mix. A brand's package and the messages it communicates on the shelf are critical to its success. With today's proliferation of brands within a single product category, packaging is often the key to consumer's purchasing decision. Simply put, the package must sell the product.

Package design encompasses package structures, (the carton, bottle, or can that holds the product), materials (plastic, paper, tin, wood, etc.), and graphics (the communication of brand name, contents, use and brand positioning).

Package design is important because a poor package can result in a disaster for an otherwise good product.

A good package provides real or perceived added value to the product by creating visual impressions of superior value, quality, efficiency, taste, or convenience.

For example, Weber, maker of barbecue grills, used plain brown corrugated cartons to package their product. While these cartons were functional, they provided no visual impact or information about the product. Our analysis of their packaging led to the following conclusions:

1. There was an opportunity to use the carton as a "silent salesman" in the store by visualizing product benefits and features.

2. We could preemptively position the barbecue grills as more than just "backyard barbecues." We could convey the impression that the grills are alternative cooking appliances providing unique, exciting taste benefits. And we did that by visualizing food being prepared on the grill.

   The result? The photo on the next page shows the new packaging, which now createsan `impactful`, informative retail display. And best of all, sales increased 25 percent in just one year!

Here are 10 things you need to know to make a package design successful;

1. **Product characteristics/benefits/claims**

   What is unique about the product?

   Beyond the brand name, what do you want to communicate?

   What benefits should be exploited?

   What is the product's price point?

   Make a list of those things you want to communicate about the product, and put them in order of importance.

2. **Product Positioning**

   How is the product positioned in the market?

   For example, Snausages (see below) is positioned as a premium-priced good-tasting dog treat providing fun for both pet and owner. The gable-topped carton structure was recommended to resemble a bag, thus supporting the treat idea. The dog visual communicates fun. The product imagery conveys good taste.

3. **The Consumer**

   Who is the consumer? What are their demographics and lifestyles, and what are their *perceptions* regarding the product and competitive brands? Often, research is conducted before design is initiated to determine consumer *impressions* of product quality, usage, value, and soon. It's important to know how consumers *feel* about your product versus competitive brands. For example, when research suggested that consumers of small appliances perceived West Bend's new Mikassa China design to be something they would buy as a gift, we designed the package to look like a premium-priced gift carton.

4. **Package Equities**

   If you're redesigning an existing package, make absolutely sure you know which elements of the existing design are

important and memorable to consumers. This photo shows the old and the new design. The new package of Oscar Mayer's Packaged Meats retains the brandmark and yellow color of the old package but uses them for greater impact by retaining integrity elements.

As subtle as these changes are, volume for the brand increased significantly after the new package was introduced.

Many marketers make the terrible mistake of completely changing a package or label design with strong equities, only to find that their regular consumers either can't find the new package on the shelf or they become suspicious of changes in the product.

5. **Competition**

It's important to determine the packaging "cues" of the product category. Certain product categories dictate the use of certain colors and types of imagery on packaging. For example, many "light" (low-calorie lowfat) food products use white or light pastel background colors on packaging. It's important to stand out on the shelf and be distinctive, but it's also important to "fit in" to the category.

6. **Retail Environment**

What kind of stores will carry the product, where it will be shelved, the competitive surroundings, store lighting, the number of facings on the shelf—all play a role in package design.

For example, a product that is sold out of a "coffin" case places more importance on the top, cover, or lid of the package to communicate the brand name and product information.

7. **Objectives**

A well-thought-through set of package design objectives is essential in establishing the hierarchy of communication and providing a means to evaluate the design alternatives that will be developed by the designer.

No one can design a package without clear objectives. A typical set of objectives for designing a packaging system for a line of retail food products might include:

1. Creating strong, clear, and consistent brand recognition across all line items.

2. Increase retail impact by defining a brand section on the shelf.

3. Visualize how to differentiate between product types and flavors and price points.

4. Maximize appetite appeal by visually communicating premium quality, specific ingredients and superior taste.

5. Create packaging that is environmentally "friendly."

8. **Trade Response**

With the advent of electronic bar coding on most retail supermarket products, the trade is now in the driver's seat in determining which products gain distribution. Overnight, store management can determine which products sell at which price in which stores. They know how your product measures up on a volume-per-square-foot basis before you do.

It's a good idea to expose key retail buyers of your product to your package design ideas and find out what they think about them before you make a final design selection. Be prepared to demonstrate such things as how your package's shape and size will maximize store profit potential based on the amount of cubic space it occupies on the shelf.

9. **Consumer Input**

When you have developed a few package design ideas, take them to consumers to find out what they think about them. Find out their *impressions* of product quality, value, and so forth, for each design. By researching the concepts you can gain insight into the relative strengths and weaknesses of each design and get good direction on how to improve them and make a final selection.

10. **Selecting a Designer**

Good package designers are found in a variety of places. Generally, you're better off going to a package design agency. But there are also good designers in advertising agencies and art studios.

To find a good designer, ask a business associate or your advertising agency to submit a list of design agencies, based on your project needs and budget.

Or contact the Package Design Council in New York (P.O. Box 3753 Grand Central Station, New York, NY 10017, 212/459-4242) and ask them to suggest a few designers in your geographic area. Design firms range in size from one person shops to large, multi-service organizations offering brand name generation, research, promotion design, and corporate identity.

Invite a few design agencies to give capabilities presentations to see how they think and solve problems. Find out the background of the agency principals and project team members. Look for strong creative abilities and for designers who have worked in a broad range of product categories and for companies with substantial marketing know-how.

Most larger design firms will not provide speculative creative. But all of them will submit a proposal at no cost. Generally, the more information a designer has, the better proposal you can expect. To provide you accurate cost estimates, the designer needs to know how many SKUs are involved, the general size of the package, package materials to be used (if known), and any production constraints you may have, such as if you intend to print two color or four color. Beyond that, you may want to review with the designer the brand's history and positioning, consumer demographics, usage and attitudes, competitive environment and design objectives and parameters.

A good proposal should include:

1. A definition of the scope of the project

2. Design objectives

3. A discussion of packaging issues that need to be addressed

4. A design plan stating the steps required to complete the project

5. Detailed cost estimates

6. Biographies of the project team

7. Examples of related work the designer has completed for other clients

Good package design is a highly strategic process. Find a designer who understands that and who's not afraid to challenge your thinking.

Whomever you choose, get them involved as early as possible. A good package designer can help you think through the product positioning and can be a meaningful contributor to your marketing team.

Other Issues Affecting Packaging Design

Environment

Packaging's environmental impact has become a major issue — and one that can affect brand perception and the product's ultimate marketability.

There are four primary areas for evaluation:

- Recyclability

- Potential for the reuse of packaging materials

- Source reduction — reducing the amount of materials used to package a product

- Biodegradability — the ability of packaging to decompose after it's discarded; and toxic deleterious effects of packaging materials on the environment, such as heavy metals from colored inks, fluorocarbons from foam and dioxin from bleached papers. Environmental impact should be a primary issue addressed at the beginning of a packaging project.

Regulations that may restrict particular packaging materials should be assessed on all applicable levels: local, national and international. For example, shrink wrapping will be severely limited in the European Common Market countries. Plastic foam packaging is expressly banned in a number of U.S. localities. Recycling regulations may preclude the use of certain materials than cannot fit into a local recycling stream. In addition to societal and marketing benefits, environmentally effective packaging can also save the marketer money by helping reduce shipping weight and cutting down on material costs.

Technology

Packaging may not only help bring products to market and protect them on the shelf. New packaging technologies allow for better-tasting foods, can help prepare them (microwaveable packages), and in some cases actually defines the product (e.g., Kraft's aerosol Cheez Whiz).

Technology changes constantly. And marketers should always be on the lookout for new packaging that adds distinction and value to their product and offers a competitive edge. Among the new technologies that will drive product marketing are those that improve shelf life and product quality and may allow the marketing of products that may otherwise be too expensive or troublesome to bring to market. Growth in ready-to-serve and single-serving packages is also predicted.

Aseptic packaging is a modern updating of canning. Using highly sterile packaging machinery and materials, aseptic packaging allows the creation of shelf-stable prepared foods that come close to fresh foods in flavor and texture.

Controlled Atmosphere Packaging (CAP) gives fresh foods a longer shelf life and permits harvesting and shipping of ripened fruits and vegetables outside a limited area. Such packaging involves manipulation of various gasses produced by plant respiration or that react chemically with the food. CAP gasses and packaging materials are tailored to the requirements of specific foods.

CAP meat packaging often involves replacement of oxygen with inert gases.

CAP vegetable packaging may use semipermeable membranes to exchange carbon dioxide, oxygen, and water vapor. Beer packaging may use bottle caps with oxygen-scavenging materials embedded in them to reduce oxidation and extend shelf life.

New microwave packaging allows for transportability, single servings and helps eliminate uneven cooking in microwave ovens.

Legal

Trademarks are some of the most valuable properties a marketer can own. New brand names should be checked for conflicts and registered with the U.S. Patent and Trademark office. The marketer should also periodically search the market for products that may infringe on his or her trademark. Not only brand names are protectable. Anything unique and indicative of the brand may be registered, including graphic devices, typography, package shape, and sometimes even colors.

For example, the J.M. Smucker Company holds as a trademark the gingham pattern of its jam caps. The importance of consulting with competent trademark counsel when introducing a new brand cannot be overstressed.

Regulations

Packages and labeling are regulated—depending on the product—by several federal

New brand names should be checked for conflicts and registered at the U.S. Patent and Trademark Office

agencies, primarily the Food and Drug Administration, and the U.S. Department of Firearms.

The Federal Trade Commission regulates advertising claims that may affect what appears on packaging. State and local regulators have also become more active in policing packaging information. During the 1980s there was a laissez-faire treatment of product claims on packages by the federal government, with labeling compliance being voluntary. In the future, with the passage of the Nutritional Labeling and Education Act of 1990, there will be much stricter regulation, and marketers must be prepared.

The operations word is "truthful." Packaging and packaging information must be accurate, must not tend to mislead, and must conform to legal definitions and requirements. Claims that require particular scrutiny are those that declare nutritional or health benefits.

It is recommended that competent legal counsel evaluate final package designs and copy for compliance before the packages are put into production. New packages can also be sent for evaluation and comment to the appropriate federal agency.

A good package design works at the point of sale just like a good ad and can be a vital factor in the lowering of the cost of distribution by incorporating product sales.

Summary

A good package design works at the point of sale just like a good ad and can be a vital factor in the lowering of the cost of distribution by incorporating product sales.

CHAPTER 27

How Products and Services Are Distributed

By: Al Whitman

Distribution, along with product quality and pricing, is another key element in marketing.

There are many systems of distribution at work in the United States. The systems used vary by the category of product or services and the way products are marketed in each industry.

Peculiarly enough, the distribution system used does not often result in widely different prices as far as the consumer is concerned. The reason is that in almost every case the ultimate consumer has to pay for the cost of distribution, which varies by type of industry.

Types of Distribution Used in Different Industries.

1. Distribution by *mail.* This form of distribution is used primarily to sell goods and services via mail-order catalogs or sell them via direct- mail letters or via mail order media advertising.

   In each case, the line of distribution goes from the company marketing the product or service or from the mail-order house direct to the consumer, who pays for the product plus mailing and handling costs.

2. From manufacturer to independent wholesalers, or to chain store headquarters to the retailer to the ultimate customer.

   This form of distribution is used for many different products, but particularly for food and drug lines.

   The wholesaler charges for handling and the independent retailer adds a markup to the consumer.

   In case a sale goes from manufacturer to a chain operation like Safeway food store and Walgreen's drugstore, the chain pays the same price as the wholesaler pays, and then distributes its products to its own stores or retailers who own their stores and sell under the chain's name.

3. Distribution from the manufacturer to manufacturer's representatives, who sell direct to chains and independent retailers, and sometimes to other corporations.

    The latter system of distribution is usually used for industrial products. Naturally, the manufacturer's representative has a limited sales organization, and often just a sales manager.

4. Distribution to *brokers* to chains and to independent retailers and then to the consumer.

    The kind of manufacturer who uses this system uses the brokers as its own sales organization. This distribution system is most frequently used in the food business. You'll also find brokers used in other lines — products such as over-the-counter drugs.

    These brokers represent other firms as well and are paid a fee or commission.

    They usually have a limited sales organization that may do some in-store work, such as a manufacturer's own sales organization would be expected to do. But they usually can't afford to spend too much time for any one client in arranging for special promotions, in-store displays, and so on.

5. Distribution by *mail,* after sales have been made by phone or by personal sales calls house to house.

    The purpose of the phone call might be to get prospects to ask for detailed product information, which would be sent out by mail along with an order blank.

    This kind of system is often used by businesses such as rug cleaners, house painters, magazine publishers, house siding companies, and lumber dealers.

It's also widely used by charitable organizations asking for contributions, and to solicit national and state contributions for politicians.

Both the phone and personal calls are used as a main distribution and sales system by such organizations as insurance and brokerage houses and by firms like Avon selling door to door.

6. Distribution from manufacturers to sales and service centers. Examples are gasoline stations, repair shops, muffler organizations, and automobile dealers.

7. Distribution from the manufacturer to the discount store, department store, or other seller, to the customer. Under this system the stores are generally sold by a manufacturer's own sales organization. Eamples of this distribution system are the Wal-Mart, K Mart, and Target discount chains.

Today Wal-Mart discount stores, which compete with K Mart, J.C. Penney, and Shopko stores mostly in small towns, has built one of the most profitable discount chains in America.

One strategy it used was to build its own warehouses and thus lower prices to the consumer by being able to buy in great volume and have lower storage and delivery costs.

Wal-Mart's warehouse strategy calls for clustering stores in a 200-square-mile area around the distribution points.

Deliveries to stores can be made daily. The warehouses handle 77 percent of all the merchandise sold.

In 1983, Wal-Mart also started Sam's Warehouse Club, which soon had grown to 49 outlets doing nearly $2 billion in sales.

These strategies have made Sam Walton, the owner, a billionaire.

8. Manufacturer selling *franchises* on a state and regional basis to a person or to a

company that will then sell the product or service involved or franchise others to sell it.

9. Fast-food organizations such as McDonalds, Burger King, Wendy's, Dairy Queen. These operate using a slightly different system. The parent company builds and operates its own stores or sells a franchisor to build its own outlets.

   Generally speaking, the company that has put together the operation regionally or nationally will manufacture, or have manufactured for them, most of the foods sold in the stores and will pick up all or most of the advertising costs.

   There are almost 329,000 franchise outlets in the United States and about 2,000 franchisors in 60 industries. They do mor than $100 billion in sales.

   Today's fastest-growing segments are in *services*, such as maid services, home remodeling, painting, dry cleaning, carpet cleaning, quick oil changes and lubes, and temporary employment agencies.

10. Book-of-the month clubs. The publishing house sells consumers a deal under which they agree to purchase a certain number of books per year from the publisher for either the established price of each book (plus mailing and handling charges), or a flat price of so many dollars for so many books.

11. Credit card systems. Examples are American Express, Mastercard, VISA, Discovery.

    The consumer can use these cards to charge purchases of many different types to the credit card company.

    The company charges a fee to the retailer or manufacturer whose goods have been purchased by credit card.

12. Home shopping shows on cable television.

    The home shopping business, which sells goods and services at a discount to viewers through cable television, is still young.

Today's fastest-growing segments are in *services*, such as maid services, home remodeling, painting, dry cleaning, carpet cleaning, quick oil changes and lubes, and temporary employment agencies

The home shopping business, which sells goods and services at a discount to viewers through cable television, is still young.
Sales exceed a billion dollars and there's no annoying sales pitch or pressure to buyers

Sales exceed a billion dollars and there's no annoying sales pitch or pressure to buyers.

Seventy seven percent of the buyers are women. About half are 25 to 44 years old, and about sixty percent have attended college.

About ten percent of those who watch a show have made a purchase.

The average number of purchases have been about six per year, and the total amount spent for purchases is about $177.

13. Called *"category killers"* by retailers, huge stores feature 1,500 home furniture and houseware products.

   Most of the selling is done with signs, stickers and catalogs in the store explaining how the furniture is made.

   Many such stores offer a restaurant and nursery, plus very low prices and a wide selection of merchandise in important categories.

   In one chain, the average customer spends two to four hours shopping.

   This is a unique distribution idea and apparently it works.

14. The American Family Corporation, the world's largest underwriter of supplemental cancer insurance, markets its product through this three-tiered distribution system and collects its premiums primarily through *corporate payroll deduction programs.*

Summary

There are many different ways to employ the distribution of a product or service.

Sometimes the decision as to which system is self-evident. In other cases you have a choice.

When you can use more than one system, you're lucky, so do it.

CHAPTER 28

How to Market a Political Candidate

By: Al Whitman

In most cases, marketing a political candidate is very similar to marketing a product or service.

It makes little difference whether the candidate is running for office for the first time or is seeking re-election. The marketing fundamentals are much the same, and they include:

1. The way the candidate is positioned for the voters (see Chapter 16).

2. The *benefits* the candidate offers to the voters if elected or reelected (see Chapter 11).

3. The ideas that the candidate proposes as additional reasons to win the support of the voters (see Chapters 30 and 31)

4. The type of advertising run.

To illustrate how these principles work in practice, we'll give you two case histories of what took place in actual campaigns.

The first was waged by a Southern Democrat seeking the office of governor for the first time and in a state that for some years had voted Republican.

It should be added that this candidate had 30 years of public service to his credit and had been a United States senator for 18 years.

The second concerns a popular Republican senator from a midwest state running for reelection.

What the Gubernatorial Candidate Did to Get Elected

His Republican opponent in a Republican state was well regarded and had considerably greater funds to use than his opponent.

The Democratic candidate for governor based his campaign in substantial part on the promise that he would accept no contribution over $100 from anyone (PACS or individuals).

This concept positioned him as a candidate who did not seek support of the rich or any special interest,

The Democratic candidate for governor based his campaign in substantial part on the promise that he would accept no contribution over $100 from anyone (PACS or individuals).

This concept positioned him as a candidate who did not seek support of any special interest groups

and one who obviously could not be influenced by substantial donations.

Naturally, the Democrat advanced *other* important ideas in his campaign, including:

1. The desirability of having a smaller government.

2. The desirability of having more solutions emerge "from the ground up", so that the state government would not impose its own ideas and will on the voting public.

3. The importance of budget reforms. The candidate knew the state was badly in need of tax reform, but budget reform was needed first. In his state, a major part of tax revenues were generated by sales taxes, which are vulnerable to recession. He believed the public has lost confidence in parts of its government and would applaud serious budget reforms.

The Strategy of the Senator Seeking Reelection

The senator seeking re-election faced a Democratic challenger who was unknown to the general public.

The challenger had no political experience, and in many people's opinion, had only a couple of attributes that might be important as a senator: He was quick on his feet and had a good sense of humor.

The senator was running for his third term. He was recognized as having handled himself well in the senate. Even though he was a conservative Republican, he appealed to many voters in the Democratic party and was well liked at home and in Washington, where he was quite influential.

He was experienced in the areas of finances, nutrition, and farm policy.

He worked hard and did a good job of answering letters and suggestions.

As the campaign started, he seemed to be a shoo-in, strongly preferred by a majority of the voters in his state.

When the campaign started the polls showed he was anywhere from 15 percent to 25 percent ahead of his very liberal and relatively obscure opponent.

However, on election day, the latter obtained 52 percent of the vote, and the Republican, good as he was, received only 48 percent of the vote.

What Happened?

Any knowledgeable marketing man would tell you the Republican was ill advised (probably by out of state consultants). Consequently, he made almost every marketing mistake in the book and violated several basic principles of good marketing.

Mistake Number One

He ran a very *negative* campaign. This campaign backfired in two ways.

- It publicized his opponent by using his name and his picture in the Republican's ads.
- It created sympathy for the underdog, because people don't like negative campaigns, unless they are clearly justified.

Mistake Number Two

He positioned himself improperly (see Chapter 15).

- Long before the campaign started, he built up huge financial reserves for advertising.
- There were many heavy contributions from individuals as well as from PACS.
- It was obvious to many voters that here was a man with almost unlimited funds waging an unpopular, negative campaign against an unknown, inexperienced, super-liberal opponent who had little money backing him.

Mistake Number Three

When it came to advertising, he not only used the wrong kind (negative), but he and or his advisors put the power of money ahead of the power of *ideas* (see Chapter 30).

Mistake Number Four

He forgot all about the importance of benefits (see Chapter 11). Most of his advertisements just attacked the opponent. Few, if any, told voters what advantages they'd receive if they reelected him to the senate.

In fact, during the last two months of his campaign, he hardly ever mentioned the contributions he'd made as a United States senator.

When the conservative Republican was beaten in a tremendous upset, it may have come as a surprise to most voters. But, if you were an experienced marketer who realized the senator had violated almost all the key principles of good marketing, it came as no great surprise.

If you were an experienced marketer who realized the senator had violated almost all the key principles of good marketing, it came as no great surprise

Summary

1. The basic principles of marketing products and services applies to political candidates.

2. The starting point is the quality of the candidate. This involves such characteristics as character, integrity, stature, speaking ability, sense of humor, and political knowledge.

3. The platform of the candidate must be spelled out simply, clearly, and concisely.

4. There needs to be an understanding that advertising is only *part* of marketing and doesn't replace it.

An understanding that advertising is only *part* of marketing and doesn't replace it

5. Knowledge of the importance of benefits to voters and the ability to use benefits properly in the campaign is important.

6. So is the way the candidate positions himself or herself, that is, is the candidate liberal, conservative or middle of the road? How does he or she stand on controversial issues and why? What are the two or three changes he or she believes in strongly, and why?

7. The way the candidate handles the opponent in public is vital. Note: If a candidate is smart, the opposing candidate will never be named unless he/she has done something disgraceful or illegal.

   However, the candidate will make a point to correct certain things that have taken place during the opponent's candidacy, for example:
   » How many people have been added to the payroll?

The candidate must understand that ideas are much more important than money. If he has better ideas, he doesn't have to spend as much money as the opponent does

» How much of the various taxes the voters have to pay has increased during the opponent's regime, compared to increase in cost of living?

8. The candidate must understand that ideas are much more important than money. If he has better ideas, he doesn't have to spend as much money as the opponent does. Ideas, not money, are the most important force in the world.

9. The candidate's ability to come up with at least one important or memorable idea (such as the southern governor's promise not to accept any contributions from any individual or organization of over $100).

Two Idea Possibilities for Future Candidates

1. If you're running for office and plan to make some highly popular appointments, tell the voters during your campaign whom you will appoint to specific offices.

2. Take out an 800 number and encourage voters during the campaign to use this toll-free number to call in with their ideas, suggestions or complaints. Put each conversation on a computer tape, which will be printed out and analyzed.

   Such an idea not only is proof that the candidate cares about voters' opinions, but should result in some very favorable publicity after all the suggestions are analyzed and the candidate has reported on them.

CHAPTER 29

Marketing and the Small Business Owner

By: Al Whitman

You'd be amazed at the number of small businesses in the Unided States and their importance to the economy.

The 1989 government data from the Small Business Administration defines a small business as a company with a net worth of less than $6,000,000 and net income of less than $2,000,000. Most small businesses generally have fewer than 500 employees.

It's estimated that approximately 32.4 million people are employed in small business. The total annual sales of small businesses amount to approximately $2.1 trillion, which represents 38 percent of the gross national product of the country!

In a general way, small business divides itself into a couple of categories:

1. There are those relatively simple businesses for which a person has been specifically trained.

    Some examples in this category include a person who studies to be a pharmacist, a doctor, or a dentist.

    It also includes people who've been immersed in a small family business at a relatively early age, such as a person whose father and grandfather ran a restaurant, a haberdashery, a shoe store, or other type of specialty business.

    Most of these businesses require relatively *little* technology, and they don't need a great deal of modern marketing to have a reasonably good chance of being successful.

It's estimated that approximately 32.4 million people are employed in small business. The total annual sales of small businesses amount to approximately $2.1 trillion, which represents 38 percent of the gross national product of the country!

Note from the publisher: We're indebted to Daniel Haggarty, who runs Norwest's Venture Fund, a very successful small business investment company, for much of the material in this chapter. Dan has been in this business for many years. Few people are more experienced in and knowledgeable about small business than Dan.

2. This second group of business are those run on a somewhat larger scale by entrepreneurs, usually people who have come up with an idea that can be translated into a reasonably important new product or service aimed at a substantial market.

   To be successful, these businesses require a lot more know-how in financing, marketing, etc. than the businesses in the first group.

   Quite a number of these kinds of businesses are helped by the Small Business Administration in Washington, D.C. and regional and state offices, and quite a few are associated with Small Business Investment Companies (SBICs).

During the past 20 years the businesses in group two have changed considerably. They're much more *technically oriented.* They require better staffing and greater financing. Some are run by people with an instinct for doing the right thing and making the right moves.

But unfortunately, the woods are full of small businesses in group two that fail.

For example, we estimate as many as 15 to 20 percent of small businesses fail within the *first year.*

Some are refined and restructured so they can stay in business. Others fail because they made too many mistakes or lacked specific kinds of know-how.

In many small businesses it's rare for the owner to be a well-trained marketer and to be knowledgeable about sales organizations, distribution, selling, promotion, packaging design, pricing, and other important marketing fundamentals..

Many small business owners lack all or most of these.

In today's environment, technology changes rapidly. To capitalize on an idea, it's imperative to reach a market as quickly as possibly to avoid being leapfrogged by competition and to have as long a time as possible to recover costs and generate profitability.

This requires a major up-front financial investment to bring together a management team with the necessary skills to do a fast rollout.

Sales and marketing people should be in place to help with product development, market assessment, pricing, distribution, and promotion.

Investors who've been through the process before are a great source of guidance and counsel for an entrepreneur in a fledgling company. So is an SBIC.

Selected Criteria for Today's Successful Small Business

1. People with ideas for a new or revolutionary product or service that addresses a *significant market*. It may start out small but can have the *potential* to be a large company of up to $100 million or more.

2. A patented or proprietary product or technology.

3. A large, growing market.

4. A market or customers who recognize they have a need (or can be convinced they have a need) that is unfulfilled.

5. Capacity and willingness to pay for a solution because it makes good economic sense for them.

6. A product or service that can be expanded to a family of products over time.

7. A management team (versus individual) that's knowledgeable, experienced and driven by a desire to succeed.

8. Adequate capital.

Our experience indicates that more small businesses of the type we're discussing are started by technical or financial people than any other category.

Many entrepreneurs start a business in the following way:

- They develop an idea for a product.
- They build a prototype.
- They rent space and build an initial batch of products.
- They talk to engineering friends in companies (potential customers) and try to sell product.

- However, they often get frustrated or have to redesign their product or often they run out of money.

One shortcoming in the above process is lack of attention to customer needs or desires and a lack of understanding of *market size, and competitive products.*

(This is not meant to be a criticism of the entrepreneur, but to recognize strengths and weaknesses and anticipate where help will be needed.)

The Importance of Customer Needs

Early on in any project or idea, the entrepreneur must evaluate the need for a product or service.

This is best done by talking to potential customers about their problems and soliciting feedback on the product idea to see if it addresses customer needs, wants, and requirements. This can be done by the entrepreneur or by consultants.

The next step, assuming the meetings with potential customers were positive, is to attempt to assess market size.

The need must be large, recognized, and solvable.

If you want your company to grow to $100 million in annual sales, a need must exist or the product or service must be able to solve a big problem. The product idea must not only be capable of meeting the need or solving the problem, but should be distinguishable from competition.

Ideally you'd like to have an idea that's patentable so you can have a market to yourself for some time.

Customer feedback helps one to define or refine a product and aid in determining product pricing. It also should offer insight on who will make the decision to purchase the product or service.

This feedback will help to position the product with potential customers and should provide insight as to how to sell or distribute the product.

Most Entrepreneurs Need Help

Many entrepreneurs don't possess all the necessary skills needed to build a product, market it, and run the company. They need to rely on partners, investors, consultants, and service providers to fill in the gaps.

Early on in any project or idea, the entrepreneur must evaluate the need for a product or service.

If you want your company to grow to $100 million in annual sales, a need must exist or the product or service must be able to solve a big problem

Many don't raise enough money originally to get the job done, and have to go to a bank or an SBIC for a loan. When they have to do this, they usually end up by giving a good part of their business away.

Some are poor managers.

Others don't interact well with customers. Others don't recognize the needs and wants of those customers.

Naturally, there are exceptions to all of these statements.

The management of small business is improving all the time, and the SBICs help many of them understand the changes taking place in the market place, and help their small business clients be successful.

An Example of a Creative Entrepreneur Who Didn't Need Help

Some entrepreneurs have developed very successful small businesses on their own, using novel ideas

Some entrepreneurs have developed very successful small businesses on their own, using novel ideas.

Take the 110,000-square-foot emporium in Connecticut, and probably the worlds largest dairy store.

There are two very unusual features about this store that bring customers in from Massachusetts, Maine, Rhode Island, and New York. The owner has a passion for fun and for excellence.

1. This is the funniest store they've ever shopped in.
2. The prices are low and the quality is quite high.

When you enter the store, you'll find a collection of goats, hens, and geese featured in the "little farm" section alongside the 550-car parking lot.

The store's sales people are dressed in costumes. One is dressed in a Confederate gray uniform and accompanies himself on the banjo to "Dixie" and "I'm a Yankee Doodle Dandy."

Another is dressed in a bright yellow chicken suit. He picks up young kids in the produce section and gives them a twirl.

All employees are specially trained to satisfy the customer and are awarded gift certificates for $100 dinners and participation in a profit-sharing program.

Fresh flowers are placed in every restroom.

When a customer spends more than $100, the cash register says "MOO".

The store sells 5 tons of chocolate cookies a week, 100,000 pounds of chicken, 100 tons of cottage cheese, 25 tons of salad fixings, and 10 million quarts of milk.

Great attention is paid to quality, particularly the quality of meats, produce, and dairy items.

The prices of many products are almost unbelievably low.

So here is entrepreneureal small business successful at work, providing fun, great service, high quality, and low prices, mostly because the small business entrepreneur who owns and manages the establishment understands the power of ideas.

Why Did We Include This Chapter?

We included this chapter because we're confident there's a great deal of information in this book helpful to the small business owner or manager, especially:

- The chapters on *marketing* (Chapters 1 and 69).
- The chapters on *positioning* (Chapter 16 & 17).
- The chapter on *benefits* (Chapter 11).
- The chapters on *essential sales tips* (Chapter 53) and *sales management* (Chapter 55), plus chapters on the importance of *ideas* and the chapter explaining *where good ideas come from* (Chapters 30 and 31). The chapters on *pricing* (Chapter 26) and *sales promotion* (Chapter 2) and the chapter on publicity (Chapter 22).

We may be a little prejudiced, but we feel that every small business owner who invests in one or more copies of this book will get money back 10-, 20-, or 100-fold.

CHAPTER 30

Why Ideas Are the Greatest Force in the World

By: Al Whitman

We're not just talking about why ideas are such an important force in the creation of good marketing, advertising, and personal selling. We're also talking about the importance of ideas in the entire world.

Just think. Communism is an idea. So is Socialism. So is Democracy.

Religion is an idea, as are its many different types, from Christianity to Buddism, Hinduism, to Muhammadanism.

Think of peace.

You'll never have permanent peace without an idea that can make it a reality

How do you get peace in the world? You'll never have permanent peace without an idea that can make it a reality. It most certainly won't come in any permanent way from the use of guns, tanks, bullets, and bombs.

Examine the power of ideas in marketing, selling, advertising, and promotion.

You'll find that a good idea is usually worth its weight in gold and makes the difference between success and failure in the marketplace.

The material in this book features marketing, selling, and advertising ideas that were good yesterday, are good today, and will be good tomorrow.

Almost all the illustrations and case histories included are relatively recent.

But there are one or two that happened as far back as 15 to 20 years ago.

The following example falls into that category and is included for the following reasons:

The following example illustrates the truth of an old adage: "A gifted product is more important than a gifted pen."

This means the quality of the product is more important than the advertising

1. It illustrates the truth of an old adage: "A gifted product is more important than a gifted pen."

    This means the quality of the product is more important than the advertising.

2. It features a memorable name, and packaging, plus a unique advertising idea — all of which help position the new product line in the marketplace.

3. It also features a brilliant marketing countermove by an important competitor who was caught by surprise when our client introduced his new product line.

Here's the story:

An important food client assigned us to a line of sugarless powdered drink mixes. The product line was geared primarily to children. The fact it was sugarless gave it a secondary appeal to mothers.

The key competition was Kool-Aid, which had dominated the market for years. It contained sugar.

The first move our new product group made was to hold a series of sessions with kids from 5 to 10 years old.

At these sessions the kids would be served one or more of the drinks, and the account executive and the artist who were working on the plan would talk to them about different ideas.

One day the artist drew a picture of an orange—a California navel orange. Under it he wrote "Belly Button Orange."

The kids in the group broke into laughter. The same thing happened in the follow-up groups.

So the line of drinks was given the name, Funny Face. And each flavor was given a unique and memorable name that would appeal to children and stood out in the store.

Here are some of the names:

- Loud Mouth Punch
- Goofy Grape
- Freckle Face Strawberry
- Choo Choo Cherry
- Rootin Tootin Raspberry

The name "Belly Button Orange" was changed to "Jolly Olly Orange."

The sales manager told me that when the line was packaged and the advertising and in-store material was ready for distribution, the company sold virtually every wholesale and chain in the country on its first call.

LOUD MOUTH PUNCH ®

GOOFY GRAPE ®

FRECKLE FACE STRAWBERRY®

CHOO CHOO CHERRY ®

ROOTIN TOOTIN RASPBERRY ®

Funny Face® Drink Mix is a Registered Trademark of The Pillsbury Company©

In this case the client, in his haste to market a product with a terrific idea, blind product tested the product only on a *one-time* basis

Actually, they obtained *on their first call* distribution in chains and stores that did 82 percent of the food business!

When the Funny Face line of products was introduced in stores, the product literally "walked out the doors" being purchased eagerly by the kids and their mothers.

But there was a big drawback.

The product was sweetened with calcium cyclamate, which didn't have great taste.

Many of the kids became less and less enthusiastic about the taste of the product, and sales dropped.

It was an example of a situation in which the advertising and marketing were great, but the product was nowhere near as good.

In this case the client, in his haste to market a product with a terrific idea, blind product tested the product only on a *one-time* basis.

The testing didn't indicate that the taste of the product would not stand up after repeated use

The testing didn't indicate that the taste of the product would not stand up after repeated use.

This weakness was bad enough, but during the winter the competition came up with another brilliant counter move. It *bought up* all the calcium cyclamate in the country. At the same time, it introduced a competitive sugarless product of its own under the Kool Aid label.

So this little story illustrates the following marketing principles.

1. It takes more than a great idea for a product and its marketing to be successful.

2. The quality of the product must be right and have staying power.

You must never underestimate your competition...

3. You must never underestimate your competition.

Another Example

Historically, many advertising agency executives give Christmas gifts to one or more members of their client's organizations. A typical gift would be a lovely tie, a quart of Scotch, or some good wine or golf balls. No matter how welcome, such gifts are prosaic and unimaginative.

Here's how one agency solved that problem. The chairman of the board and one of the key copywriters came up with an idea. They reasoned that the

Christmas season is connected with angels, and angels are great communicators. If they could obtain a supply of lovely angels and use them as Christmas gifts, it would fit with the season and their business.

The agency assigned one of its brightest women, who worked in the personnel office, to interview suppliers who had access to companies throughout the world and who manufactured angels. She found an attractive small angel from Switzerland. When the base was wound it played "Silent Night." She also obtained the history of the artist who created it and arranged to have the company in Switzerland give the agency the exclusive rights to use it in the United States only.

The chairman and copywriter then wrote a glowing description of the angel and had it printed on a gold paper insert that included a profile of the angel's creator. It also explained the fact that the agency had chosen an angel as the annual Christmas gift because angels were "communicators."

The agency also made up a list of clients' personnel who would be eligible for the angel, and instructed its people to make no personal gifts to anyone on the list. Several people from the agency would sign the insert so it would be both a gift from management and from the individuals who worked regularly with the client.

In previous years, gifts from the agency's employees to client's employees hardly rated an acknowledgment.

After the people on the list received angels, letters of appreciation were received from over half of the recipients as well as numerous phone calls.

So the Christmas angel became an *annual tradition* of that agency, and should you go into homes of recipients, you'll find a display of all the angels they received during the holiday season over a period of years.

You can be sure that most of the people who receive these angels as gifts truly admire the good taste and imagination of the agency and look forward each year to adding another beautiful angel to their collection.

After the people on the list received angels, letters of appreciation were received from over half of the recipients as well as numerous phone calls.

So the Christmas angel became an *annual tradition*

188

CHAPTER 31

How Do You Come Up with a Good Idea?

By: Al Whitman

Most everything you see sprang from an idea.

The telephone — electricity — light bulbs — carpets — linoleum — books — synthetic products — cameras — pictures — mattresses — furniture — frozen foods.

Some ideas *just occur* to people.

Some, like this book, are the product of personal experience.

Others come from *observation*. That is, someone sees a product or takes a recipe and decides to market it. (See the story at end the of this chapter on how the world's most popular root beer was created.)

Still another source of good ideas is the individual's imagination and the ability to associate with various aspects of life, such as beauty, color, gracefulness, and fragrance.

The process is called association, and with it lies another source of good ideas.

Here are a few examples:

1. When you think of beauty and color; that thought process may lead to the development of new designs for dresses, carpets, linoleum, curtains, or some other item.

2. When you think of gracefulness and color, such a process may lead to a package design, the shape of a new container, or even a line of cosmetics.

3. When you think of fragrances, this can lead to the development of a new line of perfumes.

The association powers of most individuals are not well developed.

But a truly creative person with well-developed powers of imagination and association can usually be counted on to come up with good ideas time and time again.

A limited number of people have, at times, *dreamt* about a new product or service and then developed it.

A great many new products result from new product groups in corporate marketing or in advertising agencies or outside firms specializing in new product work, i.e., the famous A.D. Little firm in Massachusetts.

Formalized Programs for Creating New Product Ideas

You've heard of *brainstorming* — carefully selected groups of imaginative people meeting to discuss ideas. They discuss:

- New product ideas
- Product improvement ideas
- Ideas for new uses
- New flavors
- New forms for existing products

Someone in the group comes up with the gist of an idea, and the others expand and improve on the idea.

Have you ever heard of *synectics?*

This is a formalized form of brainstorm conducted by a leader trained to use certain techniques and procedures to open up minds, and then help coax ideas out of those minds.

In both brainstorming and synectic sessions, one key rule is always observed. *No one is allowed to criticize a thought advanced by someone else.*

Consumer Research — Another Source for Ideas

Ideas for new products, product improvements, and packaging spring from different kinds of research, such as, blind product testing and different kinds of market research.

In blind product testing (see Chapter 9), a marketer discovers how a product compares with the leading seller in the product's category.

Also, the questionnaire completed by the people who test the product at home, usually asks why one product was preferred over another and whether

Ideas for new products, product improvements, and packaging spring from different kinds of research, such as, blind product testing and different kinds of market research

any kind of added improvement in either product is desired.

Market research studies are often used to answer these questions:

   a. How many homes use one or more of the brands in the product being studied?

   b. What do they use it for?

   c. When do they use it?

   d. What do they like or dislike about each?

Such studies frequently turn up information that leads to a good idea.

Finally, major companies and new product firms make periodic studies of how certain products in different categories are used in homes, when, by whom, how often, and for what purposes.

This kind of research is a frequent source of good ideas leading to better new product development, better packaging, better package instructions, new uses, and improved advertising.

In summary, ideas are the key to successful new product programs, which can be the key to the growth of many companies and play a vital role in marketing

In summary, ideas are the key to successful new product programs, which can be the key to the growth of many companies and play a vital role in marketing.

While these product ideas will be helpful to the development of better advertising ideas, most advertising ideas will grow out of

   a. A study of available information.

   b. A decision on how to position the product or reposition it.

   c. A study of the benefits that can be used.

A New Product Is Born

Years ago a 24-year-old couple honeymooned in a New Jersey inn. During their stay, they sampled a pitcher of herb tea made by the innkeeper's wife.

They were told that this tea was made from an old family recipe that called for 16 wild roots and berries, including sarsaparilla, wintergreen, juniper and hops.

The groom was a drugstore owner and quickly recognized that the beverage had commercial possibilities. So he obtained the recipe for the herb tea.

Together with two college professors, he developed a formula for making a concentrate of the beverage,

191

which, when mixed with water, sugar, and yeast produced a drink very close to the innkeeper's wife's creation.

The drugstore owner was a devout Quaker and wanted to sell his herb tea to hard-drinking Pennsylvania coal miners in place of alcohol, but was quite properly advised that the miners would never drink a "tea," so they decided to call it a "beer."

Thirteen years later this beverage was the largest-selling root beer in the world.

Summary

Ideas are one of the keys to successful marketing, advertising and selling.

In many cases they don't cost very much to develop, yet a good idea can be invaluable.

The right idea can help set your product or service apart from its competition and make other important contributions to you.

Remember Chapter 12 showed you ten ways to pioneer with ideas.

Ideas are one of the keys to successful marketing, advertising and selling.

CHAPTER 32

What's in a Winning Name?

By: Al Whitman

A memorable name is a real asset for products or services.

It usually makes crystal clear what a product is or does.

It usually suggests a user benefit.

It adds memorability and strength to any advertising run in its behalf.

Here are some examples:

> Frozen Entrees By George. A line of products created and promoted by Phyllis George, a former Miss America.
>
> I CAN'T BELIEVE IT'S NOT BUTTER. A vegetable oil margarine.
>
> General Mill's CHEERIOS. A memorable name for a cereal in the shape of little "o's."
>
> Kraft's VELVEETA CHEESE.
>
> DOWNEY Fabric Softener.
>
> OSHKOSH B'GOSH overalls
>
> L'EGG'S Pantyhose.
>
> REVLON'S VELVET TOUCH LIPSTICK
>
> TOPFLITE golf balls
>
> Travellers "UMBRELLA" Insurance Policies illustrated by the Red Umbrella.
>
> Kellogg's NUT'N HONEY CRUNCH. This product not only has a memorable name, but its humorous advertising with a play on "Nothing, Honey" produces terrific name recognition and recall for the company.
>
> Someone can point out that the product's advertising offers no news or obvious consumer benefit to potential customers.
>
> While such a criticism is hard to refute, perhaps it should be pointed out that "great taste" is a benefit and that "nuts" and "honey" and "crunch" all suggest a crisp cereal with a taste good enough to make consumers say yes.

Author's note: Maybe someday people will agree that a great name for a book on marketing is "HOW TO MAKE PEOPLE SAY YES". It certainly suggests in six short words exactly what this book is all about.

Summary

When you come up with a memorable, one of a kind name, you give your product a pioneer advantage and provide an important plus to your promotion.

CHAPTER 33

How to Use "Word Pictures" in Advertising and Selling

By: Al Whitman

One of the most memorable experiences I ever had while working in advertising took place when he offered bayberry-scented candles as a premium for purchasing a brand of salt.

For some months, we had been offering this premium on a daytime show on 15 eastern and midwest radio stations.

To obtain the candles, the consumer had to send in a small amount of money and the seal over the pouring spout.

The radio commercials featuring premium offers usually drew about 5,000 requests per week. Then a shrewd promotional man urged me to offer the bayberry candles as a premium just before the Christmas season.

Since I knew the bayberry candles would be a hot offer, I placed an order that was larger than any order I had ever placed for a premium, and I specified that the supplier must have an equal amount in the warehouse for use in an emergency.

We got so many orders for bayberry candles that 30,000 of them couldn't be filled before Christmas.

One of the reasons the bayberry candles were such a hot item is that they were appropriate for the Christmas season.

But in retrospect, the big reason so many orders were received was the radio commercial that had been written by the head of the radio copy department at Benton and Bowles.

For most premiums offered, we were very careful to explain all about the size, the color, and the value. The man who prepared the bayberry candles commercial didn't mention anything about any of those sales points.

His commercial went something like this:

"Picture yourself on the night before Christmas in a little village square in a typical New England town. On the edge of the square is a farm house. You approach the house and see the beautiful living room with a Christmas tree in one corner and crossed muskets over the fireplace. Suddenly little twin girls, dressed in white organdy, enter the living room. Each is carrying a bayberry candle. They cross the room and put the candles into the candleholders over the mantelpiece. They light the candles and the scent of bayberry floats through the air. Then they recite a little poem about the luck that bayberry candles bring to their users." This poem, which was then read, was written by the Benton and Bowles writer.

Then the announcer said, "If you want a pair of bayberry candles like these, send 25 cents and the label over the pouring spout to the following address."

Nothing about size. Nothing about color. Nothing about value.

What this imaginative commercial had done was to create a picture in words that the radio listeners could understand. It made them want the candles. Even if it didn't answer all the questions about color, size, and value.

Much to my embarrassment, we were swamped with orders that we couldn't possibly fill before Christmas.

What this imaginative commercial had done was to create a picture in words that the radio listeners could understand. It made them want the candles. Even if it didn't answer all the questions about color, size, and value

Four More Examples

1. Have you ever seen the commercial that shows a towel soaking up Niagara Falls? It is a great commercial, and it beautifully illustrates how to sell by using word pictures.

2. Perhaps you've seen television commercials aimed at farmers about a product called Buctril, which eliminates weeds.

   Here's what the copy says: "Buc works so fast you can hear the weeds drop."

3. Years ago, there was a great black pitcher who wasn't accepted by a major-league team until he was nearly 50 years old. His name was Satchel Paige.

Nolan Ryan, the great pitcher for the Texas Rangers, one day asked Satchel the secret of his pitching success. Satchel replied, "The 'old bow tie' is the best pitch in baseball." This was Satchel's way of saying, "Throw a hard fast one right under the chin."

4. In one of TV's great family comedies, the following remark was made: "She has such full wet lips, she could suck the paint right off a car."

CHAPTER 34

How to Sell by Association

By: Al Whitman

Selling by association is one of the oldest selling principles used in advertising and in personal selling.

Many years ago a New York advertising agency was given the job of introducing Plymouth into a low-priced car market that was completely dominated by Ford and Chevrolet.

The agency, in one of the great campaigns of all time, ran several ads, each using the headline "Look at All Three." Each ad pictured a Ford, a Plymouth, and a Chevrolet side by side. This implied that all three cars were equally good.

The advertisements sold "by association." Within six months, Plymouth was established as a solid third in the marketplace, picking up a substantial share of the market previously enjoyed by Ford and Chevrolet.

Advertisers who use testimonials are selling by association.

When a great golfer, like Curtis Strange or Tom Kite, tells us that he uses a certain golf ball, the commercial sells by association.

The Ford Motor Company ran a commercial for its Continental car. The ad featured Jack Nicklaus as the best in his field and compared him to Continental as the best in its field. This is selling by association.

This whole concept of selling by association is built around creating believability.

You say a couple of things that consumers know to be true, then you make a third point about your product. When they believe the first two points, they accept the third as being true "by association."

Another Example

Readers are perhaps familiar with the television commercials advertising a woman's hygenic product named Gyne-Lotrimin.

The commercial goes something like this:

> *Isn't modern medicine wonderful? It gave us marvelous new products to use when we first became a woman.* (True)

> *Then other new products for us to use at childbirth.* (True)

> *Now for vaginal yeast infection, they've given us Gyne-Lotrimin, which your druggist has right now. It's available without a prescription.*

This commercial is an excellent example of selling by association. Women who recognize the first two statements as true will tend to believe the third also.

CHAPTER 35

The Five Key Elements in a Good Print Ad

By: Al Whitman

There are five key elements in each good print advertisement.

The most important elements are the *headline* and *main illustration.*

After seeing them, the average reader goes to the bottom of the ad and looks at the product "logotype" which may or may not have a selling idea attached to it. Example: "You're in Good Hands with AllState." By logotype we mean the name of the product or service at the base of the ad.

The fourth element is the main subhead, and if the copy is fairly lengthy, you break it up by including short, secondary subheads as the fifth point.

Readership surveys have shown again and again the relative importance of these five elements.

Here are a couple of additional observations.

Ideally the main illustration should fit like a glove with the headline and visa versa (see chapter 14).

In addition, some ads may contain secondary illustrations with captions for each.

When secondary illustrations are used they are usually read by more people than the main subhead.

Ideally the main illustration should fit like a glove with the headline and visa versa (see chapter 14)

The Importance of the Headline

Some years ago, after I retired from Campbell-Mithun, I was the director of marketing and part owner of what today is the 19th-largest travel agency in the United States.

I put together for the company a travel school to train new agents for employment in our agency and in other travel agencies.

Just before the school was opened I started running ads in the travel section of two Sunday newspapers. I tested 8 or 9 ads. In each the body copy was almost identical as was the coupon at the base of the ad.

The essential difference from ad to ad was the headline.

The winning ad pulled nine times as many coupons as the weakest ad, five times as many as the average of all ads and three times as many as the second best ad.

The headline which accounted for the difference was either "How Can I Get a Job in a Travel Agency?" or "How to Get a Job in a Travel Agency."

The winning ad pulled nine times as many coupons as the weakest ad, five times as many as the average of all ads and three times as many as the second best ad

CHAPTER 36

How to Write a Good Print Ad

By: Al Whitman

1. Learn as much about the product as possible, particularly the specifics on the people you want to reach (see Chapters 5 and 6) and the benefits such people receive when they use your product (see Chapter 11).

2. Decide how to "position" the product or service you're advertising. (see Chapter 15)

3. Write a headline that:
   a. Catches attention.
   b. Features news or a benefit, or both.
   c. Suggests a picture that dramatizes the headline.

4. Write a subhead that expands on the headline. Add a logotype with a basic selling idea.

5. Use secondary subheads if the copy is long and needs to be broken up.

6. Ask for the order in the very last paragraph, repeat the benefit and then say, "So don't wait another moment. Buy it today."

CHAPTER 37

How to Dramatize a Product Name or a Selling Idea

By: Al Whitman

In advertising or personal selling, it's a very good idea to dramatize the product name or a key sales point.

Just make sure that the way you dramatize is truly pertinent.

Here are a few tips on this subject which illustrate the idea featured in this chapter.

1. In a print advertisement always make sure that the main illustration and the headline say the same thing.

2. You can dramatize a name by an unusual, memorable selling idea. Example: TV commercials for Miller Light Beer campaign, "Tastes great - less filling."

The Marlboro man dramatizes the thought, "Here's a cigarette for real he men."

The "Ho Ho Ho" commercials of the Jolly Green Giant dramatize the name "Green Giant" by sound and the trademark dramatizes the name.

The little giggle of the Pillsbury "doughboy" is equally memorable.

The famous hands commercial and selling idea, "You're in good hands with All State" is perhaps the very best example.

CHAPTER 38

The Importance of Sound in Radio and Television

By: Richard Wilson

Dick Wilson is an advertising man, a song writer and a playwright.

He wrote his first musical when he was a student at Colorado College and has been a prolific song writer ever since, authoring hundreds of advertising jingles and half dozen musicals.

He's been an excellent copy writer and idea man for several leading agencies. At Campbell-Mithun, Wilson teamed up with Steve Griak (see Chapter 44) as a prolific two man creative team.

A few years later they formed their own agency, Wilson & Griak, specializing in creating and producing television commercials.

However, the urge to write musicals was so great that Dick sold his interest to Steve and went on his own. Since that time he has written a half dozen plays and several popular record albums, including the religious album, "He Lived The Good Life," a musical about the life of Christ.

We learn most of what we know through three of our senses. Our eyes, our ears and our sense of touch

What's the job of advertising? It's to sell products and services. Some companies use very little advertising because the best way for them to sell is directly to the prospective customer in his or her home.

But most of the corporations in America have found that to sell their product or service, they need to advertise. They have sizeable sales organizations making calls and obtaining distribution for their products, but they still need advertising to make customers aware of important and unique benefits the advertiser has to offer.

We learn most of what we know through three of our senses. Our eyes, our ears and our sense of touch. We learn from smelling and tasting too, but not to the degree of the other three. And it's the sense of *hearing* we're addressing in this chapter.

We think the job of advertising is to make the customer aware of your best benefit…the best reason he or she might buy the product, so that he or she will "*want* to do what the advertiser wants them to." We want to get our product's name and benefit stuck in the customers mind, like a fish hook. We want to gain "share of mind." That's our main purpose.

So how do we do it with sound?

As you know, sound plays a major role in *two of the media we use to advertise*…television and radio. Most of the sound we hear is the human voice. But if your maiden Aunt called you on the phone and you hadn't seen her for years, you'd probably know it was your maiden Aunt, because voices are so individual.

So when searching for the right voice for your commercial, do it right. Listen for the kind you'd like to have for your product. It can be a strong equity in building the awareness you need.

Many small town radio stations have a problem here because they usually have only one announcer read all the commercials. So, if any of our readers are involved with smaller cities, don't settle for that one person. Find a voice that can be your own. If you really work at finding your voice, you should get one you'll like.

Another way to build equity for your product and get awareness is the smart use of *sound effects*. Some years ago Stan Freeburg, a wild creative man who specializes in the unusual, did a radio special. He created the sound of a big cherry dropping into Lake Michigan with appropriate radio sound effects. It was remarkably effective.

One of the great sounds was used in 1990 by McDonalds for its "sub" sandwiches.

The sound they used was the emergency sound subs use. It goes like this: AH OO AH. It's almost unforgettable.

The bubbling sound of coffee percolating (one of Ogilvy and Mather's famous commercials) was a memorable sound effect for Maxwell House Coffee. When you heard it, you thought immediately of that brand.

Much the same is true with the restaurant commercial frying bacon. You can almost *smell* it. The same is true with the commercials of popping corn.

When Northwest Airlines used to be called Northwest *Orient* Airlines…every time the announcer said the name, you heard the sound of an oriental gong between the words "Orient" and "Airlines." It was a great and memorable sound.

But what we believe gets the message of the advertiser into the heads of customers faster than anything is the right use of memorable and well-produced *music*. Songs…good songs, are simply more memorable than anything else we've got in our advertising tool chest.

We think you'll agree that these two commercials have great sounds. The first is Kellogg's® Raisin Bran, package shown at right. The music behind the "two scoops" claim in the commercials is memorable and outstanding.

The same is true of the song Diet Coke uses in its "Just for the Taste of It" commercial.

What we believe gets the message of the advertiser into the heads of customers faster than anything is the right use of memorable and well-produced *music*

Music is memorable, durable (it can last for years), it's very acceptable because people like good music and it sets a mood for your product, especially in television.

The trick to getting good advertising music done is to find a music company you trust. Why? Because very few people in this business know much about making music. What you need to ask for is a demonstration tape of their past works.

With today's synthesized music, this shouldn't cost over $500.

Because music has the ability to get into customers' minds, it's important that any "jingle" writer you hire can put your main thought into the most memorable part of his song. Years ago many of the finest commercials featured jingles. Today you seldom hear one on the air.

The 10 Commandments of music in advertising:

1. Thou should not use music when you have a newsy 3 for 1 sale, 25 cents off or a special of the day. Music needs to be played more often than such retail ideas would allow, and familiar music is not newsy.

2. Thou should not use music when running *short* campaigns of less than four weeks. Music needs time to work most effectively.

3. Thou should not use music when thou does not have a *good idea* to sing about. Good music has never yet saved a bad idea…and it never will.

4. Thou should use music when you are planning to stay with one idea a long time. But good words in the music can go on and on.

   It's good to vary the song if you plan to run it for a long time, but keep the same tune.

5. When thou uses music, you should *not* try to say too much. Consumers can remember one idea together with the name of your product or service, rather easily. But multiple ideas can confuse your selling ideas and get in the way.

6. Thou should fit thy music to your market, because different people like different music. There's *young* music and the great music of the thirties for today's elderly. You need to know the demographics of your customers and the kind of music they want.

7. Thou should use music to *set a mood.* We've mentioned this before. Nothing sets a mood better than music. Just ask the folks that make movies.

8. Thou should not covet thy neighbors music, but originate your own. (Too many songs are connected to the original words. So find new territory that can be your own.)

9. Thou should *strongly* think of using music when your product or service makes people *feel good* because music makes people feel good. ('nuff said)

10. Honor thy client, but not necessarily thy client's *taste in music.* He/she may have a "tin ear." Trust your best creative people and the musicians they trust. If they really believe in what they're doing, the music should be right. If the client doesn't like it, find a way to research it fairly.

So what is selling through sound?

It's uncovering those wonderful ideas that build unique sound equities.

Sounds that hook the customer through his ears and stay in his mind.

The three tools you have are voice, sound effects, and music. Listen more intently to these sounds now, on T.V. and on the radio, and determine who you think is doing a good job.

Then start doing it yourself.

Thou should fit thy music to your market, because different people like different music. There's *young* music and the great music of the thirties for today's elderly

CHAPTER 39

Using Memorable Trademarks and Selling Ideas

By: Al Whitman

You may remember that earlier in this book we mentioned that the logotype was the third most important element in a print advertisement.

In a glance the reader understands what company or product is being featured. If a selling idea is featured along with it, so much the better.

There are many great companies who feature memorable trademarks, with or without selling ideas, in everything they do, including advertising, literature, letterheads, annual reports, etc. Here are a few examples:

1. The Prudential Company's use of the famous trademark "Rock of Gibraltar." The selling idea is, "Be sure you own a piece of the rock."

2. The little Dutch boy, which dramatizes Dutch Boy paint on the package and in its promotion. No selling idea.

3. The Leo Burnett Advertising Agency in Chicago uses a hand reaching for a star. People in advertising understand this is Burnett's way of saying, "Everyone who works here tries to excel and to do their very best."

   Leo Burnett himself had something to say about his corporate trademark. "We don't always get to grab hold of the star, but we never come up with a handful of mud either."

4. The "Mr. Peanut" trademark for the Planter's Peanut Company.

5. Early in 1991 my wife and I took a vacation and stayed at a guest ranch in Wickenburg, Arizona, about 60 miles northwest of Phoenix.

This guest ranch, RANCHO de los CABAL-LEROS had a distinctive trademark of a wrangler riding a prancing horse.

You'd find this trademark on almost anything associated with the ranch.

- their stationery and envelopes
- placemats
- napkins
- golf score cards

This is one of the finest use of trademarks you'd ever expect to see from any organization.

CHAPTER 40

For the last three years, Sonja Larsen has been President of a consulting company, Fawn Creek, Inc.

Previously, she spent ten years with Target stores, primarily as Senior Vice President of all its advertising, sales promotion and merchandise presentation.

She has had officer responsibilities with various quality department store chains in New England and the Midwest. She has worked as a copy writer in a leading advertising agency and currently is on the board of another.

Her consulting clients include nonprofit arts organizations, food and hardware stores, small start-up businesses and established retail chains.

She has just published a book on the art of retail merchandise signing called "Signs That Sell."

In 1987 she was elected to the Retail Hall of Fame.

Today's Retail Advertising and How to Create It

By: Sonja Larsen

Retail Advertising — Immediate Results

There are four basic differences between retail advertising and general manufacturer's advertising:

1. **Pressure to perform short term.** Retail advertising has tremendous pressure for immediate short-term results. Often advertising is created quickly (overnight!) to create sales necessary to support the retail store's overhead.

2. **Pressure to offer recognized in-demand product.** Retail advertising contains proven product — merchandise that the retailer knows the public wants at a price that's attractive enough to increase customer traffic.

3. **Pressure to use vendor support.** Retail advertising is supported in part by manufacturers' money, which is called "co-op" or vendor-paid advertising. This pressure is often in conflict with pressure #2 (to present most-wanted product).

4. **Pressure to keep "mining" current customers,** versus marketing efforts to reach new customers.

Let's discuss each difference.

First, retail advertising's *pressure to perform.* Retailers analyze their sales, day by day, year by year. Plans are made to insure that last year's sale figures are at least met and preferably exceeded.

Every day of lost sales is simply a loss. They don't get "made up."

So there's heavy pressure on advertising plans to bring in more customers than you brought in last year, and have them spend more while they're in your store.

This pressure translates into promotional price advertising. Sales!

Storewide sales at strategic times of the year.

Departmental sales at periods of peak interest in certain merchandise.

Sale prices on specific products in high demand. Retailers' theory of "Shoot while the ducks are flying" means that paint and home repair supplies are always on sale just before peak do-it-yourself weekends.

Unlike manufacturers, who may wish to promote in a down cycle, retailers are interested in the up cycle. It's necessary to maintain share of market and stay competitive.

Recognized product. The successful retail operation stays very close to its customers. It constantly brings in new products to stay exciting and find out what will become staples in the future.

Large retailers have sophisticated procedures to test customer acceptance of new items, in order to project future sales and prices. Once a product has tested well, it's a candidate for advertising.

Retail profit margins are thin. The advertising must have some guarantees built in. Product rate of sale and past performance are the guarantee.

Vendor incentives and coop. Manufacturers understand that their image advertising and brand identity programs do not sell product the way a retail ad can.

Part of a manufacturer's advertising is aimed as much at retailers as the potential customer. To get their product into the retail distribution system in quantity, manufacturers offer advertising incentives. Usually 50% of the ad cost, up to a percentage of the total product shipped. It could be 2% of sales, or 4%.

This range changes from industry to industry, and can change by manufacturer from product to product.

A manufacturer may pay 100% of the ad cost for a new product introduction, or only 25% for an older item.

This investment in retail advertising is a wise one for most manufacturers.

The successful retail operation stays very close to its customers. It constantly brings in new products to stay exciting and find out what will become staples in the future

First, the retailer has a lower ad rate because of the quantity of advertising it negotiates locally.

Second, the retailer has a local reputation to put behind the product.

Third, the local retailer's advertising gets read with more attention than national ads. (people have a tendency to read ads by stores they frequent.)

If the retailer is a large chain, its circular with full-color photography will cost the manufacturer much less than the same space in black and white ROP.

A retailer must use good judgment to balance the desire for the vendor support to help pay the advertising bills, and the need to present the very best, most-wanted merchandise to lure the customer into the store.

Another interesting fact about retail advertising.

When a well known retailer with broad consumer confidence advertises an individual item, consumers will be more convinced about the advantages of using the product.

Generally after reading about it in a department store or popular discount store's ad, there's greater acceptance than if the same claims were made by the manufacturer's own advertising.

So it's to the selfish advantage of the manufacturer to have their products advertised by a good retailer.

Mining current customer base.

Retailers with charge accounts have a gold mine of customer data. They can find out who shops for what and target their advertising to that customer. Catalogs, sale announcements and letters can be personalized as well. It's called database management.

Traditionally, retailers establish a trade area and keep hammering it. They see their charge customers as the primary target for their direct mail efforts — with good reason. Research has shown that the 80/20 rule applies here. Almost 80% of sales can come from 20% of the total customer base. Charge customers make up most of the 20% group.

Pressure on ad results means that the retailer will spend most of the ad dollars against its best customers — the ones "guaranteed" to respond.

A retailer must use good judgment to balance the desire for the vendor support to help pay the advertising bills, and the need to present the very best, most-wanted merchandise to lure the customer into the store

Retailers with charge accounts have a gold mine of customer data. They can find out who shops for what and target their advertising to that customer

Efforts against new customers need to have enormous reassurances built in. Invariably, homes with profiles that fit one's best customers' profile, and a low-cost delivery system for the advertising message, are selected.

If a retailer does not have charge card customers, research can create a customer profile, which is useful in trying to enlarge the customer base and make one's advertising media more effective.

Here's where sales promotion tools are used. In-store events: contests, sweepstakes, fashion shows, personal appearances are all designed to bring new customers into the store.

A sharp retailer will count customers, check sales results, and balance these against the cost of the promotion. A "cost per customer" is established to identify the best promotions, which will be repeated; and the worst, which will not.

The use of names and addresses in sweepstakes has not been well executed. Follow-up mailings or promotions to new names is rarely done. The bits of paper languish in storage.

Retail Advertising – How to Create It

1. **Select the product.** Is it new and exciting? Will its introduction add luster to your store's image? Will it be in demand by fashion-forward customers, or the general public? If it isn't new, is it still in increasing demand?

   If demand has leveled off, is your price the news? How dramatic a price cut can you make?

2. **Select the audience** for the product. A fashion-forward product could be aimed at just the customers in your fashion-forward departments.

   However, you may want the "halo" such an ad gives to your customers in general — the idea that you're an exciting place.

3. **Select the media** according to your audience and your budget. Newspaper is the primary medium for most retailers. Either ROP or free-standing circular inserts. It certainly isn't the only medium.

Radio can be used to reach a specific demographic audience.

Direct mail can be targeted to a specific type of customer or neighborhood.

Television can reach a large audience, and present a great opportunity to demonstrate product uses or advantages.

4. **Secure your pipeline** of merchandise. Get guarantees of deliveries to fit the ad plan. If the merchandise is in short supply and retailers are competing for it, how sure are you that you'll receive adequate goods in time for the ad break? Nothing ruins your advertising credibility faster than not having the merchandise

5. **Create an ad that fits your store image.** Use the media, graphics and all the elements of the ad to convey your store's mission.

A store known for superb quality must never compromise its graphic quality in any ad. No matter how quickly it must be produced. Because of the time constraints, and because a campaign has more strength than a string of single, different ads, most retailers have "formats" or standard balances of graphics and type, into which the individual product can be fitted.

This allows several different art directors to create ads with a single "look" that's the store's image — not theirs.

Superbly organized retail ad departments may even have 5 or 6 art directors working on one catalog — with a seamless total look.

See to it that all ads including the TV sign-offs feature the same logo, ideally with an accompanying selling idea.

6. **Communicate the information about the ad internally.**

Make sure you have signs ready in all stores.

A store known for superb quality must never compromise its graphic quality in any ad. No matter how quickly it must be produced

Make sure the employees know the ad is coming, and how to present the merchandise.

Make sure the price and all the barcode information is in the price-scanning system so sales will be recorded correctly, and the customer will pay the right price.

7. **Measure the results.** What was the cost of the ad; what were the total sales for the product, and what was the "halo" effect of the ad on the department? Incremental sales are an important factor. Document the information, including any odd weather quirks which might have affected sales.

8. **Assume your ads will be copied by competition.** Retailers "borrow" shamelessly from advertising leaders. New type faces, formats and creative approaches remain unique for a limited period. The pressure to change, improve and to innovate is a daily one.

A few comments on retail advertising departments and their staffs.

Retail advertising departments pride themselves in being on the firing line every day.

Sales results are an immediate measure of success or failure. Hundreds of ads are created during a time period in which an advertising agency grinds out one campaign for non retail accounts.

It's extremely fast-paced and full of changes, as the retailer adjusts to new trends, new customer desires and new competition.

A successful career in retailing takes creativity plus flexibility and the ability to juggle many ads, several campaigns and a host of changes all at once. It's exciting!

The retail advertising industry attracts generalists — people who can understand research, customer profiles and hard-headed business decisions, and balance that with creativity and sensitivity to changing fashion.

All this, plus attention to detail. ("Retail is detail" is an old maxim). It's a daily attempt for perfection in

Retail advertising departments pride themselves in being on the firing line every day.

Sales results are an immediate measure of success or failure.

Hundreds of ads are created during a time period in which an advertising agency grinds out one campaign for non retail accounts

Most people who work in the creative departments of ad agencies have never written an ad in which the price of the product is featured

an imperfect world full of change. If this excites you, it's right for you.

What kind of creative people do best in a retail environment?

Many creative people who write print, radio, TV and outdoor advertising for non retail accounts are not very good at creating good advertising for retailers.

They often don't understand the difference between retail ads and ads for a manufacturer.

Most people who work in the creative departments of ad agencies have never written an ad in which the price of the product is featured, nor are they accustomed to having to write a half dozen ads the same day, usually for different products.

Finally they're not accustomed to having the results of their work measured by actual sales results in the marketplace. This can be a very *humbling* experience for a writer who tackles retail advertising for the first time.

These recent Target ads follow the best advertising rules to create full-page drama. Ideally, *one* product per ad.

Next best: *one* tight category of merchandise. The ads don't scream "price" but the savings are clear and easy to see. The quality of the total design and execution supports Target's image of brand and quality.

They are as exciting as any top department store's R.O.P.'s, yet they get the price across.

They are successful at mixing quality and price, which is what an upscale discounter is all about.

Timely merchandise, presented with photography is part of Target's philosophy of honest-dealing with the customer and its desire for a quality image.

They are as exciting as any top department store's R.O.P.'s, yet they get the price across.

They are successful at mixing quality and price, which is what an upscale discounter is all about.

There are several subtle messages in these ads.

1. That a woman who buys expensive clothing also shops at Target, which is a low price discount chain.

2. That Target has fashion savvy.

3. That Target understands women shoppers.

4. That Target's merchandise has the quality that will satisfy a discerning fashion customer.

All that, without saying it and boring the customer. These ads are all part of a series of mid-week run-of-paper newspaper ads. They were developed at Target after the author's retirement as Senior Vice President.

CHAPTER 41

How to Write Advertisements for Classified News Sections

By: Al Whitman

Classified newspaper advertising on homes, cars, appliances, rentals, and other items is big business. One good sized newspaper tells me that the weekly and Sunday classified ads amount to 30% of its revenue and for some newspapers up to 50%.

Just as in other advertising, there are good classified ads, fair ones and poor ones. At times someone comes up with a sensational one based on results.

To write a classified ad that works in the market place, you should follow the principles covered in this book:

- Benefits
- Positioning
- Eye-catching headlines
- Active verbs
- Word pictures
- Reader involvement

You don't judge a classified ad by sales alone. You have to measure its real worth by the number of legitimate prospects it turns up. If the prospects don't like what they see or what's for sale, the ad didn't measure up to what it said and won't produce sales. Yet it could have been an excellent ad.

The Importance of Believability

If you want people to respond to your ad and buy what your advertising features, be believable. Never exaggerate. Usually it's far better to undersell than oversell.

A Specific Example

Some years ago my wife and I bought a lovely old farmhouse and guest cottage on four acres in the country. We had four young children and needed help to care for our kids, do the cooking, and take care of other chores, so I wrote several ads that produced scores of inquiries but *no good prospects.*

Here's a typical ad which I wrote:

"Want a home of your own and a job in the country?

"We need an individual or couple to work on our place. Job includes cooking, cleaning, outside jobs. Fair pay and you get a charming house to live in."

At the time I thought this was a good ad, but I was wrong. The individuals and couples who applied for the job were far more interested in the house than in the job. We hired several, but none were satisfactory.

So my wife decided to write her own ad.

It read something like this:

"WANTED: An individual or couple to work in our home.

"Must have happy disposition, love young children and animals. Like cooking and cleaning. Modest but fair salary and small home of your own to live in."

This ad drew only *one* response. Two days later, after the ad appeared, the door bell rang. There was a petite, cheery middle aged woman with ruddy cheeks. She had a box under her arm and a suitcase.

She said, "My name is Nursema Skogland. When I saw your ad, I baked cookies for your kids and packed my bag. I do hope the job is still open."

We had "Nursey" for about 10 years. She was a jewel in every way. She loved us and we loved her.

So I learned my first lesson about writing classified advertising that works; *never over promise.*

Another Example

During World War II, in Washington D.C., there were thousands of people who came to the city.

Some were military men who were stationed temporarily in Washington. Others came to work for government agencies. Living space of any kind was in short supply. The classified sections in the Washington papers bulged with ads placed by people and families looking for a place to rent.

This ad drew only *one* response. Two days later, after the ad appeared, the door bell rang. There was a petite, cheery middle aged woman with ruddy cheeks. She had a box under her arm and a suitcase.

She said, "My name is Nursema Skogland. When I saw your ad, I baked cookies for your kids and packed my bag. I do hope the job is still open."

A man I knew, who worked for the office of War Information, wanted to move his wife and two young children to Washington for a few months. He sat down to write a classified ad to rent a small home. A co-worker saw what he was doing and said, "Don't waste your money. No ordinary ad will work in *this* town, but we have an ad that will work."

So at a time when thousands of people, including one congressional medal of honor marine, did not get a single answer, my friend at the office of War Information ran the ad recommended by his co-worker and got 16 letters from homeowners saying they'd consider renting their house to him and his family.

This is what the ad said:

> "IF YOU LOVE YOUR HOME —
>
> Responsible OWI executive with wife and two young children wishes to rent a three bedroom home for three months. We'll care for it as though it were our own."

Why did owners respond to this ad and not to others?

They didn't want to run the risk of renting to people who liked to party, who might not be responsible and who might not take care of their home.

So my friends "tested" ad worked like a charm.

Houses for Sale

Here's a classified ad on houses that appeared in the paper recently:

> GREATEST BUY - $165,000
>
> 5 Acres in Birch Bluff
>
> Charming rambler - 3 bedrooms, 2 baths, family room, laundry. Large living room.
>
> 515 Peach St. Call Pat Smith 717-3624

We picked this ad because, in our opinion, it is somewhat better than average. Its headline implies a good value. It's specific as to what the house offers and where it's located.

Now, let's see if this ad can be improved in one or more of four ways:

1. By including benefits.

2. Through the use of word pictures.

3. By positioning it for a specific market segment.

4. By using meaningful adjectives and active verbs.

Here's an example of each:

1. WANT A CHARMING RAMBLER THAT'S A DELIGHT TO LIVE IN?

   - On 5 usable acres in Birch Bluff
   - 3 charming bedrooms, 2 baths, family room, large living room, laundry.
   - Easy to clean and move around in. Save you time and work. Great for children. A home you'll be proud to live in.
   - Priced a little below market.
   - Call Pat Smith at 717-3624 and compare.

2. PICTURE YOUR FAMILY IN THIS CHARMING COUNTRY HOME

   - The whole family in a spacious living room. Your kids playing in a great family room. An easy to use laundry with the kind of quality appliances you like. 2 baths, 3 bedrooms with views, 5 acres in Birch Bluff ready for gardens and playing fields for your kids, great views. Priced for value at $165,000
   - Call Pat Smith today at 717-3624 for showing.

3. THE PERFECT HOME FOR A FAMILY OF 4 WHO LOVE COUNTRY LIVING

   - Charming living room, family room, 3 bedrooms, 2 baths, laundry, 5 acres, ideal for gardens, playground for kids. Fairly priced at $165,000. Call Pat Smith today at 717-3624.

4.   WANT A CHARMING COUNTRY RAM-
     BLER? THE HOME THAT GIVES
     YOU:

> – 3 lovely bedrooms?
>
> – Beautiful living room?
>
> – 2 large baths?
>
> – Great family room?
>
> – Plenty of space outdoors for a garden and kids to play in?
>
> – All are yours on 5 beautiful acres in Birch Bluff.
>
> – Almost a steal at $165,000. Call Pat Smith at 717-3624. SEE IT TODAY.

Another Key Selling Idea

My son, John, who has owned and sold three houses, plus a number of cars, outboard motors, boats, etc., has a key idea, which he has used time and time again, with considerable success.

MUST SELL BY (DATE)

He uses this idea in a headline whenever permitted to do so by the paper involved.

He follows up on the headline with a description of the item for sale. He closes with this reminder, "Remember this (name of item) must be sold by (date.)"

He says this approach almost always works.

CHAPTER 42

How to Multiply the Effectiveness of a Good Selling Idea

By: Al Whitman

When a company or its advertising agency creates a key selling idea for a product they naturally use it as a key idea in the headline and/or logotype of every ad, as well as on radio and television commercials.

But that's only the beginning.

If the product is a consumer item, the company or agency should include the idea on the front of the package. It should also go on the company's stationery, all brochures, annual reports, and on other items such as calling cards.

In ways like these, you multiply the sales effectiveness of the idea and at virtually no cost.

Today there are companies who do not take advantage of this opportunity, although a great many do.

It is a sure way of getting something for nothing, so it's well worth remembering.

To dramatize the above, Ray Mithun came up with the phrase, "cogwheel idea."

Do you know what a cogwheel is? It's a center wheel connected by spokes to a series of smaller wheels. When you turn the central wheel all other wheels connected with it turn as well.

You can see what an apt phrase "cogwheel idea" is. The center wheel is the wheel with the key idea. The other wheels are the advertising, the packaging, company stationery, annual report, brochures, publicity, and sales literature.

This thought illustrates again what a great teacher Ray Mithun was and is.

He actually had a cogwheel put together by a carpenter and used it in his explanation of the idea to our people.

If the product is a consumer item, the company or agency should include the idea on the front of the package. It should also go on the company's stationery, all brochures, annual reports, and on other items such as calling cards

CHAPTER 43

How to Use Advertising to Do Both the "Inside" and "Outside" Job

By: Al Whitman

Under certain conditions smart advertisers run advertising for a twofold purpose:

1. Influencing the performance of the people who work for them.
2. Selling customers and potential customers, i.e., outsiders.

A beautiful example of promotion designed to do a job inside the company and outside with customers is the famous Avis Rent-a-Car campaign, "We Try Harder."

Advertising designed to accomplish both the inside and outside job is of particular importance to service companies, such as, banks, insurance companies, advertising agencies, travel agencies, and brokerage firms.

A beautiful example of promotion designed to do a job inside the company and outside with customers is the famous Avis Rent-a-Car campaign, "We Try Harder."

Another Example

A chain of banks featured the following line in all their promotion, i.e., advertisements, envelope stuffers, signs at deposit windows, etc.

The line was: "WE'RE HERE TO HELP YOU GET WHAT YOU WANT."

Obviously, this was a great line for the bank's customers. But it also made everyone at the bank from president to office boy *live up to it!*

Are you in a service business? Is there an opportunity for you to offer your customers what they want, and help insure your employees will give it to them?

CHAPTER 44

After a ten year stint at Campbell-Mithun, where he worked in both print and television creation and production, Steve teamed up with Dick Wilson (see Chapter 38) to found Wilson-Griak Inc. When Wilson left the firm a few years later, Griak ran the company with his own team, creating and producing excellent and modestly priced commercials for many important agencies and clients.

In the 1980's The American Federation of Advertising elected Steve as its "Man of the Year in Minnesota." Steve has also received many regional and national creative honors for excellence. His awards include four CLIOs, perhaps the most important creative award an advertising man or woman can receive.

In an hour of TV viewing you could see 30 commercials

How to Create and Produce Good TV Commercials

By: Steve Griak

If there are any rules to creating a TV commercial idea, they are the same rules you'd use in making a print ad or a radio script. What we're attempting to do is *sell something.*

Advertising is selling and to sell a product or a service you have to know all about it (see Chapters 5 and 6).

How good is it?

What kind of person is going to buy it?

Who is presently buying it?

And, what kind of product advantage, if any, does it have?

Why Television?

Maybe the best way to sell a product is to go door to door...bring the "vacuum cleaner" you're selling into the living room, throw some dirt on the rug and "demonstrate how beautifully the cleaner works."

Other possibilities are magazines, newspaper ads, radio, or the current hot salesman...the TV commercial.

Great! Moving pictures, not a still photograph. Sound...you don't have to read, somebody will tell it, or better yet, *sell it.* Average viewing time in America's households is seven hours per day...television is a great *demonstrator.* What an arena to sell in! How can you miss?

But there are always some negatives. For one, in an hour of TV viewing you could see 30 commercials. Multiply that by the average viewing time of four hours per family member and an average viewer sees 120 commercial messages per average day.

To really work, your commercial must stick out of the crowd.

Also, the magic of television production makes miracles commonplace. People can be made to fly, animals can talk, mom or dad dance on the ceiling, and dirt can disappear off the rug without the "vacuum cleaner."

The viewer of the 90's has seen it all and knows all the tricks.

So, the next time you show egg disappearing off a dish, or dirt off a rug, you'd better do it in a new, amazing, dramatic and convincing manner.

Remember, your customer has seen it all.

Getting Ready to Find An Idea

First you must know your product.

Second, you must know your customer.

Then you're ready for step three, creating a communication that'll not only catch the eye of the viewer, but make him/her feel more positive about your product or service.

And if you really do your job, some of your viewers may even want to buy your product or service.

Before we start creating, let's throw the rule book away. If there ever was an area where the old expression "rules are made to be broken" applies, it's here.

First, we want to *get the audience's attention.*

Remember, your audience is being bombarded with attention-getting devices, so the ideas we invent have to separate us from the pack.

Second, we want to *make it simple.* The viewer doesn't have intrinsic interest in commercials. The message you send needs to be quick and easy to understand.

In television "one idea per commercial" is the axiom. Don't let your key message get lost. Don't let your client's desire to say everything allow the communication to get complicated. Leave the viewer with a simple, clearly stated message.

Finding an Idea

Where do we find the "idea?" How do you "have an idea?" (see Chapter 31). There are as many ways to generate an idea as there are people trying to find them. We've arrived at the key moment in the

Also, the magic of television production makes miracles commonplace. People can be made to fly, animals can talk, mom or dad dance on the ceiling, and dirt can disappear off the rug without the "vacuum cleaner."

In television "one idea per commercial" is the axiom. Don't let your key message get lost

advertising process, and maybe the best. If we could just find the right good idea.

Where do we start? By putting down every idea that comes into our head that relates to the product or service or its use. (see chapter 15 on arriving at alternate positions for new products)

Reject nothing. No idea is bad right now.

During this horrible/wonderful time some people work alone, others in groups or in creative teams. As the process begins, keep reminding yourself and your team what makes the product or service unique, and what kind of people use it.

Inspiration can come from anywhere. Keep the thoughts coming out. One writer called this process "snowballing." Make the ball bigger and bigger.

Somewhere along the line, stop and take a look.

Pick your best idea and "flesh it out" in commercial form. Does it work? If not, try another idea and flesh it out.

Finally, it's a good idea to walk away for a time.

Appropriate ideas can come into your head at dinner, out jogging, or even in your dreams.

Not all ideas come out of a conference room of creative thinkers.

Be willing to think freely, and *give it time.*

Ideas can come in five minutes or five days — many creative projects evolve over weeks or even months.

Ideas can come in five minutes or five days — many creative projects evolve over weeks or even months. Finally, remember the idea business is a fragile one. Tread lightly on anyone's ideas, including your own. Be prepared to look for what *you like* about an idea, *not* what's wrong with it.

Presenting your Idea

Once you and your team have an idea you like, you have to present it to your agency and client.

A storyboard is the most common communications tool used to present a TV idea. It's a series of drawings, not unlike a comic strip, that visualizes the idea with copy and description to clearly define the idea. A storyboard is sometimes only one picture — other times it might be 30 pictures or more.

Commercials are made in 60, 30, 15 and 10 second lengths. The length is dictated by the budget, difficulty of communicating the idea and the advertising strategy.

Producing the Idea

Once sold to your client, your idea is ready for production. Your agency production department will help you locate outside resources to make your idea come alive: production companies, talent, music, animation and the like.

You'll now have the opportunity to review samples of Commercial Directors work. Ask yourself, is the work similar to the production techniques you're looking for? Look for someone to "plus" your idea by taking it to the next level.

Based on your screening of samples, select three or more production companies who you feel might do an outstanding job of producing your idea. Get their thoughts and ideas, and request their bid.

Based on the returned bids, the director's comments and his/her "feel" for your idea, award the production.

Production

Production is a myriad of details — casting, set design, props, wardrobe, locations, scene timing. The director and production company will bring in additional experts to assist in these areas.

The actual shooting of the commercial is the culmination of a totally complete and thoughtful process. Your job is to protect the idea you started with.

The final step, after photography, is called editing and finishing. Film elements, along with dialogue, voice over, music and sound effects, animation and title elements, all are married into a finished commercial. Your job, once again, is to protect your idea.

Rules of the Road

Here are some "rules of the road" for commercial production, learned after many years of bumping into them:

1. Make sure you double check everything at least 24 hours before you shoot! "Trust me" and "no problem" are warning flags. You can avoid a lot of trouble by checking everything for yourself.

2. If you're producing a 30-second commercial, make sure you have a 30-second idea.

Select three or more production companies who you feel might do an outstanding job of producing your idea. Get their thoughts and ideas, and request their bid

234

Not 20 seconds, not 60 seconds. Most client approved storyboards need major surgery at the production stage.

3. "A funny script is a funny script…A funny commercial that sells a product effectively is a miracle!"

    The written word can be very different when it gets to the screen.

    Make sure to visualize your script in your mind. Can you really illustrate what you want to say?

4. In the production of a television commercial, there are an unbelievable number of decisions to be made, so you'll make mistakes. Make sure they're not big ones! Managing the successful resolution of mistakes may be more important than not making any mistakes at all.

"Producing a 'champagne' commercial on a beer budget often results in bad champagne instead of good beer!"

5. "Producing a 'champagne' commercial on a beer budget often results in bad champagne instead of good beer!"

    Learn to work within the constraints of time and money you've got to work with, instead of trying to do too much and ending up with nothing at all.

    Remember, the simple and the obvious is the best (see chapter 49).

6. "GOOD - FAST - CHEAP"—you can't have all three! You can have quality at a bargain price, but chances are you won't get it quickly. You can also get a job done quickly and cheaply, but it will likely not be very good.

7. Manage your vendors for success, by inspiring them and putting them in a position to win. Don't ask for the impossible.

8. "The bitter taste of poor quality remains long after the sweet taste of low price has been forgotten." Manage your client's money like you would your own. Demand the best value…and pay fairly for it.

Remember, all of these rules have been broken at one time or another with wonderful results. Good Luck!

Wrapping it All Up

In summary remember these key points:

- Know your product
- Know your audience
- Find a product advantage
- Get the right idea
- Create the story board
- Take all the necessary steps to create and produce the commercial the right way and at the right price

236

CHAPTER 45

Why Simple and Obvious is the Best

By: Al Whitman

This is one of the most important thoughts in this book.

In my life in advertising, I've taught a great many subjects, but few have been remembered and used more than this one by those who worked with me.

It all started with a professor who taught politics during my sophomore year at college.

He lectured once a week and opened every lecture with the following remark. "Remember fellows, as Woodrow Wilson used to say, 'In business, as well as in politics, the simple and the obvious is the best.'"

If you were to ask me what I learned in college that was really helpful, this single thought is about the only important idea I can come up with that was truly worthwhile.

In my opinion this was worth the price of four years education at a very expensive college.

I'm sure you've heard many talks that beat around the bush and never came directly to the point. What the speaker had to say wasn't either simple or obvious.

Now if you're a student in a college or high school, ask yourself how many papers you've written or read that get right to the point.

If you're a salesperson, don't you always try to say what you want to say in the shortest possible time?

Isn't it true that you can't stand people who have "diarrhea of the mouth?"

At a recent board meeting I heard an incentive plan described by its author. His description was so complicated that it was difficult to understand exactly how it worked.

Another member of the board spoke up and said, "Isn't it possible to prepare a plan, the gist of which

If you're a salesperson, don't you always try to say what you want to say in the shortest possible time?

your wife would understand if you explained it to her in thirty seconds?"

As a result the plan was greatly simplified and improved so that it could be understood in an instant.

Chapter 14, "Some Thoughts and Convictions of David Ogilvy," certainly indicated his belief in this thought, i.e. use short, easy to understand words, short sentences and short paragraphs.

Apparently a great President of the United States believed "the simple and the obvious is the best."

He wrote the Gettysburg address using about 265 words and delivered it in about three minutes. Don't you wish today's politicians would and could do that?

Why not take a few minutes and ask yourself how you can take the idea that the simple and the obvious is the best, and use it to your advantage?

You'll be glad you did!

Apparently a great President of the United States believed "the simple and the obvious is the best."

CHAPTER 46

How to Write and Use Direct Mail Letters

By: Carol Clemens

Carol Clemens is the owner of Media Management Corporation.

This corporation specializes in direct mail letters.

Carol has over 20 years of background in advertising and research ranging from marketing consumer packaged goods to computers. The latter led to the development of Media Management Corporation in which she has established an experienced team of advertising, creative, and account people.

Carol has an extensive marketing background in consumer and business to business accounts working as media director and vice-president for two well known agencies and has been instrumental in the integration of new products ranging from computer software to new appliances.

She has worked for such companies as Pillsbury, General Mills, A.C. Nielsen, Toro, 3M, Control Data and Coca-Cola Bottlers.

We are using Carol to create, develop, and test a direct-mail program for this book.

In many ways the advertising and selling of goods and services through direct mail letters is the essence of direct marketing activity.

What could be more direct than a seller contacting a potential buyer, one-on-one with no middleman, seeking a positive response to a sales pitch? Unlike television with its program environments, magazines' editorial atmosphere, or even the personalized immediacy of radio, direct mail must generate its own interest levels.

The direct mail practitioner has little third party interest to borrow upon. A direct mail sales solicitation stands or fall on the communications contained in the envelope. Its success is directly linked to the recipients favorable response to the overall mailing package.

Direct mail is just one aspect of direct marketing.

Its close relative is direct response advertising, wherein print or broadcast media is used either to solicit an inquiry for more information or sell something right from the advertisement.

The latter usually contains either a mail-in coupon, an 800 telephone number, or both of these response devices. The interested readers or viewers do respond via mail or phone and they soon receive either the goods they ordered or the requested information.

In contrast direct mail is pure, unadulterated, "in your face," selling. It doesn't rely on you noticing an advertisement because you happen to read a particular magazine or local newspaper. Direct mail does not complicate a sales call by filtering it through any third-party medium.

Like most other marketing activities, successful direct mail requires that a plan first be developed. At its most elemental, this plan will set goals, determine strategies, and select the executional tactics to be used.

The following outlines the elements of a comprehensive direct mail plan.

Situation Analysis

The situation analysis serves as background. This useful opening section might include how and why the decision to pursue direct mail was made in the first place. A historic recap of previous direct mail efforts, if available, can set the stage for creating an even more effective new mail package.

Describe the product or service to be sold via the mails in layman's terms first so that the reader will have a better grasp of the technical descriptions to follow. Technical descriptions should include any recent testing results, strengths and weaknesses, and details on how the product or service works.

Be Sure You Know Margins and Costs

Be sure you know what kind of margin your product offers. This knowledge is vital. The greater the margin, the more you can spend.

Also know your handling, postage and credit card costs so you can price your product properly.

Current product positioning in the minds of both the various customer segments and internal company personnel should be included. Review any pertinent research on current positioning or perceptions.

Dramatize the benefits of the product or service offered from an end-user, decision maker and other influencer vantage points.

Point out if benefits will differ among different segments of the customer base. Describe benefits in terms of both what the service will do for the user (such as make a person's life easier or save time) and of the emotional pay-off (such as it will enhance their self-image or promote peace of mind).

An important section of the situation analysis is a review of the environment in which your product or service must compete.

This should include a competitive products or service descriptions, promotional spending, price points and distribution data. Also collect direct mail

Describe the product or service to be sold via the mails in layman's terms first so that the reader will have a better grasp of the technical descriptions to follow

Dramatize the benefits of the product or service offered from an end-user, decision maker and other influencer vantage point

packages, packaging and collateral materials on your primary competitors. Examine what has worked in mail order media advertising, i.e., both media and copy.

In addition to providing valuable product information, these materials will give insight into creative strategies and positioning. Ultimately they will help you develop the points of difference between you and your competitors which can be used to build your strategies.

State the Objectives

A clear statement of objectives will drive the strategic planning for your direct mail plan. State precisely what is to be achieved.

For example, are you trying to generate sales or leads (inquiries)? Are you trying to build a database of future prospects or just creating immediate sales?

Direct mail objectives are inherently measurable. Quantify the degree of response you want to achieve. Include the time frame in which you want to achieve your goals.

For example, "produce $500,000 worth of sales in the fourth quarter" and "build a database of 10,000 future prospects in three months" are both measurable objectives.

Make sure your goals are achievable given past experience, size of target market, budget and other factors. It's also recommended that an overview be presented on how the direct mail objectives will work in conjunction with the overall marketing plan goals or other promotional elements.

Set a Timetable

The timetable should include target dates, timing for testing and rollouts, lists and creative lead times, timing for telemarketing and fulfillment activities, production schedules, analysis time and follow-up or back-end timing.

If there's an extensive delay in one or more areas, it will inevitably impact another even seemingly unrelated area.

Establish a Budget

A financial operations plan including costs and expected performance results should be discussed in the budget section of the direct mail plan. There are a number of methods for establishing budget levels. For many companies, budget is set based upon percent of sales or a figure which is affordable. For these methods, results which can be expected are somewhat dependent on the size of the budget. Other methods of setting budgets start with plan goals and work in reverse. This includes the task method, i.e., what will it cost to create the desired response rate. There are several other break-even or analysis methods that can be utilized.

Estimating response rates for a first time offer is especially tricky. Without a historical response history, pretesting is often required to establish whether or not the direct mail letter will be profitable.

Identify Target Audiences

The most valuable source of information in helping to identify target markets exists in a direct mailer's knowledge of current or potential customers—what are their demographic characteristics, where do they live, what lifestyle or other psychographic traits do they have in common, what are their occupations. Customer profiling, based on data collected directly from customers or derived from demographic overlays purchased from a service, can be an important first step in identifying characteristics of groups of people who are currently interested in your product or service. The task then becomes how do you find more people like them.

Lacking a current customer base or sufficient knowledge about current customers may require using syndicated research to identify broad characteristics of persons who are using products or services similar to your offering.

Whether trying to define the most likely target audiences for a new customer base or trying to develop niche markets beyond the current customer base, the key question to ask is, "Who needs the benefits offered by this product or service?"

As your customer base grows and your knowledge about your customer segments is developed, you may want to turn to more sophisticated techniques such as predictive response modeling to identity characteristics which predispose an individual to respond to your offer.

Direct Mail Lists

In direct mail, appropriate lists are vital. Each is also a market in itself. Whom we reach is limited by the lists available to reach them.

Often the first step leading to a list recommendation is the establishment of a universe which is a compilation of the lists which might be relevant to your particular target audience and product/service offering. This listing should include pertinent data about each, such as selections available, cost, closing lead times and use by competitors.

The greatest degree of selectivity is available through the world of mailing lists. There are over a billion names available on more than 50,000 different mailing lists.

Many lists offer segments within the basic list which allows selectivity based upon demographics, geography, product usage, past response behavior or a number of other options

Many lists offer segments within the basic list which allows selectivity based upon demographics, geography, product usage, past response behavior or a number of other options.

Among the lists you consider for product/service offerings, your current customer list is the most valuable.

It's often easier to sell additional products or services to an already satisfied customer than it is to prospects. This is particularly true for products or services which have a good repeat value.

Your past experience with various lists is the most objective and accurate prediction of future results with it.

When a response history by list is not available, or when looking at expanding your current lists, *testing becomes essential.* In fact, testing of new lists should be built into any on-going direct mail program. Most lists are available in test cells as small as 5,000. If your test samples are large enough to be projectable and each test cell is reasonably representative of the whole list, you can be relatively confident as to the outcome when you expand your list with additional names. Even with disastrous test results much can be learned about formulating subsequent tests.

Lists vary in cost from a low of $50 per 1000 names to as high as $250.

Create the Offer Strategy

A key driving force behind the direct mail offer strategy will be positioning. (see chapter 15) Positioning involves the commitment to a decision on what your product or service is and does, how you want it perceived and finding a credible way to plant that perception in the minds of consumers. The essence of positioning is to make the reader say, "That's *my* kind of product or service." This is one of the key ways to establish empathy with the reader.

Positioning requires focus. You cannot be all things to all people. You need to select and focus on the benefits which will motivate your target audience to buy. Actually, benefits (see chapter 11) are more important than positioning in the creative process. Benefits are the key to persuasion—the key to motivate a prospect to want to buy your product or service.

The offer is comprised of the product or service and price and how they are presented and expressed to the prospect. Price decisions include the establishment of price points, charges for shipping and handling, volume discounts and credit and payment terms. The product includes the physical product or service and added-value offers and guarantees (if any).

Changes in the direct mail offer and the way it's stated can significantly affect response rates significantly, so this is a key and valuable way to test alternatives.

Develop Copy and Art

The product or service are the keys to the creative elements which should be used and to what benefits should be offered and how to use them. The unique selling proposition must be translated into a creatively arresting presentation of the offer. Making different offers can affect the number of sales made with the readers.

The first goal of all direct mail is to get the right people to open your mail package or envelope. You'll need a device to get their attention and pique

The essence of positioning is to make the reader say, "That's *my* kind of product or service." This is one of the key ways to establish empathy with the reader

The first goal of all direct mail is to get the right people to open your mail package or envelope. You'll need a device to get their attention and pique their interest or curiosity

their interest or curiosity. You create a desire to obtain the product or service by focusing on the benefits and the emotional satisfaction the product or services can deliver to the individual.

For example, Toro sells lawn mowers, but more importantly they sell good looking lawns to proud homeowners. (benefits)

Lastly, you give the prospect a *call to action.* You cannot be shy about telling the prospect what he/she has to do to accept your offer. And you make it easy for the prospect to accept your offer by the careful construction of the response device.

Creative tactics should also address the need to build credibility for the product or service offered and for instilling a sense of urgency in the prospect to respond immediately.

Implementation

Key decisions must be made concerning which lists, creative executions and offers will be tested. Setting up a viable test grid, determining sample size and a coding structure for 800 numbers and extensions are vital steps in direct mail selling.

A number of other decisions must be considered prior to the starting date for your direct mail including the following:

Approved copy and layout concepts will be submitted for production bidding and production and lettershop facilities contracted for material completion.

Lists must be selected and purchased to coordinate with overall production schedule and desired mailing dates.

Telemarketing firms must be contracted if an 800 number(s) will be part of the response mechanism.

Fulfillment houses must be selected to handle orders and see that orders are filled properly and that adequate inventories of the product are always on hand

Fulfillment houses must be selected to handle orders and see that orders are filled properly and that adequate inventories of the product are always on hand. In-house or service bureau data bases need to be prepared for the recording, tracking, and retrieval of information gathered from respondents.

Where appropriate, communications must be imparted to the sales force or other company personnel to build internal awareness, ensure cooperation and/or guarantee timely follow-up of sales leads.

Analyze Results

With the proper construction of test grids, key codes and databases, the analysis of test results will be simplified. Results must be compared to original objectives to determine overall success rate for the campaign.

Results should also be analyzed by test cell to compare differences in response rates between offers, creative executions, lists, or other designed test factors.

15 Tips on Creating Profitable Direct Mail Letters

1. As previously recommended, put something on the envelope of your letter which makes the person receiving it want to open it. The greatest letter in the world is useless unless the prospect opens the envelope. Pretesting different ideas is highly desirable.

2. For your letter, say something in your very first sentence that captures the reader's attention. Here are a few "for instance" examples:

   a. Do you want to solve this problem?

   b. This letter is designed particularly for people over 60 or under 30. These are excellent examples of "positioning."

   c. What we offer will not only save you time, but will save you real money. (benefits)

3. Never say anything in your letter that makes them say or think "no."

4. Make them say "yes" by putting ripe, juicy benefits under their nose.

5. Be sure to use testimonials to convince people that what you have to offer is great.

6. Be sure the letter has a "freshly typed" look.

7. Expand on your opening paragraphs with additional sales points.

8. Use copy that's as long as it takes to tell the whole story.

9. Write colloquially as though you are talking to the reader face to face.

For your letter, say something in your very first sentence that captures the reader's attention

Be sure to use testimonials to convince people that what you have to offer is great

10. Use easily understood words, short sentences and short paragraphs.

11. Break up the copy with appropriate subheads, or even line drawings, or use a second color to emphasize key sales points.

12. Be sure to ask for the order and give them a reason or incentive to act immediately.

13. If you use an 800 number for orders charged to American Express, Visa, Master or Discovery card, always add an extension number or letters, i.e., ask the buyer to call 1-800-123-4567 Dept. A2 or 101.

Wherever possible use a P.S. at the end of the letter to accomplish or reemphasize some important objective

14. Wherever possible use a P.S. at the end of the letter to accomplish or reemphasize some important objective, such as another benefit or a temporary discount if ordered before a certain date.

15. Never under any circumstance use a letter a second time if it was *unprofitable* the first time!

An Example of a Successful Promotion Via Direct Mail Letters

Description: Develop and execute a direct marketing promotion to generate funds for the IRA (Individual Retirement Account) product line from the current IRA customer base, as well as the public at large.

Goals:

- Attract $20 million in new funds from the current client IRA accounts.
- Generate new funds for client through the rollover of funds from non-client accounts.
- Encourage customers to visit client branches to make deposits in person.

Strategies:

- Position a client IRA account as a fast and safe way to build retirement savings, despite the recent tax law changes.
- Create a sense of urgency and the need to act on an IRA deposit now.
- Direct promotion at the following target groups:

Current IRA customers (the best potential prospects).

All income-earning adults age 35-54 in the client trading areas. People who are aware and concerned about saving for retirement.

Execution:

- A direct mail package containing a double-sided letter and IRA newsletter in a #10 envelope sent to current customer list.
- ROP newspaper ad scheduled to support and call attention to the mailing arrival in the respective markets.

Results:

- Achieved 170% of goal or $34 million in new IRA funds.
- Generated over 1,600 new IRA accounts.

The 17 Steps Needed to Develop and Execute the Test Market Mail Order Plan for This Book

1. Carol Clemens and Al Whitman first prepare the mail order test plan using direct mail letters and mail order advertising.

2. Carol Clemens buys the mailing lists she wants to use for the test plan from list brokers.

3. A fulfillment house to handle orders from customers is chosen. In our case, the house is the Promotion Mailing Center, where Mike Gretzin is the sales manager and our man.

4. We apply for an 800 number that customers will use to call in their orders, i.e. 1-800-123-4567.

5. We have the book printed by a company like the Banta Co. in Menasha, WI, which company submits the costs of printing per book in different quantities such as 25, 30, or 40,000.

6. We negotiate with Banta on the time it will take them to put the book back on the press and reprint follow-up orders. We negotiate the minimum lead time.

7. The head of the mail order house estimates the orders that will be received during the first month.

8. We order from Banta the number of books needed, plus a reasonable reserve so that customer orders can be filled almost overnight.

9. We have our direct mail letters prepared by Media Management and the mail order advertising prepared by the Ruhr/Paragon advertising agency.

10. We agree on extension numbers for all letters and all ads using 1 for the first time an ad appears, 2 for the second, etc. We also use initials for each market such as SB for ads that run in small business publications like *Inc.* and *Entrepreneur.*

11. We mail out the letters and run the ads.

12. From the orders received, we determine if one or more letters or ads is going to make a profit.

13. If so, we establish a new budget, considerably larger than the original test budget, send the profitable letters to far more people, reprint profitable ads and add new media, run the ads more often, or both.

14. We computerize our operation as much as possible, keeping track of inventory, setting up automatic reorders and, if possible, using a software program that will forecast future sales.

15. We estimate our orders for the next month or six weeks.

17. We reorder a new supply from the printer for whatever we estimate we will sell, plus a reserve.

CHAPTER 47

Important Facts About Mail-Order "Media" Advertising

By: Al Whitman

Mail order media advertising is a very important form of marketing.

It differs from direct mail advertising because it appears in advertising *media;* whereas direct mail advertising uses *letters* mailed to selected lists of consumers (see chapter 46).

Each form of advertising has identical goals:

1. To create enough interest to persuade consumers to part with their money and order a product, or to send for additional information about it.

2. Each can be *tested* for profitability *before* the expenditure of large sums of money.

3. Each either pays for itself in creating enough sales to pay all costs and show a profit or is discontinued.

Who Uses Mail Order Media?

Companies and individuals sell via mail order media advertising and direct mail for at least two good reasons:

1. It requires no sales organization.

2. It produces far greater gross profit margins than more "traditional" marketing because it requires no sales organization, no commissions for brokers or manufacturers representatives, and no markup for wholesalers and retailers.

Let's examine the typical costs involved in marketing a food product:

a. Production, packing costs, plus overhead will usually amount to 35% - 40% of the selling price.

b. Then you add the costs of distribution, wholesalers, chains and retailers mark ups, plus the costs of trade and consumer promotion.

By contrast in mail order media advertising, you have these key costs:

1. The cost of the media advertising including production costs.

2. The cost of handling and mailing out orders plus the credit card company fee. These can be substantial but are covered by adding them to the price charged to the customer.

Most successful mail order companies will tell you that to make a profit, the cost of the product, packaging and company overhead should never exceed 20 percent of the sales price, and that 16 percent or less is a much safer percentage.

What Kind of Products Use Mail Order Media Advertising?

Two major users are *books* (Time, Life), also *records* and *cassettes*.

But there are many other products and services including financial services, books on health, recipe books, etc.

Also sets of small appliances, automobile seat covers, magazines, book of the month clubs, travel clubs, and even frozen steaks.

It's big business.

What are the Key Advertising Media Used?

Some print media, such as specific magazines like *Entrepeneur* and *Inc.*, are published for small business.

Generally speaking, newspapers have not been considered as a good direct mail medium. The exceptions would be the *Wall Street Journal* and the mail order sections in the *New York Times* and other major papers in cities like Los Angeles, San Francisco and Denver.

Radio advertising, according to our informants, is generally not a good direct mail medium.

Regular TV and cable TV are excellent mail order media.

Most mail order advertising on cable TV appears on sports and news programs and on late evening

To make a profit, the cost of the product, packaging and company overhead should never exceed 20 percent of the sales price

movies. Much of this advertising appears late at night when lower time costs permit the use of 90 second to two minute commercials. Commercials in old movies can be a good buy.

It should be noted that direct mail media advertising can sometimes be purchased at lower rates.

What is a Good Mail Order Ad?

One that returns a profit every time it runs.

How do you Write a Good Mail Order Ad or Commercial?

If one reads and understands certain chapters in this book and is a good writer, it's not too difficult to write an ad that has a chance of being profitable.

Its purpose is clear. Your ad has to make prospective buyers "want to do what you want them to."

To bring this about and make them say "yes," follow the principles laid down in:

- Chapter 11 on benefits
- Chapter 14 on creating great ads and headlines.
- Chapter 15 on positioning.
- Chapter 31 on how do you come up with a good idea.
- Chapter 44 on creating television commercials.

Other chapters may give you some worthwhile ideas, particularly:

- Chapter 12 on pioneering.
- Chapter 46 on direct mail letters.
- Chapter 35 on key elements in a print ad.
- Chapter 33 on word pictures.

Take These Steps

1. Know the taraget audience(s) you have to sell.

2. Even if you're going to use TV, write a print ad first.

3. Try to write at least a dozen good headlines, and then think about them before choosing the one you want to use as is, or with changes.

4. Then write your subheads and body copy, using the least number of words needed to tell the whole story you need to tell.

5. Remember the key elements in an ad are the headline and main illustration.

6. Remember the importance of the words "New," "Free," and "Only" (see chapter 14).

7. Use Benefits in the headline (see chapter 11).

8. If you use an illustration other than the product itself, be sure it tells the same story as the headline.

9. One of the most common systems used in direct mail media purchases is to charge the purchase on a credit card (American Express, Visa, Mastercard or Discover Card after calling on a toll free 800 number displayed prominently in the ad or featured in television.

10. If you also use a coupon take these steps:

   a. Have a finger pointing at the coupon with such words as, "Cut out and mail this coupon today."

   b. Place an illustration of a scissors next to the coupon, outside the top left hand corner.

   c. Include a tiny picture of what you're selling *inside* the coupon in the upper right hand corner.

   d. Include space for the customer's name and address.

   e. Make the coupon large enough to be readable when it's filled in.

   f. Be sure you specify the price of what you're selling and specific handling and mailing costs or say they have been included in the product's price.

   g. Provide a simple P.O. Box number for the mailing address.

11. Why write the print ad first?

   a. It should help you write a better TV commercial

b. You may want to test the profitability of print versus TV to see which medium is the most effective.

Quick Summary - Key Points

1. You use direct mail media advertising for one reason only: to make a profit.

2. All direct mail media advertising must be tested on a small scale to learn whether it will return a profit.

3. Never run an unprofitable ad more than once.

4. In creating the advertising, follow the basic principles spelled out in this book.

5. Pay attention to the suggestion made about the toll free 800 number and the no-risk coupon.

6. Price your product as high as the market will bear and include handling and postage charges in the price.

7. If you wish, test at different price levels before deciding on the final price.

A leading mail order house recommended we show these ads as excellent examples of profitable mail order advertising. These ads were run over and over again because of their success.

CHAPTER 48

What Do People Remember?

By: Al Whitman

When there are no differences to talk about it's hard to get the public to remember anything about the product or service or company or people you're talking about

Differences in products or people or companies stand out like a light and are easy to remember.

When there are no differences to talk about it's hard to get the public to remember anything about the product or service or company or people you're talking about.

Here's an example that helps make this point:

Years ago I was having lunch at a club with a friend and noticed a stately, white haired gentleman enter the dining room.

I asked my friend who the man was, but when my friend looked around the man had disappeared. "Can you describe him," he asked. I said, "He's about 70, has a slight build, a friendly face, and he also wears a *carnation in his buttonhole.*"

My friend immediately identified the man because he was the only one in the club who always wore a carnation in his buttonhole.

When you single out, in your advertising or selling, a certain type of person, such as a gal who likes her coffee black or specific group of people, such as a member of the Elks or Kiwanis Club, or a specific marketing segment, such as people over 65, you automatically make it easy for people interested in that person, group or marketing segment to identify themselves with what you're advertising or what you're saying.

For example, years ago, in New York City, one of the most successful campaigns featured a brand of rye bread advertised as "The Jewish Rye."

If you're a Prudential policyholder, you're more likely to remember what the Prudential ad has to say. And, if you're overweight you'll find it easy to identify yourself with a diet like the "Slim Fast Diet Plan."

In parts of the U.S. there's a company called Pearle. This company makes prescription glasses in an hour. Its commercial asks, "Are you wearing your

'Pearles' today?" This play on words is obviously memorable.

Another way to get people to remember a product or service is to feature a simple thought that's easy to remember because of its aliteration. "DON'T BE MAD, GET GLAD" (plastic bags).

CHAPTER 49

How to Create Advertising for Patent Medicines and Related Non Prescription Products

By: Al Whitman

There are four secrets for writing profitable ads for patent medicines and related products. They are:

1. Always feature the name of a specific ailment in the headlines.
2. Always describe the ailment in the harshest possible terms.
3. Always use active verbs and memorable adjectives.
4. Use a memorable illustration wherever possible.

Here are some specific examples of what not to do and what to do.

> Don't write something like, "How to treat your backache." Do write something like, "Stop that awful backache pain."

> Don't write, "What to do when you have a cough." Do write, "Stop that miserable cough this easy, soothing way."

> Don't write, "How to lose weight." Do write, "Slash off that excess fat."

In each of the above cases we have used the ailment in the headline. We have described it so that it sounds like an "active enemy of yourself." We have done so using active verbs and memorable adjectives.

For years, in the advertising business, most advertising similar to the above, appeared in type in a small space newspaper ad of approximately 50 lines. Today you're more apt to find it in 30 second television commercials, and occasionally 60 second commercials.

It might interest you to know that years ago patent advertisers used one headline that worked and repeated the ad for as long as 20 years.

Example

Carters' Little Liver Pills (sold by the maker of Arrid deodorant) used this headline for many years: "WAKE UP YOUR LIVER BILE WITHOUT CALOMEL"—followed by the line in smaller type "and you'll jump out of bed rarin' to go."

After two years of testing, a new agency found a headline that beat the original. The line, "UN-BLOCK YOUR DIGESTIVE TRACT." I do not remember the "benefit" line which followed but the ad worked *most* successfully and turned out to be more productive than the "liver bile" ad.

Memorable Illustration

Today the makers of MICATIN, an athlete's foot remedy made by Ortho Pharmaceutical, use a TV commercial which talks about this ailment in terms of "burning feet" and shows the toes of both feet *on fire*.

It's one of the most memorable and effective patent medicine commercials you've ever seen. Truly outstanding.

CHAPTER 50

How to Judge a Proposed Print Advertisement or Campaign

By: Al Whitman

I'm sure there are a number of different ways to judge advertising.

For what it's worth, here are some of the questions I asked myself when I looked at a new, proposed campaign:

- Does the ad feature *news* or a *consumer* benefit in the headline?
- Is the idea featured really *pertinent* to the market for the product?
- Is the main illustration interesting, and does it clearly and *readily illustrate the idea* featured in the headline?
- Does the main subhead expand on and *develop* the headline?
- If secondary illustrations are used, does each have a caption (as it should)?
- Does the ad *ask for the orde*r?
- Does it have a good *logotype* with a selling idea?

There are excellent reasons for questions like these. Advertising research has shown again and again that the best read parts of an ad are in this order:

1. The headline
2. Main illustration
3. Logotype
4. Secondary illustrations
5. Main subhead
6. Body copy (broken up with appropriate subheads)

NOTE: The above thinking applies to print. Many of the points pertain to television as well.

CHAPTER 51

Evaluating Results

By: Richard Rundle

Dick Rundle, who authored this chapter has a research and marketing management and teaching background.

He started his business career at Campbell-Mithun and spent 4 1/2 years in its research department.

He then became research and media director of BBDO, Minneapolis.

The next 14 years were spent at International Multifoods, where he retired as Vice President and Business Group Manager, in the Consumer Products Division.

Dick is currently marketing manager of the Master of Business Communication Program at the University of St. Thomas in St. Paul, Minnesota, which offers unique and broadly based instruction in marketing communications, public relations and corporate communications.

After a marketing plan that includes an advertising campaign has been introduced in the marketplace, the results should be evaluated.

- How well did the marketing plan work?
- Were the objectives achieved?
- How well did the advertising work?

Generally, it's easier to evaluate the overall marketing effort than it is to evaluate the advertising alone. The advertising is just *one part* of the marketing program.

Evaluating Marketing Results

Marketing program results are usually evaluated in various ways:

1. The marketer's sales results. You look at sales changes overall and by individual chain and wholesaler account. You compare sales against sales made in comparable periods. This should indicate if sales have or have not been satisfactory. Comparison is usually made with "shipments" from the same period of the previous year.

2. Major advertisers of food and drug products often subscribe to marketing services that show actual consumer purchases in retail outlets in dollars and units and also provide information on market share, distribution levels, and sales by package sizes, among other things. A.C. Nielsen is a service that regularly measures sales of products sold through food and drug outlets.

Another source that shows usage levels, brand sales, market share, and other statistical information is Info Scan, a division of the Behavior Scan Co. in Chicago. This service is directly competitive with A.C. Nielsen.

This information tells the advertiser and its agency what progress is being made and how the results compare with projected goals.

The quality and scope of the information obtained by these services is very good, but the cost is high.

Many large companies developed their own systems for tracking sales, market share, and brand awareness. But for the smaller or average company, the cost of developing equivalent data systems may be prohibitive. They may have to rely on government reports, trade associations, research figures and their own sales records, but these sources do not include all the important data.

Evaluating the Advertising

Evaluating advertising effectiveness is a different and often much more difficult task than measuring overall marketing results. With some marketing programs it's possible to conclude that the advertising program used in the overall marketing plan was totally or mostly responsible for a successful marketing effort.

Al Whitman tells me that years ago, when he was the management representative on a regional beer account, sales began to increase within four to five weeks after switching from the old campaign, "Gold Standard Of Fine Beer" to the new campaign, "Refreshingly Yours, From The Land Of Sky Blue Waters."

He also told me that when Campbell-Mithun was the advertising agency for a line of refrigerated doughs that lent themselves beautifully to demonstration, sales increased almost immediately when television advertising was used for the first time.

Finally, Bill Whitman, who wrote chapter 59 in this book, tells of a client who enjoyed an almost immediate increase in sales when cable television was used in its behalf for the first time.

However, the availability of such information is the exception rather than the rule, so in most instances we have to use research to tell us whether or not advertising has been effective. To do this, several questions must be addressed before research can begin.

When should the evaluation be made? Before the advertising schedule is run, after the media budget

Evaluating advertising effectiveness is a different and often much more difficult task than measuring overall marketing results

264

has been spent? Or both? Many companies and their agencies do both pretesting and posttesting.

Which research techniques best measure what we want to measure?

The *first step* in measuring advertising effectiveness is defining the result or "effect" you expect the advertising to have. Sales? Increase in awareness? Attitude change? Brand preference? Or just *recall* of the ad and its primary message?

Many advertising experts believe it's not appropriate to evaluate advertising effectiveness by observing sales response. Advertising is only one of many factors at work in a well-developed marketing effort.

As a criterion of advertising effectiveness, it may be more appropriate to use changes in awareness of the brand name, or of a theme or slogan, or of a specific product feature or benefit emphasized in the advertising. The important thing is to decide what's reasonable to expect the advertising to achieve and use that as the measuring stick.

It's usually necessary to interview a number of people, either in person or on the phone, to get information about the advertising. At times, interviews are done in stores or shopping centers. In the interviews, the researcher questions a cross section of prospective customers to learn whether they are familiar with the advertising they're presented. They may also be asked about their familiarity with advertising claims or benefits of *other* brands in the same product category.

The interviewer may also collect information on products in that category that the person has tried or uses regularly.

The professional researcher decides which research techniques are best to use. But whatever techniques are chosen, they should be used repeatedly to develop norms of performance.

A word about "focus groups." Small groups of people (usually 8 to 10), who are paid to come to a central location to look at and react to advertising materials, are widely used for research; perhaps too widely.

While they may be helpful in developing the range of interpretation and reaction that an ad or commercial may generate, focus groups are *not* a valid way to measure an ad's effectiveness. If several different group sessions are held, and if the reaction tends to be *consistent* from group to group (mostly positive or mostly negative, for example) the results may have greater validity.

Example of Measuring Results

Let's assume that a life insurance company has initiated a costly campaign to advertise its policies and services. The campaign has run for several months at a cost of several million dollars.

The research shows that the typical prospects interviewed can name four insurance companies. These companies are AllState, State Farm, The Prudential, and the advertiser financing the research.

When asked whether they are familiar with the advertising being run by any of these companies, and if so, what it says, the research reveals that fifty percent of the prospects respond, "You're in good hands with AllState." Thirty percent respond, "Like a good neighbor, State Farm is there." Twenty-five percent respond either, "The Rock of Gibraltar" or "A piece of the rock" for The Prudential, and fifteen percent respond, "We've got you covered," the key line of the company for which the research is being done.

If this percentage equals or exceeds the goal set up in advance for the new advertising campaign, then the results would be considered favorable. If it falls woefully short, it might mean that the advertising would have to be drastically changed.

In setting the goals, the amount of money that has been and is being invested in advertising by each life insurance company has to be carefully considered, as well as the period of time each company has used its campaign. And, to some degree, the reaction of our life insurance sales organization is included in the total evaluation.

In setting the goals, the amount of money that has been and is being invested in advertising by each life insurance company has to be carefully considered, as well as the period of time each company has used its campaign

CHAPTER 52

How to Write a Good Sales Letter

By: Al Whitman

Before you start to write, make a list of known areas of interest of the person or company to whom you're writing

1. Before you start to write, make a list of known areas of interest of the person or company to whom you're writing and include any business problems you think they face.

2. Write from the recipient's "side of the table."

3. Highlight quickly what you're going to say in your letter.

4. In your first paragraph, say something that grabs the attention and stimulates the interest of the reader.

5. Show ways you can help solve any business problems, and capitalize on existing opportunities.

6. Offer as many benefits as possible.

7. Close by summarizing what you've said and ask for the order.

Here is a sample letter, written by an advertising agency to a prospective client, who has invited the agency president to compete for part of his business.

"Dear Mr. Barnes:

Thank you for the invitation. We know of no other advertiser we would be happier to work with than your company, and with our reputation and unique knowledge of advertising, we are confident you'd enjoy working with us.

We feel we know what you're looking for in your new agency:

    A. Great creativity, particularly in television.

    B. Unusual skills in designing 24 sheet posters.

    C. Substantial strengths in marketing, including sales promotion.

We're looking forward to showing you our reel of TV commercials and telling you the results our clients have received from them.

We're very strong in outdoor design because three of our better art directors are from California, America's number 1 market for posters and painted billboards.

We'll prove to you rather quickly and easily our skills in marketing. As you may know, we have our own sales promotion subsidiary headed by Alex Jones, whose ability in sales promotion is known throughout the industry.

In short, we're very anxious to work with you. We know what you want in television, outdoor design, marketing and sales promotion.

We're confident we can help increase your profits and lower your costs of distribution.

Thanks again for the invitation.

Sincerely yours,

Ralph Gustafson, President

P.S. We'll be in your office on Wednesday of next week to make our presentation to you and your associates."

CHAPTER 53

Dean Thomas is the head of his own consulting firm, Dean F. Thomas, Inc.

For years Dean was the Sales Manager for the Pillsbury Company, now called Grand Metropolitan Pillsbury Company.

Pillsbury's former Chairman, who also had been the Company's Sales Manager, called Dean, "The finest Sales Manager Pillsbury has ever had".

Essential Tips for Selling

By: Dean Thomas

This chapter is written for salespeople, by a salesman. Its purpose is to present proven essential tips that help make the prospective customer say "yes."

The selling profession is one of the world's highest paid professions.

My father once told me that the people who produce products and services never make as much as the people who sell them — and he was right!

A company may have a sales force of 1 or 1,800, but the size of the average sales force is 60.

Their statistics are listed in the table at the bottom of this page.

Companies around the world rely on their sales forces to sell their products and generate profits. According to one corporate executive, "We've come to realize that salesmanship is our most important factor for increasing profits."

So what are those essential tips behind powerful selling, the principles, techniques and the ideas that create success?

Many are found right here in this book:

- Chapter 1 told you that marketing is based on offering and selling known needs and wants of customers and prospects.

- Chapter 11 explains the importance of using *benefits* as a way of demonstrating the value of a product or service.

Type of Selling	Compensation Range	Calls/ Day	Costs/ Call
Consumer	$20,400 - $140,000	2 to 6	$116.26
Industrial	$20,500 - $160,000	2 to 5	$244.87
Service	$16,200 - $120,000	2 to 8	$165.85
Note: These figures do not include bonuses.			

- Chapter 12 tells you 10 different ways to pioneer.
- Chapter 14 gives you some "magic words" to use in selling.
- Chapter 15 describes what "positioning" means. Present your story one way and you fail; present it another way, and you close the sale.
- Chapter 19 tells you how to sell successfully by phone.
- Chapters 30 and 31 reinforce the importance of ideas.
- Chapter 52 tells you how to write a good sales letter.
- Chapter 55 tells you what it takes to be a good sales manager.

Planning the Sales Call

What techniques do good sales people use to make people say "yes" to their product or service? Before you make a sales call, you must have a good *sales plan*. Good sales presentations are planned.

- Set the goals you want to accomplish.
- Personalize your presentation to fit your target.
- Use data that fits your target market.
- Know what you want to say and how to say it, and support your statements with facts and examples.
- Set up your presentation as you would tell an interesting story. Build it point by point.
- Use an attention-getting introduction such as "How would you like to make an additional $500,000 profit this year?"
- Use significant data in the body of your sales presentation.
- Close your presentation with a strong message of conviction.
- Ask for the order and ask for the size you believe is in your customer's best interest.
- Test your plan on others. Get ideas to improve it.
- Whatever you do, don't try to "wing it" without a good sales plan.

Whatever you do, don't try to "wing it" without a good sales plan

270

Making the Sales Call

Make an appointment and confirm it before you appear.

Be sure you get to see the *right person* who can say "yes."

Make sure the buyer will agree with your opening remarks; never start by saying something he or she may disagree with. Your buyer has to have confidence in you. So sell yourself first. Buyers respect knowledgeable salespeople to whom they can turn for information.

If you already have the buyer's confidence, improve on it with each call. Cherish that trust.

Empathy and Enthusiasm

The very best salespeople I ever had were the ones who always believed they could be of service to their customers. One particularly knowledgeable salesman always took the time to learn about the other person's problems. On calls he always brought ideas with him to address or solve those problems.

His style always dealt with the other person's point of view.

Use visual aids. Some will come from your company, but you'll make many yourself. Adapt your company's ideas to your customers. Make no two presentations exactly alike.

One good technique calls for the use of a miniature easel, 10 to 12 inches high and 8 inches wide. Build it with a ledge that'll hold a dozen 3-x-5" cards featuring your sales points in proper sequence. This presentation idea is easy to use and different enough to interest buyers.

Always sell with enthusiasm, no matter what the situation might be. In a real sense, enthusiasm is conviction in motion.

One of my greatest lessons as a sales manager came from working with salespeople who were having no success. On call after call, they would sell little or nothing.

I would then step in to do the selling so they could observe what happens during a good presentation. It always worked. I would always sell goods. After each call, I'd point out that both the unsuccessful

The very best salespeople I ever had were the ones who always believed they could be of service to their customers

271

salesperson and I were saying the same things, but I was saying them with an enthusiasm that created conviction.

One of my salespeople called it "selling on the balls of my feet."

Today's key selling word is "empathy." The trouble is, quite a few salespeople don't know what it means and how to use it to sell goods.

Empathy means putting yourself in the other person's shoes. It is described as *selling from the buyer's side of the table*.

It's saying the things the customer wants to hear; it's putting things in terms of what your product will do for your customer.

Example: Some buyers believe most salespeople are liars. They don't say so, but they think so.

Back up everything you tell a buyer with facts. "My product will sell to 7 out of 10 consumers when displayed." "Test market results in 10 stores with exactly the same demographics proves my point."

Empathy is selling, fine-tuned to the person whom you want to say yes.

The Value of Listening

Stop talking and listen. Listen *very carefully.* The sensitive salesperson knows when to listen. If you listen well, you'll find the lead that will close the sale.

One man I knew likened this technique to playing the piano.

By this he meant mentioning different subjects until he found one that interested the buyer. He then talked about that subject.

All the great salespeople I've known have been their own special person. One was a young man, fresh out of a great midwestern school, who really wanted to *learn* to sell. He made it very clear that I was there to help him learn. He asked me to do at least half of the sales calls.

We were selling a major program and had done our planning well. I was informed that my first call would be his largest and toughest account. If he was to make his sales goal, he absolutely had to make this sale.

Empathy means putting yourself in the other person's shoes. It is described as *selling from the buyer's side of the table*

That customer was new to me, but hard as I tried, I did not sell him very much. We did, however, have 30 minutes together, during which the customer did most of the talking.

The young salesman was listening with great interest. As I was about to leave, he promised me he would achieve his goals with that customer shortly.

He made his promise good, and that customer soon became his number one account.

Later he wrote a letter thanking me for my efforts, and particularly with the tough customer. Listening carefully taught him what it would take to make that customer say yes.

And this salesman went on to become our number one producer.

So there you have some of the essential tips on what it takes to do the job of making your customers and prospects say, "yes."

CHAPTER 54

How to Create and Make a Good Presentation

By: Al Whitman

This subject covers several possible situations or occasions, some of which may be important to you including:

- A presentation to your associates.
- A presentation to a client.
- A personal sales pitch to a present or prospective customer.

Here are some specific tips you should find valuable.

A. In creating your presentation:

- Know your stuff.
- Keep it simple.
- Be believable. Never make any points which are exaggerated or debatable.
- Stick to pertinent facts and recent findings and statements by recognized authorities.
- Have an associate review it.
- Make a list of possible questions and come prepared with the answers.

B. In giving your presentation:

- Talk from your listener's side of the table.
- Use benefits (see chapter 11) if you want your audience to do something or support a point of view.
- Decide which type of presentation to make:
  - a. A straight talk
  - b. Flip over pages
  - c. Slides or a videotape

C. In preparing your presentation:

- Write out your presentation, keeping it as simple and clear as possible.
- Collect any materials you need and use as examples or exhibits.

- Decide what kind of equipment you need to make the kind of presentation you want.

- Do you want the material prepared for use in a projector?

- Do you want overhead transparencies?

- Do you want the kind of equipment that lets you make changes on the transparency while presenting a page?

- Do you want the presentation to be put into slides?

NOTE: You'll need to know if you have to take the equipment with you or whether it's available at the location where you'll be making your presentation. If you're going out of town you may have to rent equipment.

Once you make the decision on the type of equipment, prepare your presentation in the form the equipment calls for and carefully review it on the equipment, page by page.

The Importance of Rehearsing and Making Sure of What you Say

Some years ago, I was the account manager of a relatively large and well known client. One week we were going to make a presentation on a specified product the following Monday. Early that week the top account executive came down with appendicitis.

His assistant, who was a young and rather inexperienced assistant account executive, assumed I would make the presentation instead of his boss. He was quite surprised when I told him *he* was going to do it.

I asked to see the first draft of his presentation on Thursday. He had it ready. It wasn't very good and I tore it apart. He showed me his first revision on Friday. It was better, but still had some real loopholes. I asked him for a revision on Saturday. He got rather disgruntled at this because he had plans for the weekend.

On Saturday he brought in a fairly good revision...but still, far from perfect.

I asked him to come in on Sunday to make all the necessary final changes. He did this, but his nose was out of joint because I'd spoiled his weekend.

On Monday, he gave the presentation. It was excellent. It was so good that when he finished, the client group in charge of marketing the product *broke into applause*

On Monday, he gave the presentation. It was excellent. It was so good that when he finished, the client group in charge of marketing the product *broke into applause*. He had done something he didn't think he could do, and the client didn't think he had it in him to do it.

About a half hour later, he came into my office, quite excited. He was very pleased and appreciative.

He made one comment I'll never forget. He said, "It just occurred to me last night that I spoiled your weekend. I'm sure glad you're such a demanding boss and were so helpful."

I might add that this young man, some years later, became the head of a branch office of one of the largest agencies in the country.

If you were to ask him today if he believes in rehearsal and perfectionism, he'd answer with a resounding "yes."

CHAPTER 55

How to Be a Great Sales Manager

By: Dean Thomas

The primary responsibility of a sales manager is to get things done through the efforts of other people

The primary responsibility of a sales manager is to get things done through the efforts of other people. The specific objective: to develop within each salesperson a complete and understandable knowledge of:

1. The company for whom they work.
2. The markets in which they sell.
3. The products they have to sell.
4. The competition they have to sell against.
5. The planning designed to sell our products.
6. The techniques of salesmanship that put it all together, to attain the goals they have agreed to reach.

Without this knowledge and these abilities, salespeople are no better than the plumber who brings all of the right equipment but can't stop the leak.

The sales manager's job description reads very much like the ones being used for marketing management, the educated profession of MBAs.

In fact, the job itself has the same requirements, and perhaps a few more.

Professional sales managers are college graduates with skills in general sciences, economics, finance, human resource management, information systems, marketing, communication, and administration, to name but a few.

Strong "People" Talents

Recruiter, trainer, teacher and *leader* are the words that best describe today's sales managers.

Each of the following statements represents the convictions of a successful sales manager:

"I am no one without the strong support of my selling team."

"People who need people and know how to direct them are sales managers."

"The strongest part of sales management is the people who do the selling."

Hired to be the leader, but humble in the realization that he or she can win only through the skills of the sales team.

Authority and control are necessary traits for any sales manager to possess. A successful sales manager must also hire the right people, train them to perfection, teach them the important ways to use that training, and then be the leader they all respect and believe in.

Any sales manager who wants to attain his or her objectives, must provide his or her people with:

- Motivation
- Quality decisions
- Selling leadership by example
- Challenge
- A driving desire to win

Communication

Through communication, people share knowledge and information.

For the salesperson, who deals primarily in words and impressions, the ability to communicate effectively is basic.

One of the greatest communicators I ever met was an Army colonel. His methods were as follows:

> "I'm going to tell you, then I'm going to tell you what I told you, then I'm going to tell you what I told you I was going to tell you, and then, you are going to tell me."

He communicated well; we all understood.

Communication is a two-way exchange of views.

1. Talk *with* people, not *to* people.
2. Make people feel important.
3. Give the other person a sense of participation.
4. Stop talking and listen.
5. Don't communicate from the attitude, "I'll tell you."

Know and accommodate the problems of listening:

1. Realize that many hear only what they want to hear.

For the salesperson, who deals primarily in words and impressions, the ability to communicate effectively is basic

Realize that many hear only what they want to hear

2. Listeners need a permissive atmosphere to hear what is being communicated.

3. Don't assume that you are being heard. Check it out by asking questions.

4. Don't take the position of the listener lightly.

5. Remember, prejudice diverts hearing what is being said. So, to disagree will impede hearing.

Working the Sales Plan

No salesperson can successfully generate volume sales without effective sales planning.

A sales plan is a carefully developed presentation to accomplish a determined goal. It must be presented enthusiastically, with logic, facts, and conviction, and it must create acceptance.

It must be done with confidence, interest, and professional sales skill.

To accomplish this, a salesperson must be trained to communicate a natural talent of salesmanship that *does not stress "selling" but stresses "value."*

Sales Management Contributions to the Marketing Process

As an important member of the marketing team, the sales manager carries the responsibility to ensure that the marketing plan is not only feasible, but saleable.

- **Sales Forecasting** To generate forecasts of sales volumes based on solid knowledge of markets, sales and sales trends, the strength of the sales organization, distribution, and related information often put into a company's computer.

- **Advertising** The ability of sales to effectively use advertising as a major strength in the selling message.

- **Sales Promotion** To be involved in the planning of promotional supports and to use the sales promotion plan in selling (see Chapters 2 and 4).

- **Production** The logistic between sales and production and available supply must be coordinated. You can't sell what you can't get.

A sales plan is a carefully developed presentation to accomplish a determined goal. It must be presented enthusiastically, with logic, facts, and conviction

- **Commercial Research** A vital part of the marketing plan and the selling presentation.
- **Pricing** A tremendous "secret" weapon of our times, in which sales management plays a major role in determining, on a market-by-market basis. Remember, proper pricing creates the competitiveness the product must have to sell in the marketplace at a profit.
- **The Marketplace** Knowing the geography, demographics, and customers in a selected marketing area.
- **Incentives** Those that help make customers and prospects say yes in keeping with company dignity and the market requirements.
- **Leadership** The ability to provide a competitive edge for the company and the sales team.

Perhaps the best way to explain this attribute is with an example, accomplished by a sales manager.

His company was a major manufacturer of consumer products sold through retail food stores.

It was an extremely competitive marketplace with three major companies fighting for market share, which could happen only through product distribution and support by those retailers doing the major share of the grocery business.

One major retailer clearly was the leader, operating over 1,300 stores.

This sales manager knew he had to dominate in this chain, yet his company had not made that important "sale" and needed a "competitive edge" to win.

Knowing that need, he put together a plan to call on the chairman of that company's board, with the request he bring to a meeting his top executives, to hear a presentation that promised accelerated profits throughout their entire chain.

This was a bold and ingenious effort, but the sales manager was up to the task.

He got that meeting. It lasted only 30 minutes, but in that time his plan was accepted throughout that entire chain of stores. It obtained leadership for his company that continues today.

Selling Intelligence

The five "knows" of selling intelligence:

1. Know the competition: their current status, and projected plans, which could stand in the way of success.

2. Know selling strategies: the ones that work today and tomorrow. Also, know the ones that do not work.

3. Know the customer: their people, their ways of doing business, their requirements, their potential, their policies and their demands.

4. Know selling intuition: Fix only what is broken, and maintain enthusiastic salespeople.

5. Know yourself: your people, your products, and your market.

Selling intelligence, fundamental for a sales manager, comes from understanding many things.

Knowledge and Wisdom

There was once a great book written by Og Mandino entitled "The Greatest Salesman in the World."

In this story, Mandino reveals ten scrolls, upon which are inscribed life's principles. These principles, when followed, prescribed a living philosophy for success to become the greatest salesman in the world.

Certainly, knowledge and wisdom must be a part of a sales manager's great strengths.

Selling is, and shall always be, a combination of art, science, and skill. Their role, in the ever increasing demands for selling effectively, shall continue to reflect the sales manager's importance as a key member of the marketing team.

The Power of Professional Sales Management

Strong people talents

Communications

Planning the work, working the plan

Leadership

Selling intelligence

Knowledge and wisdom

CHAPTER 56

How to Write a Speech

By: Al Whitman

Almost everyone has to write and give a speech now and then.

Some, like sales managers and ministers, have to prepare and make many talks during the year.

This chapter wasn't written for the relatively few "professional" speech makers who've learned to write and give a great speech, or have a natural instinct for doing so, and are "stem winders" at the podium.

It's for the majority of people who need or want to improve their knowledge of the basics of creating and giving a speech.

We can't tell you how to write a *great* speech because so much depends on the *content,* which must come from you, and on the way you *deliver* it.

However, if what you have to say is interesting and important to your audience, here are specific steps that'll help you to create a speech that's good and possibly great.

Decide the *key point* you want your listeners to get from your speech

1. Decide the *key point* you want your listeners to get from your speech.

Make sure your opening sentence or paragraph you write has something of genuine interest

2. Make sure your opening sentence or paragraph you write has something of genuine interest, which "something" your listeners can *relate to*, often news, a benefit, or something that piques their curiosity.

Example:

   a. Do you believe the strength of a nation depends on the *characer* of its people?

   b. Do you believe the most important asset in a good company is the *ability* of its employees?

   c. Today I'd like to talk to you about how to *double your salary* in the next three years.

d. Do you feel as I do that one of the most important problems most individuals face is *stress*?

   e. So today, let's discuss how to *eliminate stress* and replace it with peace of mind.

3. Tell them the *gist* of what you're going to say to them. Never forget the simple and the obvious is invariably the best (see chapter 45).

4. Make sure your speech sticks to the single key point, and *doesn't wander* into other subjects, even closely related ones.

5. Remember a good speech should "march" step by step toward your objective. So make an outline to arrange its development.

6. Write the speech as though you're writing a sales letter (see chapter 52) or as though you were writing an ad as David Ogilvy explained in chapter 14, i.e., with simple, easy to understand words or thoughts — short sentences and short paragraphs, etc.

7. Read chapter 65 on how to be a great teacher. Great teachers *know how to write and give* great speeches.

8. You phrase your talk, using simple words as though you were talking to an individual face to face.

9. You say what you'd like to hear if you were in your listener's place.

10. You offer benefits, benefits and more benefits so your listeners will want to say "yes" to what you have to say.

11. If possible or practical, tell them a story or a very short case history, or read a quotation that backs up your key point.

12. If possible, include some *humor* in your speech. If you can make your audience laugh, you get them with you. Humor also provides a change of pace for your speech. When you alternate between humor and seriousness you're employing

an ancient and fundamental way of capturing attention.

13. Close with a quick summary of what you've said, and a reminder that helps your listeners want to do what you want them to, if that's the purpose of your talk.

Some additional pointers:

   a. Never read a speech.

   b. Use notes if you have to.

   c. In delivering your speech let your audience know when you are moving from one point to the other through use of such words as, "in the first place," or "secondly," etc.

   d. Emphasize any thought or word which deserves it.

   e. Read the speech out loud at least twice. As you rehearse, read it to someone else if you can.

   f. Ask him/her to tell you if there was any part of your talk he/she didn't under stand or agree with, and why.

   g. Deliver your speech in as convincing a manner as possible, making it evident that you believe in its content.

So there you have some basics about speech writing and delivery. We're confident that if you put them to good use they'll make your listeners *want* to do what you want them to.

CHAPTER 57

How to Win the Battle... and Lose the War

By: Al Whitman

I'm sure you've heard the old saying, "It's far more important to win the war than it is to win every battle."

If you try to win every battle you can lose your best friend.

Or you can lose your wife or vice versa.

We lost a major account one time by reacting much too quickly to a criticism which the client wouldn't accept even though it was correct. So he fired us.

The above is a short introduction to a true and somewhat humorous story which makes a very important point.

We believe you'll like and appreciate both.

This story involves a close friend who was unbelievably capable in many areas.

Even though he plays the piano with only one finger, he had at least five songs approved for publishing by Ascad. He invented many products which were marketed successfully by different companies.

He told funny stores all day without ever repeating a single one.

He was a terrific master of ceremonies.

He was a marvelous advertising man, who supervised an important part of the business of a major advertiser.

Later he became president of a large agency.

He told us the following story.

One day, the executive vice president of his client called his boss, who was the chairman of the board. The client had a new product which he had not assigned to any of his agencies. The client also had a *packaging problem* that needed to be solved before the new product could be marketed.

The client asked the chairman to call together a few of the agency's finest creative brains to whom he could explain the problem in the hope they'd come up with some ideas that would lead to a solution to the packaging road block.

The chairman set up the meeting. As soon as the executive vice president of the client had finished his presentation, my friend exclaimed, "I've got it."

He then excused himself to go and have an artist make a sketch for him.

When he returned to the room and showed the sketch, it was obvious that he *had* solved the packaging problem in a very few minutes.

So the meeting broke up and my friend went home, feeling he had done a great day's work.

When he arrived at the office the next morning, there was a note on his desk from the chairman saying, "See me please."

He arrived at the chairman's office and was told to close the door and have a seat. Suddenly the chairman, who was a short portly man, and a little awkward on his feet, stood up and started to circle his desk, snapping his fingers, and exclaiming over and over again, "I'VE GOT IT," "I'VE GOT IT," "I'VE GOT IT."

Then he turned to my friend and said, "You certainly were stupid yesterday."

My friend replied, "What do you mean? I solved the client's problem, didn't I?"

The chairman replied, "Yes you did. But in doing it so quickly, you made our client look stupid in front of a lot of our people and several of his."

My friend asked, "What should I've done?"

The chairman said, "You should have waited until after the meeting was over and showed me the answer to the problem. Then I wouldn't have gotten in touch with the client for at least a week. At that time I'd write and say we had worked hard and long on the solution to the problem, which was a difficult one, and had come up with an idea that seemed to make good sense.

Then I'd outline the idea and ask him for a response, which we would know would be favorable. In that way the client would have the feeling that he, in large part, had been responsible for the solution and would put it into effect immediately."

As soon as the executive vice president of the client had finished his presentation, my friend exclaimed, "I've got it."

He then excused himself to go and have an artist make a sketch for him

In that way the client would have the feeling that he, in large part, had been responsible for the solution and would put it into effect immediately."

My friend said, "Well we solved his problem, didn't we? Don't you think he'll assign the account to us?"

The chairman replied, "I don't believe he will, and he may not even use the idea."

He was right on both counts!

CHAPTER 58

When You Want Someone to say "Yes," Use the Pronoun "We" Not "I"

By: Al Whitman

This chapter is short, to the point and addresses an important issue.

There's one pronoun you should never use to get someone to "*want*" to do what you want them to. We're talking about the pronoun "I."

Obviously there are times when it's quite proper to use this *pronoun*. Examples: "I agree." "I see." "I'm going someplace," etc.

But when you want someone to say, "yes," you should use the word, "we."

"I" is singular. "We" is plural. When you're selling something to someone, isn't it far better to say. "*We* believe this is so," which implies strongly that two or more people or even a team believes the statement, than to say "I believe it's so," which says clearly that the belief comes from a single person.

Here's a true story which illustrates this point:

> Some years ago we had a talented creative leader who created unbelievably great television commercials. One day he presented three or four brand new commercials to an important client.
>
> He never used the world "we," just "I," despite the fact that others had taken part in creating the ideas.
>
> After the meeting, even though the creative man had all the commercials accepted by the client, we went to his office and congratulated him for his work. Then we chastised him for his use of the word, "I." The creative man got madder than a hornet and wouldn't accept the criticism.
>
> A week or two later, he accepted a good job with another agency.

When you're selling something to someone, isn't it far better to say. "*We* believe this is so," which implies strongly that two or more people or even a team believes the statement, than to say "I believe it's so"

293

We felt confident that our criticism contributed to his decision to leave us.

About six years later he returned to our agency in a very important capacity.

On his first day back he said to us, "I want you to know how big a favor you did for me when you told me I should have used the world 'we' some years ago. I was mad at the time, but after thinking about it, I realized how right you were.

"As a result, I never used the word 'I' again."

Remember: When you want someone to say "yes," the word "we" beats the pants off the word "I" every time.

CHAPTER 59

Today's Advertising Media

By: William Whitman

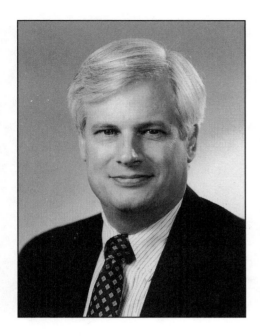

Bill Whitman is a Senior Vice President and Account Director at the Leo Burnett Company, where he has worked since 1972. Currently, he is responsible for the domestic portion of the Kellogg account. In his 18 years at Burnett, Bill has worked with a variety of businesses, including Nestle, Pillsbury, Phillip Morris International and Dean Witter.

He is a graduate of the American Graduate School of International Management and Williams College and served as Lieutenant Junior grade on an aircraft carrier in the U.S. Navy. His ship picked up the first, or one of the first, astronauts to fly in space.

Bill is married with two children and lives in Evanston, Illinois.

To some, the planning and placement of media are two of the more mundane steps in the advertising process. But from my experience, they are often critical to the success or failure of an advertising program.

To make my point, consider the experience of one of our food clients. For one of our smaller brands, we recommended reapportioning our advertising weight slightly to add a newly defined daypart. With that one adjustment, we increased our business in Year 1 by 13 percent. Our client continues to use that media mix to this day.

At this stage, the answers to the following questions begin to take shape as media plans and eventually as media purchases:

- Who: Target Audience
- When: Seasonality
- Where: Regionality
- What: Advertising Objective(s)
- How: Selection of Media

In Chapter 6 ("How to Prepare a Fact Book"), the discipline of asking and answering fundamental questions like *who, when,* and *where* was discussed. In this chapter, I'd like to touch upon the *how* (selection of media), as in "How can you reach your target audience in today's advertising media?"

Three interrelated trends influence today's media:

1. Advertisers' desire for greater selectivity, i.e., ability to pinpoint their target
2. Increased media options
3. Increased audience fragmentation.

When I began my career in the early 1970s, national advertisers and their agencies could achieve most media objectives by using vehicles like network television and national magazines, which were geared toward delivering mass audiences efficiently.

Today, that's changed. In the last decade, given on-going media cost escalation and marketers' demands for greater media selectivity, media alternatives have flourished. The following are examples:

- In television viewing, the growth of
  - » Independent TV stations (not affiliated with the 3 networks)
  - » Fox
  - » Syndicated programs
  - » Cable (basic and pay)
  - » VCRs
- In radio listening, gains in
  - » Format-oriented stations
  - » FM
- In reading, the rise of countless narrowly targeted magazines.

With these options, there has been a resultant rise in audience fragmentation, thereby reinforcing the need to consider media alternatives.

While a thorough discussion of each medium would require an entire textbook, here are a few thoughts on several media, with special emphasis on television.

Magazines

Magazines have become an increasingly segmented medium.

Circulation of most mass-audience magazines (e.g., *Reader's Digest, Time, Woman's Day)* has declined and a raft of new magazines has been launched each year.

Today, increased competition between existing and newer magazines has created opportunities for advertisers, including:

- Better targeting
- Improved efficiencies (e.g., willingness to negotiate prices)
- Merchandising options
- Positioning advertising next to related editorial.

Typically, magazines are used to:

- "Target" a given demographic group (e.g., adults 50 and over via *Modern Maturity*) or certain lifestyles (such as car enthusiasts, skiers, and travelers)

- Provide related editorial (such as seeing Fiber One cereal in *American Health*, and storage bags in *Family Circle*)
- Accommodate special creative needs (e.g., lengthy and factual copy for cars, multipage insert to showcase a line of activewear, or an insurance ad with an attached application form).

Radio

Radio can be an especially effective medium for local advertisers and those with highly selective targets.

Used often as a supporting medium, radio is:

- Highly targeted via program formats such as top 40 and classical
- A frequency builder (15 to 20 commercials per week on several stations in a market)
- very efficient.

Additionally, out-of-pocket costs are low for both air time and the production of commercials.

Outdoor

Long a favorite of advertisers restricted from using other media, outdoor advertising is also used extensively as reminder advertising.

By necessity, outdoor advertising is limited to simple copy and graphics.

Outdoor advertising offers advertisers:

- High frequency (providing repeated exposure due to daily traffic patterns)
- Geographic flexibility with showings near or in supermarkets, airports and sports arenas.

Newspaper

Newspapers are used primarily by local advertisers (such as retailers) and by some national advertisers with variances by market (such as airlines). They are also used frequently to carry promotional offers including coupons.

Newspapers allow advertisers:

- Flexibility
    - —Short lead times
    - —Market by market purchase
- Timeliness: One can respond to major events such as natural catastrophes or competitive moves like reductions in airline rates.
- Geographic concentration: Little circulation "waste" outside intended market.

Television

Despite the significant upheaval of traditional viewing habits, TV still provides several key benefits to advertisers:

- Intrusiveness.
- Ability to build reach rapidly.
- Broad reach of both mass and selective audiences.
- Cost efficiency.

There are four primary vehicles to buy TV: network, syndication, cable, and spot television.

Network

Although network viewing audiences have eroded substantially and continue to decline, network TV still provides the highest reach potential of any media vehicle (It can deliver a share of TV viewing of 60 percent or more on a given night).

At the same time, it can be used as a selective or targeted medium through the use of specific dayparts. The following are some generalizations about daypart audiences:

1. Prime

    All-family

    Working adults

2. Late Night

    Young adults

    Balance of women and men

    Light TV viewers

3. News

    Older adults

    Balance of women and men

4. Daytime

> Primarily female, especially homemakers

5. Sports

> Primarily male
>
> Light TV viewers
>
> Some income skew by sport

Syndication

As the number of independent stations has soared, so has the need for programming. Syndicated programs (e.g., "Jeopardy," "Wheel of Fortune," "Oprah") have been created to fill this need. Syndicated programs are typically sold individually as a "prepackaged" network of independent stations.

In the past decade, syndication has grown to become a major factor in today's media environment.

Syndicated programs offer an advertiser a number of benefits, including:

- National coverage (usually 70 to 90% of U.S. homes)
- Strong ratings (often comparable to network programs)
- Efficient pricing (up to 50% less than network)
- Lower out-of-pocket costs, which affords a "small" advertiser the opportunity to run in higher-rated evening programming.

Cable

As cable provides homes with more viewing options, it has grown tremendously and accounts for a sizable portion of the networks' audience decline.

Today, while ratings of cable programs are a fraction of network or syndicated programs, cable offers advertisers distinct advantages, including:

- Highly selective programming
- Price efficiency
- Slightly more upscale audiences
- Homes with children.

With improved programming, especially in sports and news, cable ratings have grown steadily. A recent example is Cable Network News (CNN),

With improved programming, especially in sports and news, cable ratings have grown steadily. A recent example is Cable Network News (CNN), whose ratings, while below those at the peak of the war in the Persian Gulf, remain above their prewar levels

299

whose ratings, while below those at the peak of the war in the Persian Gulf, remain above their pre-war levels.

Given its growing stature in today's environment, how do advertisers generally use cable in their TV purchases? It depends, of course, on a given advertiser's objectives.

For a financial services client, we used cable to supplement our network and syndicated purchases for three reasons:

1. To balance delivery of our national TV schedules in cable versus non-cable homes.
    » Since cable homes tend to watch less network and syndicated TV, we purchased cable to compensate for our national plans' underdelivery in cable homes.

2 To generate increased frequency efficiently against our target audience.
    » Typically, cable is only 40 to 50 percent of the relative cost of other TV options.
    » Its small ratings and low out-of-pocket costs enabled us to deliver multiple exposures to the same small audience (i.e., frequency) at a reasonable cost (which helps explain why cable appeals to direct-mail advertisers).

3. To reach highly selective targets.
    » Cable offers a variety of programs that appeal to narrow audience segments such as The Nashville Network (TNN), The Weather Channel (TWC), Financial Network News (FNN).
    » Against our upscale, highly educated adult target, cable offered selective programming alternatives such as CNN, ESPN, FNN, and Arts and Entertainment.

Spot Television

"Spot" refers to the purchase of commercial time in programs on a local market basis.

Clearly, "spot" is advantageous for local advertisers, but it is also used by national advertisers who desire to pinpoint their support by

- Market
    » Isolate additional support in a key business
    » Test new copy
    » Test a new product

- Daypart
    » Purchase those times not available nationally (e.g., late news, local sports, children's daytime).
- Target audience
    » Buy the most efficient and selective local shows against a specific target (such as late afternoon or early evening for teens).

"Spot" also affords an advertiser budget flexibility because of shorter lead and cancellation times.

The main drawback of "spot" TV is cost. Usually, an advertiser will pay a premium of 30 to 50 percent relative to national alternatives for adult dayparts. The premium for kids' programming is far less.

The following are some hypothetical uses to provide a sense of how television might fit into various advertisers' plans.

1. A salty snack, positioned against older kids and teens, might use a mix of television vehicles: cable (e.g., MTV), network (late afternoon or early evening network reruns such as "Gilligan's Island" or "The Brady Bunch,") and Fox ("In Living Color").

2. A vitamin supplement targeted against mature adults (aged 50+) with a limited budget might focus its weight in several efficiently priced vehicles like network TV (e.g., "Hee Haw" or game shows) and cable (e.g., CNN).

3. A regional marketer of women's hair-care products is launching a combined shampoo and conditioner in two test markets, targeted to women 18 to 34. It's likely that the advertiser would purchase spot

TV (e.g., daytime, late night, and perhaps some prime time) and possibly local cable (e.g., selective shows such as "Lifetime").

Earlier, I mentioned that today's media environment is in a state of flux. Here are four trends I believe will have a profound influence on the shape of media planning and buying in the future:

1. Continued erosion of network television.

2. Even more targeted programming/vehicles.
   » More cable channels
   » Potential for programming via phone lines and fiber optics
   » More selective magazine titles

3. Pay-per-view TV will become economically viable.
   » Its potential will reach far beyond the occasional heavyweight title

4. Interactive TV will become a reality.
   » New technology will provide viewers with complete control over a wide variety of viewing alternatives, including:
      – Selection of personal camera angles
      – Viewer controlled broadcasts
      – 1-900 numbers

Now, more than ever, in light of the ever-changing nature of today's media, media planners and buyers must stay on top of developments to recognize how best to reach the intended target audience.

Note: The author of this chapter on advertising started his very successful career by working for two years in the media department of one of America's great advertising agencies.

Today's media environment is in a state of flux

Now, more than ever, in light of the ever-changing nature of today's media, media planners and buyers must stay on top of developments to recognize how best to reach the intended target audience

Bill Dunlap is currently the CEO of Campbell-Mithun-Esty, a $750,000,000 agency.

He joined Campbell-Mithun with a rather fascinating background.

He spent a few years in the U.S. Postal Service, then joined Ralston Purina Company and later Procter & Gamble, where he worked on detergents, paper diapers and cosmetics.

Then a stint with IBM in the computer field, followed by new product work at Gillette.

He then became the director of new products at Procter & Gamble in Cincinnati. He rejoined the Post Office as Assistant Postmaster General. He became President of MCA (Market Corporation Advertising), an agency in Connecticut, all before joining Campbell-Mithun-Esty offices in Minneapolis, Chicago, Detroit and New York.

Bill lives in the country, outside Minneapolis. In that city he is active on the United Way, Chamber of Commerce and is chairman of the advertising task force promoting the Super Bowl in 1992.

How to Get New Business in Today's Market

By: Bill Dunlap

In the advertising agency business, there are fewer and fewer new business prospects available and more and more agencies scrambling for what business there is.

Ten years ago it was sufficient to wait for new business presentations to come over the transom and to prepare presentations for them as they arrive. Today that simply isn't enough.

New business prospecting requires a *plan* as disciplined as your agency's fine year growth plan, or the marketing plan you've written for your client. It should include objectives, criteria for identifying prospects, exactly who within the agency is responsible for the prospecting and finally the procedure and administration of the prospecting process.

Prospecting Objectives

Like any good marketing plan, your prospecting plan should be centered around achieving set objectives.

Your objectives for a prospecting plan should include exactly how many prospects you expect to contact and how many *capabilities meetings* you expect to obtain during the year.

In setting your objectives, it's critical to remember that the purpose of prospecting is simply to develop a relationship with your prospect in the hopes of being asked to present if and when that client's advertising is up for review. If your going-in expectation for a new prospect is to get that client to hire you within the next 12 months, you'll be frustrated, disappointed and your prospecting will ultimately fail.

Identifying Prospects

The criteria upon which you identify prospects to pursue should be fairly strict and well thought-out, but totally flexible. While the criteria you select should closely reflect your agency's situation, you may want to include the following:

- *A minimum billing criteria.* This will depend largely on the size of your agency, but you should have a good feeling for what your minimum billing threshold is to run an account profitably.

- *Uncovered industries.* Look closely at your current client portfolio and you'll easily be able to identify industries in which you don't currently have a client. These could include the automobile industry, electronics, medical, food, other package goods, etc. Concentrate if you can, on a few industries so that the learning you do for one prospect in an industry can be transferred and related to other prospects in that industry.

- *Identify vulnerable agencies.* It may seen like you are a vulture picking over the remains of a dying animal, but the fact is that when clients are bailing out from an agency, the remaining clients lose faith in that agency's ability and are more open to solicitations from other agencies.

- *Conflicting clients.* NEVER solicit a client that would be a direct conflict with an existing client, no matter how much bigger the prospect is. While it may make all the sense in the world to trade up from a $1M local restaurant to a $50M national chain, by openly soliciting their business you have demonstrated a lack of trust which can probably never be repaired.

Who Prospects?

One of the most ill-conceived notions in agency history is that new business should be left entirely in the hands of upper management. Everyone who works at the agency should be responsible for new business.

Of course, everyone doesn't have the resources to draw upon to make an impact.

But if an "everyone is responsible" philosophy is part of the corporate culture, people who do have the resources will draw upon them more readily.

One of the most ill-conceived notions in agency history is that new business should be left entirely in the hands of upper management

What I believe works particularly well is a process where every account person, account supervisor and above, is responsible for one to two client prospects in addition to their on-going client responsibility

Some agencies employ a strategy where one person is singularly responsible for the solicitation of clients, and nothing else. While this "rain-making" strategy has had isolated cases of great success, I favor a strategy where you spread the prospecting process around middle and top management.

What I believe works particularly well is a process where every account person, account supervisor and above, is responsible for one to two client prospects in addition to their on-going client responsibility.

It is their responsibility to initiate, develop, and nurture relationships with prospective clients. Their success in this area should be as much a part of their performance assessment as their ability to manage an ongoing piece of business.

How to Prospect

You can't expect people to perform a task for which they are not properly equipped and trained. They must be provided the prospecting tools and the confidence they need to do it successfully. Here's what you need to give them:

- *The big picture.* Share with them the agency's philosophy toward prospecting and their role in it.

  Make them understand that prospecting is part of their job responsibility and they will be judged accordingly.

  Most importantly, make them understand all they need to do is get and keep your agency on the prospect's radar scope. Getting the business itself is an entirely different matter.

- *How to cold call.* This can be one of the most intimidating and difficult parts of the prospecting process. Most agency people like to service existing clients, not generate new ones. So the easier you can make this for them, the better you'll be.

  Historically, we've held telemarketing seminars for the prospectors.

  They learn how to identify the decision maker at the prospect company, how to get through the switch board and make contact with that person, how to generate initial interest in your agency and how to engage that person in an ongoing dialogue.

- *Don't re-invent the wheel.* It's critical that your prospectors have at their fingertips a portfolio of existing agency materials to draw upon for use with their prospects.

  They should have a portfolio between 5-15 different pieces of literature, case histories, creative reels, etc., which demonstrate your agency's capabilities. If it's left to the prospector to develop new materials to keep in contact with their prospects, the job will become insurmountable and won't get done. The most important thing to remember in this area is that any contact is better than no contact at all.

How To Get The Meeting

This may be in many ways even more difficult than initiating and developing a relationship because it takes longer and you often don't see the results, even after years.

In many ways it's like trying to keep the weight off after a successful diet. You no longer have the tangible gratification of the weight loss; you have to be satisfied with weight maintenance.

Nurturing a relationship to get a meeting eventually is similar. You must be increasingly inventive and insightful to engage the prospect in discussions to stay top-of-mind for the eventuality that he'll call for an agency review.

You must patiently, yet persistently demonstrate your agency's understanding of their business and how your contributions can make a difference to them.

You also demonstrate the benefits (see chapter 11) they'll receive if you want them to put you to work on all or part of the account.

Wherever possible, suggest informal lunches, meetings and outings for the prospect to meet key agency people.

Keep it non-threatening, but never let them doubt your commitment to want to handle at least a part of their business.

It's critical that your prospectors have at their fingertips a portfolio of existing agency materials to draw upon

You must be increasingly inventive and insightful to engage the prospect in discussions to stay top-of-mind

The Meeting

In new business presentations, you must always "go the extra mile" and provide an added dimension of thinking.

The focus of the meeting should be on the prospect's business, and *not* on agency credentials

The focus of the meeting should be on the prospect's business, and *not* on agency credentials. Whereas it's easier to talk about one's own agency, what the prospect is really interested in is how the agency can help the prospect build his business.

The central point of a presentation should be to present one or more powerful creative ideas that help the prospect differentiate and build business and increase share of market within his business category.

In all cases, the ideas should be researched among the target audience so you have some objective rationale as to how/why the ideas will work in the marketplace

In all cases, the ideas should be researched among the target audience so you have some objective rationale as to how/why the ideas will work in the marketplace.

In most cases, it's helpful to demonstrate how the creative ideas can be executed in television, print, radio, sales materials and collateral materials.

Where possible, timing/implementation details should be provided.

It's essential to adhere strictly to time limits during the presentation, and to address the specific issues you're confident the prospect's most interested in.

We always try to provide the prospects with excellent ideas and *more than he expects* in terms of understanding and quality of work.

Lastly, a sense of humor is always appropriate in a new business presentation.

By and large, the best performers in advertising have fun in doing their jobs. The advertising business is not brain surgery.

If you employ a team of successful prospectors and presenters, there's no doubt you'll increase—overnight—the number of new business meetings you participate in by 50% and the number of success will increase dramatically.

Note from Al Whitman: I asked the agency president who wrote this chapter if he'd include a case history of a successful new business solicitation. After talking to his top executives about it, he finally refused because his agencyhad been so successful in new business. He did not want to give any of his agency's specific new business techniques away.

CHAPTER 61

Jim Fish now operates a small consulting business in Wayzata, Minnesota, called Ad-Ventures. Some years ago he was the Director of Advertising for General Mills.

Upon retirement he was asked to be the first Dean of a special new graduate program in business communications, including marketing, advertising, direct mail, etc., at St. Thomas College in St. Paul, Minnesota. Many people believe that this small school is the finest in the State of Minnesota and one of the best in the Midwest.

Jim has been a great community leader and public servant for many years helping with countless worthwhile projects.

He has done more to help improve this book than any other person except one.

Jim was elected to the Advertising Hall of Fame in 1984.

How to Get a Job

By: Jim Fish

After leaving corporate life, I became a college teacher, and I found how ill-prepared many young people are in the serious business of getting a job.

Whether I was counseling college students going out into the cold world for the first time, or counseling older people who had lost their jobs or were seeking a job change, no one seemed to have a plan. No one seemed to realize there is a process involved. That the process is like marketing a product.

This led to the development of an assignment for my senior advertising majors requiring them to write a marketing plan for themselves. The plan followed a format we were using to develop marketing and communications.

How to Market Yourself

Marketing yourself is like marketing a product or service and involves these steps or processes:

1. Know all you can about the Product (you), and your competition.

2. Identify the Market where you want to work.

3. Decide how you're going to reach that Market (media).

4. Decide how best to "package" yourself, particularly what benefits (see chapter 11) you can offer the company in the job you're applying for.

5. Evaluate your progress, refining your thinking as you go.

You As the Product (or, Know Thyself)

Here are some additional things to consider:

*   First, what kind of a person are you? Are you quiet, gregarious, a loner, creative, numbers oriented, a team person, a leader, good at relating to people? These are but a few words that describe what you take to the job market. Possibly with the help of others,

you should draw up a personality/talent profile of yourself.

- Are you a good communicator (written, oral)? Are you a good listener?

- What are your natural *talents*? What *skills* do you have from any training or experience?

- Do you have clearly defined career goals? Are they narrow, or are they broad and diverse?

- Have you considered vocational testing as a more objective way to find out about your talents?

- What do those who know you best feel your talents are? A mentor in the business can prove a wonderful help in "getting your act together."

Many young people aim at a specific career because of peer pressure, or because they think it's an easy, glamorous way to make a living. Many of these people won't make it because they have neither the aptitude nor the work ethic to succeed. So, know thyself.

The Market (Where the Jobs Are)

When I first talked to students interested in advertising as a career, I asked them what kinds of jobs they really wanted. Usually only two types of jobs were mentioned: Copywriter/art director, or account executive.

How limited that viewpoint is! That narrow focus indicates that the only jobs in advertising are with agencies. It ignores the host of jobs, both in and outside agencies, that make up the diverse advertising field.

What about retail advertising?

Or ad departments of manufacturers? Or media sales — local, regional, and national?

Or with full-service printers who provide creative and marketing services?

Or with promotional companies?

Or in the growing field of nonprofit organizations that need advertising and marketing help in selling their cause or in raising funds?

Or in marketing research, an integral part of the advertising and marketing process? Or, what about a retail sales job?

A simple look in the Yellow Pages will demonstrate the wide variety of opportunity areas for the serious job seeker. Incidentally, some of the best jobs for people who have the knack of persuading others to "want to do what they want them to" are in sales… selling for a manufacturer or a broker or a distributor in the food and drug field, selling real estate, insurance, stocks and bonds, almost any kind of sales.

How else can you find out where these job opportunities lie?

Talk to people in the business, spend time in libraries researching an industry, talk with local ad or sales clubs or related organizations. Networking is extremely important. Such analysis should lead to your development of a target company list.

Then, *who* in these identified opportunity companies is *the* person to see? Who is the decision maker? A "Dear Sir" letter to a company usually winds up in the wastebasket. But a few phone calls to that company, asking specific questions about who has responsibility, and in what areas, will often net you the names of the right person to write or call on, his or her direct-dial phone number, and probably the name and phone number of the "gatekeeper," usually the person's secretary. Incidentally, secretaries can be very important. When you're particularly nice to him or her, you'll increase your chances of seeing the boss.

Keep records so that you know who you talked with, when, and what they said.

In the job search it's important to know *where* you want to live, or where you *don't* want to live. So, don't diffuse your efforts by spending time and effort to discuss a job opportunity outside your identified geographic limits.

If you're trying to get your first job, look for *internship* opportunities with companies that offer them, or training programs. It may be smart to focus on them as a way to get your first job.

All this adds up to "Know Thy Market."

A simple look in the Yellow Pages will demonstrate the wide variety of opportunity areas for the serious job seeker

A few phone calls to that company, asking specific questions about who has responsibility, and in what areas, will often net you the names of the right person to write or call on

The Message (Your Copy Platform, and What You Need to Implement it)

The Resume

The resume is your most important selling tool.

Over the past dozen or more years, resumes have become more sophisticated in content and appearance. The availability of books and seminars on resume development, and the convenience of print shops with low-cost typesetting facilities allow almost anyone to produce a professional-looking resume. Many people have matching stationery and business cards printed at the same time. While there's no absolutely right or wrong way to prepare a resume, here are some pointers that may improve the effectiveness of your resume:

1. It should be more than a dull listing of schools attended and achievements to date.

2. It should reflect the personality and talent of the individual.

3. It should be attractive in appearance and flawless in spelling and grammar.

4. Ideally it should include your "positioning statement," like how and where you hope to fit into the broader world you seek to enter.

The Cover Letter

The cover letter is often used to get your resume to your target, lets you personalize your message, and add special emphasis to what you're applying for and what you can bring to the job.

It shouldn't be in stereotypical business prose, but can reflect more of your personality and style. It should be businesslike but not stuffy. It's important that you find ways to dramatize any benefits (see Chapter 11) you can offer the company. The fact that you really want the job for certain reasons can be a benefit. So can your saying you're a good listener, never make the same mistake twice, or that you're accustomed to working long hours.

The cover letter is often used to get your resume to your target, lets you personalize your message, and add special emphasis to what you're applying for and what you can bring to the job

The fact that you really want the job for certain reasons can be a benefit. So can your saying you're a good listener, never make the same mistake twice, or that you're accustomed to working long hours

312

The Portfolio

If you're applying for a job in advertising, show them ads you've worked on or articles you've written or ones that have been written about you. Assemble in orderly fashion things you've done to date that demonstrate the skills and capabilities you've acquired so far.

Keep your portfolio up-to-date. Throw out earlier samples that have been superseded by more recent examples of your work. If you're applying for a job in sales, describe what you've done and the progress you've made — that is, any promotion, salary increases, or bonuses.

The Interview/Presentation.

This is what all your efforts have been aimed at.

There are a number of books on interviews, but here are some fundamentals important in a successful interview.

1. Know as much as possible about the company you're interviewing. Check the business library for periodicals with recent stories about the company. If they are a public company, get their annual report and any other literature they may provide on request.

2. Be prepared for the interview situation with an orderly presentation. Materials in addition to your resume should be woven into the meeting. Even a desktop flip chart may add memorability to your interview.

3. Start off by saying something the interviewer will say yes to. If he doesn't agree with your starting remarks, you'll probably spoil your interview.

4. Try to remain relaxed. Listen carefully to questions, and don't use "overkill" in your responses.

5. Be creative. Example, a daughter-in-law of a close friend of mine read about a job opening in a top-notch nursery. She enjoys flowers and had her own garden. So she took a picture of her garden for the interview. When she showed the

Start off by saying something the interviewer will say yes to. If he doesn't agree with your starting remarks, you'll probably spoil your interview

interviewer the picture, she got the job
immediately.

6.   Dress appropriately, and make sure you are
well groomed (hair, nails, jewelry,
makeup, etc.).

7.   Always thank your interviewer in person,
and drop him or her a note immediately
after the interview. Keep records on
what the interviewer said.

The Media — How To Reach Your Market

You've defined the product (you), you've developed the target markets (your list), you've got your selling materials, and a number of ads and articles about you in hand (resume and portfolio), so we address the delivery system.

While your selling package and your list of prospects are the foundation of your effort, how you get these to your targets is your next challenge. This effort is aimed at getting you the first interview, and then the subsequent interviews, which are usually required before you get the job.

The Telephone

The telephone is of most help during the development and sharpening of your list. Intelligently used, the phone can save a lot of postage and shoe leather (see Chapter 19)

Direct Mail

 Direct mail is the most useful in getting your materials to the decision makers, and in all the follow-up (see Chapter 46). Be sure your mailings are error-free and professional. And, again, maintain copies and records. Follow-up mailings are usually involved, so build this into your planning. For some good tips on how to write good direct-mail letters see Chapter 45.

Other media

If you're extra creative, and have your target defined sharply, you could use a number of fun approaches: a small outdoor sign opposite the entrance of the building in which your "target" works using copy with his or her name on it, or small space ads in trade publications or in the business pages of the Sunday or classified ad sections of the local newspapers. Or have special kits prepared and delivered by messenger or mail service. The sky is the limit when it comes to unique ways you can deliver your message. This approach underlines the need to differentiate wherever possible you and your message from "all others" who are after jobs in the same area or even the same job. The trick is: How can you be different? How can you be memorable? How can you do these things and still maintain a serious, businesslike image?

Evaluation

In the real world, marketing people are continually evaluating what they're doing, refining and improving their selling tools and techniques as they gain experience.

It is no different for you when you are selling yourself. Be willing to make *changes* in your resume or your other selling materials. Refine your "market" as you learn from your calls. Look back over your records to see whether somewhere along the way was a promising opportunity that may have ripened since your last contact. Timing is an important element in the job search. You want to be there when the job opens up.

Discuss your progress with a friend or mentor. Sharing your experiences can lead to some new ideas, (and perhaps pump up your spirits).

Summary

- Organize your efforts, and pattern them after a real-world marketing plan.
- Talk to lots of people in the business to get a good fix on what's current.
- Differentiate yourself through your selling materials.
- Try to find a mentor.
- Keep records.
- Thank everyone along the way who has given you time.
- Keep up to date on what's going on in the world around you.
- Attend relevant seminars or courses as a means of honing your skills and for the networking they provide.

A final note: While many of these thoughts were developed and proved in the context of the graduating college senior, experience has shown that the principles apply equally to those who are already in the business world, who've lost their job, or who want to make a job or career change.

So just remember: Marketing yourself is like marketing a product or service (see Chaper 1).

CHAPTER 62

How to be the Best Advertising Agency Account Executive

By: Al Whitman

The account director's "job description" will vary from agency to agency. It will also vary as a function of the way the agency works and the client involved

A really good executive or account director who learns his/her job and does it right can be a key person in an advertising agency.

The account director's "job description" will vary from agency to agency. It will also vary as a function of the way the agency works and the client involved, but generally the key elements in the job are:

1. Understanding the client's needs and wants and communicating them accurately to the agency's management and working associates.

2. Understanding the agency's client information requirements, obtaining the information and relaying it along with other key thoughts to the proper people within the agency.

3. Work with the client's representative to arrive at the key elements that'll be used in the marketing plan. The account executive is responsible for working out any differences of opinion.

4. The account executive is responsible to determine what jobs are to be done by the client and what jobs are to be done by the agency. He'll then prepare a time table reviewing the tasks and indicating when, where and who will do them, making sure that everyone has the right signals and understands their role.

5. Put together in memo or fact book form (see chapter 6) all the available data pertinent to the marketing of the product or service. If key information is missing the account executive and the client agree to get it or forget it.

6. Participate with the agency group on such subjects as:

    a. what alternate "position" (Chapter 15) should be considered for the product or service if it is new?

    b. what kind of "repositioning" opportunities are there if the product or service is already on the market?

7. Spell out to the creative team what customer benefits (chapter 11) are available - what the competition is, and what advantages, if any, the client's product has over competition.

8. Directs the creative team to prepare preliminary creative efforts for one or more specific media.

9. Communicates to the creative team *what to say,* but never *how* to say it.

NOTE: Remember in creating advertising, the "what" that should be said is the account man's job. The "how to say it" belongs strictly to the creatuve team.

Spell out to the creative team what customer benefits (chapter 11) are available - what the competition is, and what advantages, if any, the client's product has over competition

Remember in creating advertising, the "what" that should be said is the account man's job. The "how to say it" belongs strictly to the creative team

CHAPTER 63

How to Motivate People Who Work For You

By: Ray Mithun

Here are eight tips on this important subject.

1. Make sure each person knows exactly the job he/she is expected to perform.

2. Whenever possible, have each individual define his/her own job in writing.

3. Never hesitate to ask for their advice. This compliments them and shows that you care what they think. They might also come up with a good idea.

4. When you communicate with them don't just say, "Do this." Instead turn on your powers of persuasion to make them want to do what you want them to. This calls for your pointing out the *benefits* they'll receive in doing what you want them to.

   Benefits, as explained in chapter 11, are the key to persuasion and motivation for all people — not just the ones who work for you.

5. Both formally and informally make sure you evaluate their work at periodic intervals.

6. Before you tell your people what you think about their performance, ask them to evaluate their own work first.

7. Always listen to what your people have to say.

8. Make sure everyone understands that "the job is the boss" (see Chapter 67).

CHAPTER 64

How to Be a Good Leader

By: Ray Mithun

A good leader has the ability to *visualize the goals* for the team and make everyone in the organization *enthusiastic* about attaining them

A good leader has the ability to *visualize the goal*s for the team and make everyone in the organization *enthusiastic* about attaining them.

A good leader makes sure everyone knows *what their job is* and what's expected of them.

A good leader sets a *good example.* If you want people in the office at 9 a.m., be there when they arrive.

A good leader gives employees plenty of *responsibility* and makes them feel important and appreciated.

A good leader is *demanding,* but always fair.

A good leader *listens* to what employees think.

A good leader *gives* timely, helpful *advice,* particularly when asked for it.

A good leader is a great *communicator* and *teacher.*

A good leader finds ways to *dramatize* key concepts that you want them to understand and remember (see Chapter 10).

Finally, a good leader is one who engenders *trust* and *respect.*

Few business executives possess all 10 of these important abilities. But when a company is led by someone who possesses 7 or 8 of them, chances are that company will be very successful.

CHAPTER 65

How to Be a Great Teacher

By: Al Whitman

Most corporate owners and leaders are good teachers, and they take certain steps in their own way to pass along what they've learned to their people.

They start by requiring certain actions from their people:

- Written plans
- Fact books (as explained in Chapter 6) or their equivalent.
- Call reports covering actions taken and decisions made at meetings with each client, and in key telephone conversations with the client.
- Written memos giving directions.

These disciplines or requirements are part of how the owners expect their people to work. But actually they are **teaching** certain key disciplines to their people.

Teaching also involves understanding and doing other things including calling attention to certain actions that other people have taken, holding seminars on key subjects, bulletin board displays, etc.

How to Be a "Great" Teacher

The great teacher never forgets the teacher learns more than the pupil, so he assigns specific subjects to selected individuals and has them teach them to others

There are many **good** teachers but only a limited number of **great** ones. The great teacher never forgets the teacher learns more than the pupil, so he assigns specific subjects to selected individuals and has them teach them to others.

He also finds other ways to get his people involved. This may call for writing or preparing marketing plans etc.

The great teacher lists for himself/herself what the pupils should learn and builds a teaching program to achieve that goal.

A great teacher knows that student's understanding varies from student to student. When you make a point one way, student A will get it, but student B will not. Make a point another way and student B will get it but student C will not. That's why great teachers make the same point *several different ways*.

The great teacher appreciates the truth in the old saying, "You can lead a horse to water, but you can't make him drink." He keeps this thought in mind when he teaches.

He does his best to make his students interested in each subject and never assumes the student has fully learned a point just because the teacher made it. He or she knows that students like to have a little fun in the classroom, and enjoy the learning experience with a teacher who's unpretentious. They love a teacher who has a sense of humor.

Finally, the great teacher finds ways to dramatize certain key concepts so they'll stick in the students brains like a fish hook (see Chapter 10).

The repositioning story in Chapter 16 is the kind of a story that a superior teacher might tell because it will stay in the student's memory.

Here's another story that happened years ago:

There's an excellent preparatory school located in the same town as one of America's great universities. The school helped prepare high school students to qualify for admittance to the university.

Many of the finest teachers in this school moonlighted twice a year to teach students at the university to help them pass their Winter and Spring exams.

One teacher taught his political science students the subject of "contributory negligence." By way of example, let's take an accident. If two people get in an accident and each is partially responsible for it, then no one has a case against the other because each "contributed" to it.

Here 's how the teacher explained "contributory negligence" to the class he was tutoring.

> One fine autumn evening, a farmer was walking in the moonlight. In his pumpkin patch he noticed two young people making love.
>
> He was infuriated and he picked up a small pumpkin and threw it, hitting the man smack on his fanny.
>
> Nine months later the girl sued the farmer for "contributory negligence."

He does his best to make his students interested in each subject and never assumes the student has fully learned a point just because the teacher made it

CHAPTER 66

How to Get Ahead in Business

By: Ray Mithun

1. Become relatively indispensable in your job.
2. Understand the "Job is the Boss" (see Chapter 67).
3. Understand why every person must pay for his/her own supervision. * (see below)
4. Come up with ideas for getting new business or for saving money in some phase of the company's operations.
5. Help train your own replacement.
6. Help bring in a new employee who can really contribute to the firm.

Everyone likes to be promoted and to make more money but few of them have been given a list like the above, which tells them what they have to know, and what they have to do to get ahead in business.

* If you supervise a number of people and one or more seldom, if ever, require supervision, who should be the highest paid in the group?

CHAPTER 67

How and Why the Job is the Boss

By: Ray Mithun

It changes the whole culture of a business house when everyone in the joint understands that "the job is the boss."

According to Al Whitman, this little chapter is one of the most important in the book.

I agree, and here's why.

Because it changes the whole culture of a business house when everyone in the joint understands that "the job is the boss."

What does this statement mean?

First, let's use a simple illustration about my own family.

When our first child was old enough to learn responsibility, we made a deal with him. We'd pay him 25¢ every Saturday afternoon when he emptied the wastebadkets. This was when 25¢ was enough to buy an ice cream cone.

One day he wanted some time off and asked us if he could go outside instead of emptying the baskets. We replied, "Why ask us? The job isn't done. You made a deal, and in this home the job is the boss."

When Al Whitman and I were partners in Campbell-Mithun, we used to remind our people of certain things we believed were true, and in their best interest to understand.

Few people appreciate having to be supervised. And, actually, they shouldn't require supervision. When a person is serious about his/her job and knows what is expected, and does it, very little or no supervision is needed.

Why?

Because the person understands the job is the boss and does whatever is necessary to do the job on his/her own initiative, and does it right.

This philosophy doesn't just apply to people who work in advertising agencies.

It applies almost everywhere. In every business. In every job at every level.

CHAPTER 68

Bill Sorem is a mathematics, statistics and computer whiz.

He's a lecturer on advertising at the University of Minnesota's School of Journalism and Mass Communications.

Bill is highly skilled in all phases of marketing new products.

He has been Vice President of Campbell-Mithun and Bozell Jacobs Advertising Agencies, and is now founder and owner of Computer Obedience School in Burnsville, Minnesota.

Computers in Marketing and Advertising

By: Bill Sorem

In the last several years, computers have significantly changed the way we do business. Most of the time the change is for the better. They have produced profound changes in advertising and marketing operations as well.

Computers have also changed techniques used to create and produce advertising.

They have changed management techniques and produced totally new ways of marketing products.

In an advertising agency or similar service company, there are some functional areas where computers are nearly indispensable:

- Writing
- Design
- Account management
- Research
- Information retrieval
- Video and audio production
- Print production
- Agency management

In a marketing environment, major computer applications may be grouped into these functions:

- New product development
- Direct marketing management
- Sales management
- Forecasting
- Sales aids production
- Presentations
- Marketing management

Before discussing these areas, let's look at two *hypothetical case histories* that illustrate today's computer role: an advertising agency working on a new consumer product, and a direct marketing company.

Case History 1:

New Product Development

Knowledge about the consumer of this potential product is collected from various sources:

Library files within the agency and selected outside sources are scanned. The computer connects the seeker to samples of advertising campaigns for similar or competitive products, published articles or other studies, and similar data.

Custom research studies are processed and presented on the desktop. The decision is addressed by an artificial intelligence program that has examined thousands of other new product case histories. All such data is presented with interesting graphics that clarify critical elements.

The product design people in the client's research laboratory are following a similar path to get direction to create and test the product.

The account management staff is examining financial alternatives.

What is the likely effect of various pricing, packaging, and distribution strategies?

Preliminary budgets are produced. Desktop computers make possible examination of many more alternatives and early elimination of blind alleys.

As product development proceeds, consumer research data is made available to all who need to know. Each user gets a custom presentation of the data relating specifically to that person's area of interest.

Agency creative people see simple presentations of information that could affect the content of the advertising.

This data display is interactive and customized, any user has the ability to change it or to request additional data on a specific area.

Since the user computers are linked, information distribution is not limited to meetings and group presentations. It's available any time.

What is the likely effect of various pricing, packaging, and distribution strategies?

Agency creative people see simple presentations of information that could affect the content of the advertising

The advertising is written with computer word processing programs, designed and perhaps illustrated with other design programs

The advertising is written with computer word processing programs, designed and perhaps illustrated with other design programs.

Materials can also be submitted for client approval electronically and almost instantaneously. Client product managers and agency account managers can work together on planning documents.

The organization and style of management presentations may be standardized by client management to allow efficient comparison of alternative products and alternative strategies for a given product (see Chapter 15).

Limited test market package designs and printed materials can be produced with desktop publishing to save costs and to provide flexibility for market-suggested changes.

Finally, as the product begins selling in a test market or in national distribution, sales numbers are collected summarized and quickly made available to all people in the control loop (see Chapter 8).

Again, custom queries select the requested data from mountains of detail. A person wanting to know the sales of the 10-oz. size for the first three months in Buffalo doesn't have to paw through piles of paper or pitch a request over the transom for a special computer run.

This sales history is available as numbers or collected and presented in graphs or other visuals.

Case History 2

Direct Marketing

Consider a direct marketing company that sells a line of products by telephone (see Chapter 19). The products are advertised through a variety of media (see Chapter 47), direct-mail letters (see Chapter 46), and through catalogs published several times a year (see Chapter 24).

This scenario could apply to the direct marketing of almost any product to any area. It could be a very large company, or it could be one person with a telephone and a desktop computer.

A customer calls to place an order or to inquire about a product. When the salesperson enters the customer telephone number, the customer record is pulled up on the screen. New address, phone or credit card data can be added to the customer record. The customer asks for an item. The salesperson enters the item code and the computer reports on price, availability, and a summary of information about the product. The customer orders this and perhaps other items as well.

A customer order is prepared and the total reported to the customer, along with shipping costs and delivery date. When the call is completed, the computer creates a shipping order and a customer invoice and updates product inventory.

When the order is shipped, a charge notice is sent to the proper credit card company if the order was so charged.

As inventory is depleted, the computer generates orders to manufacturers, ordering in predetermined quantities or making exception orders if necessary.

Managers check product inventories at any time, produce statistics about inventory levels versus sales by product, by product class, or for the entire warehouse. All product sales or cost information is immediately available in numeric or graph form.

Customer data is retrieved by various demographic or geographic categories. Sales can be plotted by day, by hour, and even by minute. Performance of various sales people is reported and analyzed.

The computer reports relative profitability of various staffing levels for times of the days, days of the week, and so on.

Lead sources are tracked and analyzed, such as which magazines produce what volume of leads at what cost per lead at what total sales value.

Split-run copy (see Chapter 21) in the catalog or in the ads helps determine the most cost-effective approach.

Ads and catalogs are written, designed, and perhaps printed on the computer system. Copy input from manufacturers is gathered by phone connection directly to the computer, accepting input 24 hours a day.

Customer name lists are available for mailing direct offers.

The Computer and Advertising Agency Functions

Writing

Most writing is now done with a word processing program on a desktop personal computer. This device gives writers new power and flexibility.

Software and hardware preferences are highly personal, but the main criteria for writers are

1. Easy-to-use commands and screens that require little, if any, training.
2. On-line spell checker and thesaurus.
3. Simple editing, cutting, pasting, and formatting procedures.

Design

In the beginning, designs were created by art directors working with chalk. The introduction of the *felt-tip marker* changed that practice and helped designers work more efficiently.

Today graphic designers have the power of computer design systems. They allow a new, wider range of experimentation and exploration. These high-powered design computers significantly extend the scope and productivity of a good designer. A typical design installation includes a color scanner for capturing photos, printed material, or layouts.

Account Management

Today's account managers use many of the same tools as other service professionals. Word-processing programs produce the written word. Electronic mail systems deliver words, graphics, and perhaps sounds.

The major contributions computers have made to most account managers have come from database

Today graphic designers have the power of computer design systems. They allow a new, wider range of experimentation and exploration

The major contributions computers have made to most account managers have come from database programs and spreadsheets followed by presentation production programs

programs and spreadsheets followed by presentation production programs.

Spreadsheet programs and databases give a manager the capacity to examine many alternative solutions to financial problems:

How should an account be staffed? What fee income is needed under various assumptions? How much will a new office cost?

Often the most important use of an electronic spreadsheet is *management of the client's budget.*

Research

A research manager can now use a variety of statistical analytic techniques that were only theory 20 years ago.

"What if" analyses are now done very simply with spreadsheets and other programs. The ability to explore the financial or other consequences of various actions adds significant substance to new product, new market, and new campaign questions.

Information Retrieval

The ability to retrieve desired information quickly and easily is important to many functions in an agency. Custom database programs connect a number of information sources. The information sources can be in the user's desktop computer, in the agency's file computer, in a client's computer or in a computer anywhere in the world.

Information retrieval, organization and presentation is the largest area of computer hardware and software development in the 1990s. Advertising examples include media information from publications or stations, government census or business data, client sales data for selected products and sales areas, and library searches on a given subject.

Information retrieval, organization and presentation is the largest area of computer hardware and software development in the 1990s

Video and Audio Production

Personal computers have spawned a multitude of applications in the creation and production of music, video editing, audio shows, and multimedia productions.

Computer-assisted music and video production has become a specialized area that is beyond the scope of this discussion. The impact on advertising is the availability of many more creative options, often at lower cost.

Print Production

Word-processing and design programs can be linked directly to various printing systems. It's possible to design, write, illustrate and print a document electronically. A number of publications are produced in this way.

Approval copy, paper layouts, keylines, and other materials are still needed in some situations and are produced by laser printers, color printers, and other output devices.

With a desktop publishing program, one person can write, illustrate, lay out pages and print them with a laser printer without ever leaving the office chair.

Many individuals can easily collaborate on a project. For example, technical people can be collecting data with word-processing, database, or spreadsheet programs. A designer or illustrator working with drawing and painting programs creates visual elements.

The writer starts with a word-processing program, gathering segments from all the other people. The designer then designs the piece and uses one of the page layout programs to position and modify all the graphic and text elements.

Basic Agency Management

Agency managers have many of the same information needs as other business managers. Computers now produce more information in a more timely manner than battalions of workers in the accounting department

Agency managers have many of the same information needs as other business managers. Computers now produce more information in a more timely manner than battalions of workers in the accounting department. Spreadsheet and presentation programs are the primary information purveyors.

Marketing Functions

Many of the advertising agency examples just discussed also apply to marketing operations. Information retrieval, analysis writing, and design are all important marketing functions, but these topics are discusses elsewhere in this book

New Product Development

Most of the comments about new product marketing in the hypothetical case history at the beginning of this chapter apply to marketing management of *new products.* There are data to be retrieved, analyses to be run, statistics to be calculated, and presentations to be made, just as in an agency. The amount of raw information that can be considered for new product decisions has greatly increased, and the ability to ponder complex problems is speeded up because of today's computers.

Direct Marketing

Except for the creative ideas, computers have made possible most of today's direct marketing operations. They simply could not exist without this power.

Sales Management

The most significant impact of the computer on marketing has been their ability to allow users to retrieve and use large files.

A sales manager may track sales performance by area, by salespeople, and by product type, any possible outcomes of pricing and promotion strategies, all from the desktop. Sales results from all branch offices can be consolidated and updated minute by minute.

Prospect or customer information management, a continuing concern for sales managers and salespeople is duck soup for custom database programs.

Detailed personal and business information about sales prospects is instantly available. A salesperson can keep track of all the pieces of information that are part of effective sales prospecting and follow-up. Mailing lists, custom letters, and other communications are easily generated.

Sales Aid Production

Desktop publishing packages have revolutionized production of sales aids.

Newsletters, specification sheets, and other sales promotion pieces are created and printed faster, more accurately, and more economically than ever before. The ease of making changes means that printed support materials can be customized specifically for model types, product variations, regional variations, and customer differences, with minimum expense.

Presentations

Effective sales calls require presentation materials, whether it's a three ring binder or, more elaborate presentation. Presentation programs take otherwise dull stuff and make it glamorous and interesting. They combine elaborate, easy-to-use graphics capabilities with simple ways of including numbers:

Except for the creative ideas, computers have made possible most of today's direct marketing operations. They simply could not exist without this power

336

sales, forecast costs, and other essential details in understandable form.

Some Things to Think About in Considering Computer Applications

1. Are the dollars needed for computer applications wisely spent? If it's a cost-effective move, do it.

2. What about changing technology? Will this equipment be obsolete in a few years? It probably will, but if the dollars make sense now, it will pay off in the long run.

3. Asking the computer system to solve the entire problem may be very expensive. Often there's a solution that solves most of the problem at a fraction of the cost.

4. Bigger and faster doesn't always mean better. Taking the Concorde from New York to Newark makes little sense. Having 16.7 million colors available may not help produce better copy.

5. Get good information. The vendor salespeople and the person working out next to you at the health club may be helpful, but other more objective resources are available.

6. Train the computers, not the people. The cost of customizing the interface is often far less than the cost of "training." Marketing and advertising people should speak human lanquage, not computer jargon.

Gee Whiz

Advertising and marketing are flashy functions; without show biz glitz, they wouldn't exist. Waiting rooms, meeting rooms, office decor, and presentation techniques reflect this verve.

Computer technology offers many ways to enhance a company's image. The well-equipped agency lobby should include interactive multimedia presentations, custom information retrieval systems, computer-generated graphics, and a host of other accoutrements for visitors.

The conference room with sliding panels has been or should be replaced with computer-controlled lighting, video and audio presentations, and large-screen displays of presentation material from the same room, down the hall, or around the world.

One of the joys of working in this creative environment is the ability to dream and to make some dreams realty. This powerful new technology opens the door to new dreamlands. Enjoy!

CHAPTER 69

How This Book Is Being Marketed

By: Al Whitman

In preparing the marketing plan for the book, we've followed all the basic marketing principles you've read about in this book

In this chapter we outline for you point by point and step by step, the marketing plan that's been prepared for this book and will be executed after the book is published.

We don't know a better way of describing to you what marketing is (see Chapter 1).

You'll discover that in preparing the marketing plan for the book, we've followed all the basic marketing principles you've read about in this book.

We hope that as you go through our explanation, this chapter will give you a new appreciation for marketing, the many elements marketing entails, and the tremendous amount of work required to put together a complete marketing program for a product or service and then to commit it all to writing.

Why Does This Book Differ From Others on the Market?

You'll find the differences outlined in the preface.

For What Market Segments Has This Book Been Prepared?

See the list of occupations on the back page of this book.

How Has This Book Been Positioned?

Bearing in mind the market segments this book is intended to reach, here is how we describe the remainder of our positioning.

- It was written to help people do a better job at their place of work, make more money, and receive faster promotions.

- It was written to come as close as possible to "on-the-job" training.

- When you think of it, everything in this book was learned on the job. Almost everyone knows that when it comes to learning, the most effective method is "on the job."

What Benefits Does This Book Offer Each of These Market Segments?

- It gives them greater knowledge of the basics of marketing, advertising, and selling.

- They learn better communication techniques.

- They learn better sales techniques.

- If you create advertising, the book should help you write better ads or better direct-mail or plan better sales promotion programs, with better direct-mail letters.

Has the Marketing Plan Been Put into Writing, and What Does It Call For?

The marketing plan has been committed to writing, as well as the research plan, publicity plan, advertising plan, and direct-mail plan.

The marketing plan calls for the following:

- Making the book as interesting and helpful as possible, including good ideas suggested by those who've read it.

- Making sure it appeals to the many market segments already described on the back page.

- Making sure as many chapters as possible contain case histories or actual or hypothetical examples illustrating the basic principles outlined in the chapter.

- Pricing the book at $29.95, with quantity discounts to companies, colleges, universities, and other organizations who buy in case lots of 16 books per case.

- Giving the book a provocative, meaningful title to attract the attention of prospects.

- Designing the cover of the book and the inside pages to be as attractive and helpful as possible, using top-notch talent for

The marketing plan has been committed to writing, as well as research plan, publicity plan, advertising plan, and a direct-mail plan

the cover design and drawings or photos in as many places as possible.

- Employing a first-class public relations expert. Making sure the person heading the publicity work understands how to plan and execute a publicity program for a book like this, how to prepare fact sheets, obtain publicity in many types of media including publicity in trade papers, such as *Advertising Age* and *Sales and Marketing Management.*

- Employ an excellent direct-mail firm. This firm should know how to get the right lists, how to prepare the right "teasers" for the direct-mail envelopes to get recipients to open the letter, and how to prepare direct-mail letters for each list, as well as how to test these letters on a small scale.
Large sums of money will not be used until everything has been pre-tested and some have proved to be profitable.
It's important that the firm know how to use "800 numbers" in a way that keeps track of where every order came from, such as, extension numbers or letters after the 800 number.

- Employ a good advertising agency to create mail-order media advertisements for the book, and test different advertising approaches and different media to determine which is most profitable.

- Use a combination of selling methods for the different types of outlets or users.
  » Wholesalers, with the aid of a part-time sales manager working on commission to sell to book chains, book stores, and libraries.
  » Direct-mail to firms and individuals.
  » A tiny staff to operate and administer the marketing program. The staff will be responsible for paying all bills, keeping track of orders and submitting a weekly report on income

received from various sources, inventory control and expenses, as well as doing necessary research and follow-up work.

» In this connection get complete and accurate preliminary estimates on all expenditures, including costs involved in the preparation of the book for printing and the cost of printing itself. The costs include publicity, direct mail, advertising, travel, selling, secretarial and legal should be included.

Arriving at the Right Title.

We started by writing approximately 20 titles. We then got additional input from several people who are knowledgeable in this area.

Gradually we narrowed the list down to just a few. Then came HOW TO GET PEOPLE TO <u>WANT</u> TO DO WHAT YOU WANT THEM TO.

Finally, we arrived at a short title, which we adopted for the book, HOW TO GET PEOPLE TO SAY "YES".

This is followed by the line, And Make People *Want* to Do What You Want Them To.

What Improvements Have Been Made by Listening to Comments of Others?

The quality of the book itself has been improved tremendously by listening to what other people have to say and to their suggestions for changes and improvements.

At least a dozen people have made contributions in this area.

We've listened carefully to their comments and made a number of changes and improvements because we know the most important element in a marketing program is the quality of the product or service being offered.

The quality of the book itself has been improved tremendously by listening to what other people have to say and to their suggestions for changes and improvements

What Kind of Market Research Has Been Used for This Book?

We've printed the book by laser in black and white and using a 3-color cover. It was then sent to the following groups with a questionnaire:

20 students in colleges, universities, and graduate schools

10 teachers of marketing, advertising, and communications

5 advertising agency presidents

5 agency creative directors

4 agency account supervisors

5 marketing directors of large advertisers

3 advertising managers

4 sales managers

6 Small Business Investment Companies (SBICs)

6 small-business entrepreneurs

3 owners of sales promotion firms

Several famous marketing leaders

- We'll also send these laser-printed copies and question-naires to heads of organizations such as the National Realtors Association, American Association of Advertising Agencies, American Federation of Advertising, and the National Manufacturers Association.

- Also in the belief there should be a large market for this book in brokerage firms, real estate, and insurance companies, we'll send the same to them, not only to determine how they like it, but to what degree they feel they might want to purchase the final version after publication, for distribution to brokers, real estate agents, and insurance salespersons.

What Type of Copy Research Will Be Used?

- All advertising placed in media will solicit immediate purchases via a toll-free 800 number. Each phone order will be identified with different department or or extension numbers, so we'll know which ads were profitable in which media and which were not. Prior to this, two different campaigns will be tested via split run in one or more magazines.

- We'll do the same thing with all direct-mail letters. In neither case will we ever rerun a letter or an ad that was *not* profitable the first time.

How this $29.95 book is being distributed and sold

Sales Rep #1		Sales Rep #2	Sales & Advertising via direct mail	
Libraries	Wholesalers	Sells Firms	To firms	To Individuals
	Retail independent book stores and chains in cases of 16 at $250.00 per case, to retail at $29.95 per book.	Sells cases of 16 books at $250.00 per case.	All sales by direct-mail letter offering a case of 16 books at $250.00 per case.	All sales made via direct mail letter or by advertisement via an 800 number at $33.00 per book—including postage and handling. This includes paying the cost when the customer uses a credit card.

What Kind of Mistakes Have Been Made?

– See Case History three in Chapter 19

What About Pricing for This Book?

After studying the contents and the prices of a cross-section of books pertaining to selling, advertising, marketing, and communications, we noticed that some hard-cover books retailed for as high as $50 a copy.

Those who used soft covers offered their books at prices ranging from $19.95 to $30.00.

Because we felt we were offering a "one-of-a-kind" book, we priced our product at $29.95 and will offer discounts to purchasers of case lots of 16 books.

For purchases by individuals on a mail-order basis, we will add estimated handling and postage charges so that the price they'll pay will approximate $33 per copy.

What Kind of Publishing Strategy is Being Followed?

We've formed a Sub-chapter "S" Company with less than 30 stockholders. The company, A. R. Whitman Enterprises, Inc., will publish the book, using an outside firm to print it.

The history of publishing indicates that a publisher of a good book almost invariably makes far more money than the people who write it. Some publishing firms don't even pay authors expenses.

So by publishing the book ourselves, we have a greater margin to work with, without increasing the price to the buyer.

This larger margin, we hope, will provide the money for the advertising, publicity, direct- mail and research programs, as well as travel, editing, and operating expenses for the small staff.

Will Computers Be Used in Any Way in Connection with This Book?

Yes, we'll use a computer to keep track of expenses as well as for inventory control, and, we hope, for sales forecasting.

We're also currently preparing software programs to tell us as soon as possible:

Yes, we'll use a computer to keep track of expenses as well as for inventory control, and, we hope, for sales forecasting

a. What ads and direct-mail letters we use with different marketing segments are going to be profitable.

b. Based on the testing of ads and direct-mail letters, how many books we should sell if we increase the advertising by different percentages and increase the direct mail by different percentages.

How Will We Evaluate the Results?

a. By the sales made to book stores and libraries via wholesalers.

b. By mail-order media sales — that is by sales made through advertising.

c. By direct-mail sales.

SUMMARY

This chapter illustrates how the marketing principles called for by this book have been followed point by point.

1. We've touched on various phases of marketing (see Chapter 1).

2. We've gathered as much information as possible and have used it (see Chapter 5 and 6).

3. We've written a marketing and sales plan and specified the market segment we're trying to reach (see Chapter 7).

4. We've explained the benefits we believe this book offers to its readers (see Chapter 11).

5. We've told you how this book has been positioned (see Chapter 15).

6. We've told you about the market research we'll use to determine whether we should publish the book and how to improve it (see Chapter 20).

7. We also covered a mistake we made in trying to get people in different market segments to read a laser-printed version and answer a questionnaire (see Chapter 19).

8. We've told you our plan for testing the media mail-order advertising and the direct-mail program (see Chapters 46 and 47).

9. We've told you how we priced the book (see Chapter 23).

10. We've created a professional publicity program (see Chapter 22).

11. We've used a professional package designer to design the cover and the inside of the book (see Chapter 26).

12. We've used a firm which is expert in direct-mail letters to prepare and execute the mail-order program (see Chapter 45).

13. We've used an advertising agency to create the mail-order media advertising (see Chapter 47).

14. We've prepared a program for evaluating the results (see Chapter 51).

In short, you can see we've practiced what we've preached. We've followed every basic principle of marketing that this book has illustrated.

We hope this chapter will give you a greater appreciation for marketing and a better understanding of its scope and demands.

But most importantly, we hope this chapter wraps up for you what this book is all about and the benefits it offers you.

We hope this chapter will give you a greater appreciation for marketing and a better understanding of its scope and demands

Suppose You Don't Like This Book.

In that case you are protected by our money-back plus postage offer.

If after reading, you didn't feel this book was help-ful to you, send the book back within ten days and tell us what you paid for the book.

Mail to:

A.R. Whitman Enterprises, Inc.

1540 6th Ave. North

Long Lake, Minnesota, 55356

After receipt of such information and book, a check will be sent to you within a few days for purchase price of book, including return postage.

Does This Book Have Any Unusual or Special Uses?

We think so and suspect that either as an individual or as the head of a company, in your own interest, you may want to use one or two.

Here are uses we have in mind.

1. **Use the book as a gift item**

   It makes a great Christmas gift for employees, clients and suppliers, particularly for advertising agencies, small business investment companies (SBIC's), for sales managers, for institutions that raise money for both capital and annual giving programs. Banks should be another good market for gifts.

   Advertising agencies

   We believe quite a few advertising agencies will want to purchase enough copies of this book to give to:

   a. young creative people in each office
   b. all department heads in each office
   c. all of their people who work in the account end of the business.

   We suspect that the agency may also want to give the book as Christmas gifts to certain media people who call on them and perhaps certain suppliers such as typesetters, engravers and printers.

   Some account people may wish to use the book as a Christmas gift to certain people in their clients' offices.

   SBIC's

   We're confident that the head of many small business investment companies will want to give a copy to all or most of their small business companies with whom they work. After all, nearly 30 chapters in this book provide information that small business entrepreneurs want and need.

Sales managers

We have already discussed with a major food company the idea of having the sales manager buy a copy for every salesperson on the staff. For those who use brokers, we're confident the sales manager of their client will ask the head of the brokerage house to supply each of its salespeople with a copy. The reason:

There are 21 chapters in this book that will help a salesperson do a better job. At least a half a dozen other chapters should also benefit salespeople.

We also believe that as individuals, salespeople, particularly may wish to use this book as a Christmas gift for salespeople in other organizations who are close personal friends.

Institutions that run money-raising campaigns

We believe this book should be of great interest and help to institutions that run annual giving programs using a combination of their own small staff and hundreds of volunteer workers.

There are at least 13 chapters which should be important to the staff.

Other substantial markets

Real estate brokers and their salespeople

Brokerage firms and their brokers

Insurance companies and their salespeople

The benefits of the book to these companies and their salespeople are the same as those discussed under "sales managers."

Banks

Here we are talking about large city banks and small town and suburban banks that have computer records which can turn out lists of customers *by occupation*. When such lists exist, then there should be a substantial opportunity for banks to offer this book *as a premium* (via advertising, direct-mail and by phone). They could offer it *free* to customers who hold down jobs in marketing, advertising, selling, small business and money-raising, and to non-customers to get them to become a customer for the first time.

Travel agents — another market for gifts

Here we're talking about leading national, regional and local travel agencies using the book as a Christmas gift to clients who're strong in marketing, advertising and selling.

2. **Training programs**

Last, but not least, we believe this book offers another special use via training programs. Training programs for *salespeople*. Training programs for *service people*. By occupation, training programs for:

Small business entrepreneurs

Money-raising organizations

Marketing organizations

Advertising agencies

We also see training sessions for all kinds of salespeople in large and small corporations, including broker salespeople, real estate sales, brokers and insurance salespeople

Finally, we can see how this book can be used as the base for excellent training programs in all kinds of service companies including:

Travel agencies

Banks

Brokerage firms

Advertising agencies

Here are some of the chapters which can be used as a base for, or an integral part of, sales and service training:

For sales training

Chapters on sales promotion, sales incentive programs, how to market a sales plan, how to use benefits in personal selling, how to sell successfully by phone,

ideas, how to write and use direct-mail letters, how to write a sales letter, essential tips on salespersonship, how to make a good presentation, and how to write ads for classified news sections.

For training on service

Chapters on marketing, how to use benefits in supervising people, how to sell successfully by phone, how to use market research, how to use advertising to do both the "inside" and "outside" job, how to create and make a good presentation, how to motivate people who work with you, how to be a leader, and how and why the job is boss.

The key chapter for both sales and service training sessions is chapter 11 on benefits and an entire session on either sales or service could be devoted to this subject.

Special Thanks

We are deeply in debt to the following people who've been so helpful and who've contributed to the improvement of this book and/or its marketing:

The 17 contributing authors who wrote 24 chapters.

Elaine Archer, who did the research for and helped me write Chapter 23 on money raising.

Brewster Atwater, Chairman of General Mills, for giving us his comments and thoughts.

George Cleveland, in charge of sales and distribution of books to libraries and book wholesalers.

Jim Colville, Executive Director, United Way, Minneapolis, for his input and suggestions in Chapter 23.

Carol Danielsen, for her editing.

Tom Dolan, St. Thomas College, who had his students read and report on the book, and gave us information which has been incorporated herein.

Jim Fish, former Director of Advertising for General Mills, whose countless contributions "covered the waterfront."

Barbara Flanagan, a well-known midwestern columnist, for her ideas.

Frank Flis, who had this book printed by laser for market research (see picture and resume on this page). He also prepared the book for printing and supervised that work as well. He's been great to work with and his work has been outstanding.

Dan Haggarty, president of one of the country's best small business investment companies (SBIC) for his help in the chapter "Marketing and the Small Businessman." See Chapter 29.

Bob Hosakawa, a retired teacher of advertising and marketing, and a public relations expert, whose suggestions were vital to improving the book.

Harold King, Congregational Minister, for helping improve three chapters.

Dr. Theodore Leavitt, Professor Emeritus of the Graduate School of Harvard University, perhaps the leading authority on marketing in the United States, who reviewed this book and helped improve it.

Addison Piper, Chairman of Piper, Jaffray and Hopwood, an important midwestern brokerage firm, for his suggested improvements.

Chuck Ruhr and his agency Ruhr/Paragon for creating the mail-order media advertising.

Sue Scharf and **Sharon Mechavich**, for their secretarial and research help and **Tammy Triggs** for her work as secretary and Al Whitman's assistant.

Dean Thomas, who called on a number of sales managers in major companies and sold the book to them before it was even published.

Clara Westerhaus, for her help in making our market research questionnaire program work, and her unfailing great disposition and attitude of helpfulness.

John Whitman, who made many valuable suggestions on the content and the marketing of the book.

Diana Witt, for indexing the book.

Frank Flis, who designed this book, prepared it for printing and helped get laser prints of this book to do market research. Frank is a graduate of the Art Center College in Los Angeles, and taught there for eight years. He has worked as art/creative director on leading national accounts for major advertising agencies in New York, Los Angeles, and Minneapolis. Presently, he has his own advertising design firm.

INDEX

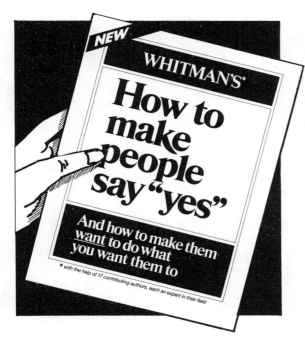

HOW TO ORDER MORE BOOKS

CALL 1-800-524-4717 Dept. B
between the hours of 8:00 a.m. and 5:00 p.m. CST

When ordering 1-15 books and using major credit cards for payment only.

If you are paying for books by check or money order, use coupon below.

Number of Books	Price	Shipping/ Handling	Price
One book	$29.95	$3.05	$33.00
2 - 15 books	$29.00	$3.00	$32.00 ea.

Minnesota residents add 6.5% Sales Tax

MONEY BACK GUARANTEE

If within 10 days you decide you're not satisified with this book, return the book to us and we'll send you your money back, plus postage. Also tell us where you purchased the book and what you paid for it.

SPECIAL DISCOUNTS
for orders over 16 books

CLIP OUT COUPON AND SEND IN TODAY

**Mail to: A.R. Whitman Enterprises, Inc.
Box #5817, Stacey, Minnesota 55079**

Please send:	Price
____ One book @ $33.00	$33.00
____ Two or more books @ $33.00 for the first and $32.00 each additional. Price includes postage and handling. ____	

Please send:	Price
____ 1 - 9 cases of 16 books @ $250.00 per case ____	
____ 10 or more cases of 16 books @ $240.00 per case ____	

Minnesota residents add 6.5% Sales Tax

Name _____

Company _____

Address _____

City _____ State _____ Zip _____